1-7-20

ARGUING ABOUT ALLIANCES

ARGUING ABOUT ALLIANCES

The Art of Agreement
in Military-Pact Negotiations

Paul Poast

CORNELL UNIVERSITY PRESS   ITHACA AND LONDON

First published 2019 by Cornell University Press

Library of Congress Cataloging-in-Publication Data

Names: Poast, Paul, author.
Title: Arguing about alliances : the art of agreement in military-pact
    negotiations / Paul Poast.
Description: Ithaca [New York] : Cornell University Press, 2019. | Includes
    bibliographical references and index.
Identifiers: LCCN 2018060432 (print) | LCCN 2019012808 (ebook) |
    ISBN 9781501740251 (pdf) | ISBN 9781501740268 (ret) |
    ISBN 9781501740244 (cloth)
Subjects: LCSH: Alliances. | Treaties—Interpretation and construction. |
    International organization. | Security, International.
Classification: LCC JZ1314 (ebook) | LCC JZ1314 .P63 2019 (print) |
    DDC 327.1/16—dc23
LC record available at https://lccn.loc.gov/2018060432

Contents

Illustrations

Acknowledgments

This project took a long time. I want to make this clear. By describing the path from initial idea to the book in your hand, my hope is that a graduate student realizes the numerous people involved in writing a "solo" project and how research projects require numerous "back to the drawing board" moments.

The original data on failed military alliance treaty negotiations were collected as part of my dissertation at the University of Michigan. My dissertation was not about military alliances per se or even about military negotiations. Instead, it was a series of connected papers evaluating the effectiveness of issue linkage as a means of reaching and maintaining agreements. I was inspired to pursue this topic after discovering the Alliance Treaty Obligation and Provision (ATOP) data in a course with Barabara Koremenos. Within those data, I found that some alliances had economic cooperation provisions. William Roberts Clark then helped me to think through the reasons states would find economics a useful instrument and James Morrow guided how I conceived of issue linkage within the context of alliances. Walter Mebane then led me through the painstaking process of figuring out how to evaluate the effectiveness of issue linkage offers. I realized that this required data on successful and failed negotiations. While evidence of the former was located in ATOP, the latter required creating a wholly new dataset. That is when, after a suggestion by Morrow, I began reading diplomatic histories with the hope of identifying failed negotiations.

I eventually submitted the core chapter of the dissertation to the journal *International Organization*. During the review process, an anonymous referee suggested that a future project could explore alliance treaty negotiation failure itself (not solely as a means of exploring issue linkages). Once that paper was accepted at *International Organization* and the other papers of my dissertation were published, I set out to write the paper suggested by that reviewer.

I worked on the paper during my first three years as an assistant professor at Rutgers University. I completely rewrote the paper on numerous occasions, but none of these drafts was ever submitted to a journal. Each new draft was leading to either a methodological or a theoretical dead end. I continued to have difficulty making the paper, for lack of better terminology, "work." Mind you, this road block was all on me. I was receiving immensely helpful suggestions from numerous individuals, namely, Jeff Arnold, Leonardo Baccini, Brett Benson, Benjamin

Fordham, Mareike Kleine, Yonatan Lupu, Michael McKoy, James Ashley Morrison, Shawn Ramirez, and Eric Reinhardt. In particular, Ashley Leeds, Dan Reiter, and Jack Levy (my senior colleague at Rutgers) offered extensive suggestions that encouraged me to continue working on the project.

Keren Yarhi-Milo eventually helped me turn the corner and produce the manuscript before you. After reading a draft of the paper, she suggested that I needed to make the paper a full-length book in order to do justice to the argument and evidence. That's when things clicked. I was coming to this realization on my own, as my inability to fit my argument and evidence into a paper seemed to be my road block. Keren's suggestion convinced me that writing a book manuscript was the right approach. Sure enough, intellectually committing to a book gave my ideas "room to breathe" and the page space to say exactly what I wanted to say.

I then moved to the University of Chicago, where my new colleagues encouraged me to focus on the manuscript. After completing a first full draft of the manuscript, Ashley and Keren, along with Scott Wolford and Timothy Crawford, came to Chicago to read and critique it. Additionally, numerous members of Chicago's political science department came to the workshop to offer suggestions and comments. John J. Mearsheimer generously chaired the all-day workshop. He went beyond simply keeping the trains running on time by asking follow-up questions of a commenter in order to clarify his or her critique or comment (and at one point summarized several lines of argument by writing them on the board). I then received additional comments (and a three hour "debrief" over coffee) from Dan Reiter. After reflecting on all these comments, I finally knew the direction to take the argument.

I then spent the next year rewriting and reorganizing the manuscript. My colleagues at Chicago continued to help me think through and refine my ideas (helped by my decision to leave a drawing of the theory's two-by-two on a white board in my office so as to facilitate on-the-spot brainstorming whenever someone stopped in). In addition to John, my international relations colleagues—Robert Pape, Paul Staniland, Austin Carson, Robert Gulotty, and Charles Lipson—were crucial in helping me to solidify the new direction of the manuscript. Paul was especially supportive with navigating the review process with Cornell. Speaking of the review process, Roger Haydon was masterful in guiding me through it. Whether helping me to craft the (numerous) response memorandums or managing the reviewers, Roger was instrumental in seeing the manuscript to the finish line. The anonymous reviewers offered immensely helpful comments, with one of the reviewers being especially thoughtful and constructive. This reviewer championed the project (while also pushing me to make much needed changes), and I am grateful for his or her support (without which, I'm not sure the book would have been accepted).

I am proud of this book. But as the above narrative reveals, this was not a work in isolation. Academia is a communal enterprise. It requires having others see and respond to your work (and lend a helping hand). Even a "solo" project is still a team effort.

ARGUING ABOUT ALLIANCES

THE FRAGILITY OF ALLIANCE DIPLOMACY

Hitler must be stopped. But how? In need of a unified plan to deter German aggression, the Soviet Union, Britain, and France met in August 1939 to negotiate an alliance, but they left Moscow without an agreement. The consequences of their failure were grave.[1] As the historian A. J. P. Taylor writes, "it is pointless to speculate whether an Anglo-Soviet alliance would have prevented the Second World War. But failure to achieve this alliance did much to cause it" (Taylor 1961, 246).

The failed 1939 Triple Alliance negotiation was not an isolated incident. From 1815 to 1945, over 40 percent of alliance treaty negotiations involving European states ended when the participants walked away without a signed treaty.[2] During the Cold War, the United States' inability to conclude a pact with Burma left a key gap in the chain of Southeast Asian anticommunist alliances.[3] Britain rejecting offers to negotiate a European army undermined French enthusiasm for the 1952 European Defense Community treaty.[4] Only after years of hard bargaining and stalled talks did South Korea and Japan sign a military information-sharing agreement in 2012 (Park and Yun 2016). And lengthy talks are often required before the current members of the North Atlantic Treaty Organization agree to admit a new member (Poast and Urpelainen 2018).

When states enter negotiations to gain formal allies, agreement is far from a fait accompli. This raises an important question: What are states actually doing and discussing when they meet to negotiate a military pact? Phrased differently, when states sit down to negotiate an alliance, what determines whether the negotiation ends in agreement, with the parties signing a treaty, or instead in nonagreement, with the parties leaving the table empty-handed? While a large body of

1

international relations scholarship investigates the formation of alliances, the actual process by which states agree to an alliance treaty is often black boxed. This is problematic. Since states have attempted but failed to negotiate alliance treaties, we should explore the process that distinguishes groups of states that form alliances from groups of states that attempt to do so but fail. Only then can we truly understand the meaning and purpose of military alliances.

Exploring agreement and nonagreement in alliance treaty negotiations requires conceptualizing the content of the negotiations. I view alliance treaty negotiations as discussions over joint war plans: the participants in the negotiation are planning a war together. While the text of the final treaty may not convey details of a war plan, war planning lies at the core of the talks. For instance, the 1949 North Atlantic Treaty does not mention a specific threat as motivating the treaty's creation. However, on numerous occasions during the negotiations, the participants explicitly identified the Soviet Union as the target of the alliance. Consider also the negotiations leading to the 1892 Franco-Russian alliance. On the one hand, the actual treaty does offer some explicit details, namely, the threats targeted. (Both Austria and Germany are mentioned in Article 1.) But key war-planning details are absent from the treaty's text, despite a large portion of the negotiations focusing on the sequence of mobilizations and maneuvers during a crisis.[5]

By studying alliance treaty negotiations and conceptualizing them as arguments over joint war plans, this book advances the alliance literature and our understanding of how alliances provide international security. Placing war planning at the center of negotiations emphasizes the coordinating function of alliance treaties. To date, the wartime coordination function of alliance treaties has been inadequately theorized.[6] While the literature acknowledges the coordinating role of alliance treaties, theoretical work mostly focuses on alliances as "costly signals": alliance treaties deter threats by informing potential aggressors of the allies' intention to defend one another (Morrow 1994; Smith 1995; Fearon 1997).[7] Our understanding suffers when we treat coordination as a secondary or even trivial function of alliances. Indeed, the coordination enabled through war planning may even explain exactly why alliances deter threats. Ad hoc coalitions often face costly delays in applying force precisely because they must pause in the midst of a crisis to negotiate the terms of joint engagement (Kreps 2011, 27), though with the benefit of the decision-making structure and terms of engagement being tailored to the task and countries at hand (Weitsman 2014, 39). Crafting a plan before a crisis can avoid delays and enable an effective use of force. In turn, knowing that a set of allies have taken steps to apply force may make the allies' target less likely to behave aggressively.[8]

Placing war planning at the center of alliance treaty negotiations also builds a bridge between existing work on the origins of alliances (e.g., Walt 1987;

Reiter 1996) and the management of alliance relations (e.g., Snyder 1997; Weitsman 2004). In so doing, my argument enhances both areas of alliance research.[9] For instance, Stephen Walt's *Origins of Alliances* theorizes about why states seek allies. But I show how states facing conditions that should drive them into an alliance can still fail to reach agreement. Similarly, Glenn H. Snyder's *Alliance Politics* primarily theorizes about relations once states are allies,[10] but my theory and evidence show that states must address concerns over alliance management even before they sign a treaty. Snyder (1997, 166) writes that "among the most prominent issues in intra-alliance bargaining are the coordination of military plans, the stance to be adopted toward the opponent in a diplomatic crisis, and the sharing of preparedness burdens in peacetime." I claim that prospective allies must begin addressing such issues before they can become formal allies.[11] Stated differently, rather than knocking Walt or Snyder off the shelf, this book should (hopefully) sit between them.

The Argument in Brief

How does placing joint war planning at the center of alliance treaty negotiations help explain when these negotiations will end in agreement? Before outlining the argument, I must define some concepts. *Alliance treaties* are documents calling on the signatories to cooperate in responding with active military force to a non-signatory's aggression.[12] The documents are written and signed by official representatives of states, and the signatory states become *allies* (Leeds et al. 2002, 239).[13] The military action specified in the document can be either *offensive* or *defensive*.[14] Defensive action entails protecting another signatory under attack, as in Article 1 of the 1851 Austrian-Prussian alliance treaty: "any attack against one party will be considered by the other party as a hostile enterprise against its own territory."[15] Offensive action entails protecting a nonsignatory by attacking its aggressor, such as when the 1832 British-French alliance treaty called for France and Britain to attack the Netherlands if it refused to remove troops from Belgium.[16] The signed documents specifying such action range from a duly negotiated and ratified treaty to a written declaration signed by heads of state to an official exchange of letters between foreign ministers.[17] Reflecting the variety of documents that can constitute an alliance treaty, a *negotiation* can be a simple conversation between diplomats or a series of formal meetings involving officials from numerous countries (Davis 2004, 14).[18] A negotiation concludes in either *agreement*, meaning it produces an alliance treaty signed by all the participants, or *nonagreement*, meaning the talks end without a signed alliance treaty and the participants have no plans to continue the talks.

With these definitions in place, I can now summarize the book's explanation for why alliance treaty negotiations end in agreement or nonagreement. An alliance treaty negotiation could touch on a host of topics, and not every detail of the negotiation will be reflected in the text of the treaty. But agreement is only possible if two items are addressed to the satisfaction of all participants: (1) *against whom* and *where* to use military force and (2) *how* to engage that target.[19] The signatories of the alliance treaty might hope the alliance deters aggression and that they never actually take military action against the threat. But even if this is the intent, hashing out the "who," "where," and "how" of joint military action lies at the heart of the negotiations leading to the treaty.

The core of my argument is that the items at the heart of negotiations for an alliance treaty are also the key features of a war plan: "who" and "where" are articulated in the strategic component of a war plan, while "how" is captured in the operational component of a war plan. This suggests that one can view an alliance treaty negotiation as an effort in joint war planning. This conceptualization of alliance negotiations evokes two variables that likely determine whether the negotiations lead to a signed treaty: the *compatibility of ideal war plans* and the *attractiveness of outside options*.

The first variable is the *compatibility of ideal war plans*. At the beginning of a negotiation, each participant reveals its ideal war plan, meaning the plan that reflects that state's preferred strategic and operational components. Ideal war plans are compatible if they articulate similar strategic and operational components. The strategic component of a war plan refers to the target of military force, which reflects a state's perception of threats. Hence, strategic compatibility means the participants in the negotiations have similar perceptions of possible threats. This lies at the heart of alliance treaty negotiations: without agreement on who to attack and where, it makes little sense to negotiate the details of military cooperation. The operational component of a plan refers to the general approach for addressing the identified threat(s), which is reflected by the state's military doctrine. A military doctrine can be either offensive, meaning the fight should be taken to the territory of the perceived threat, or defensive, meaning the objective is to stop the enemy's advance by fighting on home territory (either a state's own territory or the territory of an ally). Hence, operational compatibility means the states do not have contradictory military doctrines.

The second variable is the *attractiveness of outside options*. An outside option is the policy each participant will pursue if the negotiation ends in nonagreement. Outside options include unilateral action, an alliance with another state, or buckpassing (i.e., leaving it to other states to attack or deter the threat). The attractiveness of an outside option is the extent to which the participant perceives the outside option as offering a benefit similar to that of an alliance that follows its ideal war plan. The more attractive the outside option, the less willing a participant will be to deviate from its ideal plan. Since attractiveness is a matter of perception, it is private information and is known only to that participant. Moreover, each participant has an incentive to misrepresent this attractiveness, in order to have the final treaty more closely reflect its ideal war plan. Of particular importance is the number of participants that perceive themselves as having an attractive outside option. For example, in a negotiation between two participants, if both perceive themselves as having an attractive outside option, neither will make concessions to secure an agreement. In contrast, if neither participant perceives itself as having an attractive outside option, the participants will not want the negotiation to end in nonagreement. In this case, they are more likely to make concessions to secure an agreement.

Later in the text, I elaborate on both of these variables and show how they interact to produce negotiation agreement or nonagreement. For now, it's beneficial to see how these theoretical concepts map onto the historical record. Consider the two case studies I develop later in the text: the 1901 Anglo-German negotiations and the 1948–49 North Atlantic Treaty negotiations. During the Anglo-German negotiations that I explore in chapter 4, the British and German officials agreed that Russia was the primary target of the alliance. However, a key strategic incompatibility was the treaty's geographic scope: Should the alliance respond to Russian aggression in Europe, in East Asia, or both? Germany was primarily concerned with protection from Russia in Europe for itself and its Triple Alliance partners; Britain was concerned about assistance against Russian incursions in East Asia. Given this incompatibility and the difference between Britain's perception that it had attractive outside options and the German belief that Britian did not, the two parties failed to make the concessions necessary to reach agreement. Incompatibilities over the geographic scope of an alliance also plagued the 1948–49 North Atlantic Treaty negotiations. As I emphasize in chapter 5, debate over the geographic scope of the alliance nearly caused the negotiations to collapse: Could the parties agree on the definition of "North Atlantic"? In particular, France demanded expansion of the southern boundary of the region, to include Italy and French-ruled Algeria. The other participants initially opposed the French demand. What saved these negotiations was that the other participants lacked attractive outside options and were unwilling to hold out in the belief that France lacked an attractive alternative. The other participants capitulated to French demands, and agreement was reached.

Broader Importance

This is a study of alliance politics, but my argument and evidence furthers our understanding of international relations (IR) theory more generally. Four contributions are of note: explicitly theorizing negotiations; opening the black box of capability aggregation; rethinking how military power, level of threat, and system polarity influence international cooperation; and demonstrating how grand strategy is formed collaboratively.

First, by focusing on the negotiations leading to the creation of alliance treaties, this study helps to address William Zartman's (2010, 230) criticism of IR that "in general, IR theory and IR texts bypass [or, at a minimum, do not take seriously] negotiation . . . overlooking the fact that negotiation in its many forms takes up most of the time and effort of interstate relations, diplomacy, and foreign policy" (Zartman 2010, 230). In the area of alliance politics, specifically, there is much truth to Zartman's critique. Scholars commonly divide groups of states into two categories: groups that formed alliance treaties and groups that did not.[20] That some negotiations end in nonagreement suggests a third category: groups of states that tried and failed to form an alliance treaty. Underlining the value of taking negotiation seriously, exploring this third category—failed attempts to form a treaty—sheds light on how and why states actually reach agreement on treaties.

Second, my argument opens the black box of capability aggregation, a key mechanism in classic "balancing" arguments (Morgenthau 1948; Gulick 1955; Schleicher 1962; Dinerstein 1965; Rothstein 1968; Waltz 1979; Walt 1987).[21] Balancing via capability aggregation is the idea that allies can deploy their combined military capabilities against a threat: "throughout history the main reason states have entered into alliances has been the desire for the *aggregation of power*" (Russett and Starr 1989, 91).[22] But how does "aggregation" come about? States can take a tally of their combined military capabilities, but how does an accounting metric translate into actual fighting power? As Oliver Schmitt (2018, 6) notes, much IR work seems to "take for granted the 'capability-aggregation model'" even though such scholars as Patricia Weitsman (2004, 2) point out that "a straightforward capability-aggregation effect [of alliances] . . . is far from true." More precisely, Nora Bensahel (2007, 188, 197) observes how "although the capability aggregation model dominates the theoretical literature on alliances . . . it simply assumes that alliance members can transform a verbal or written alliance agreement into a militarily effective fighting force . . . [But] militaries in multinational operations do not automatically combine their capabilities effectively." Indeed, failure to address logistical complications (along with an incentive for allies to free ride by undercontributing) means a large coalition may not outperform a smaller but more committed group (Stam 1996, 149). John J. Mearsheimer (2001, 146) acknowledges that "putting together balancing coalitions quickly and making them function smoothly is often difficult, because it takes time to coordinate the efforts of prospective allies or member states." By conceptualizing alliance treaty negotiations as joint war planning, my argument provides a direct mechanism by which states determine whether and how they will aggregate their capabilities to jointly apply military force.

Third, my question, argument, and evidence force scholars to think carefully about how the usual variables used in explaining international politics—military power, level of threat, and even system polarity—map to international cooperation. A scholar could dismiss my findings and argument by saying, "This all might be true, but it still comes down to power, threat, and polarity." On the one hand, power, threat, and polarity do continue to set the context of state behavior and constrain leaders' decision making. On the other hand, power, threat, and polarity are far from sufficient to explain state behavior. Consider capabilities. States do not only care that capabilities are present: a simple tally sheet is only a starting point. States must also determine whether the capabilities can be brought to bear effectively against a threat. Capabilities on paper are not the same as capabilities on the battlefield. My exploration of alliance treaty negotiations shows why states will, from time to time (or even frequently), behave in a manner inconsistent with the raw distribution of power.[23]

Fourth, my theory emphasizes how grand strategizing is subject to negotiation. I presume that each state enters the negotiation with its own menu of threat priorities and guidelines for the application of force; in other words, each participant has its own grand strategic vision (Posen 1984; Kennedy 1991; Goodard and Kreps 2015). At times, these visions are in near perfect alignment—one might say that a harmony of interests exists between the participants (Keohane 1984). Since revealing compatibility in grand strategic conceptions opens opportunities for joint gains, the prospects for military cooperation between relatively symmetric military powers are greater than previously appreciated (Morrow 1991). When these visions have imperfect alignment, agreement is still possible through bargaining (Morrow 1994; Fearon 1998). This mirrors Mitzen's (2015, 74) description of collective grand strategizing, meaning states negotiate agreements "about how to act in the security domain that prioritizes threats and offer guidelines for how a state or states will use force to advance their interests (or common interests)." The fact that conditions exist where states can compromise on core components of their grand strategic visions bolsters the observation made by Mansoor and Murray (2016, 16) that alliances have been shown to be essential "to successful grand strategies throughout history." Many grand strategic visions are simply infeasible if pursued noncollaboratively.

Competing Explanations

My argument emphasizes ideal war plan compatibility as the reason for agreement or nonagreement in alliance treaty negotiations. This explanation focuses on disagreements over *how* capabilities will be used in war, but it is not the only possible explanation for why alliance treaty negotiations end in agreement or nonagreement. States may also disagree over *whether* the alliance should go to war, *when* it should, or *which* of their capabilities will be used. Stated differently, other explanations could focus on capability concerns (what), reliability concerns (whether), or entrapment concerns (when). These competing explanations could either be additional explanations (i.e., they and my argument both might help explain negotiation outcomes) or alternative explanations (i.e., they could override and nullify my argument). I will set this distinction aside for now. I will, instead, introduce these competing explanations and then return to them when I evaluate my argument empirically in later chapters.

The first competing explanation is capability concerns, meaning that the negotiations might reveal unexpected shortcomings in a participant's military capabilities. My argument focuses on the compatibility of ideal war plans, meaning disagreement over how capabilities should be used in war. What if the explanation for nonagreement instead lies with the capabilities themselves? For instance, state A may enter a negotiation with state B uncertain over the actual capabilities that state B can bring to bear against a threat. Over the course of the negotiation, state A may gain information from state B revealing that B's capabilities are far less than A deems necessary to counter a particular threat. This could lead state A to walk away. In other words, agreement could be undermined by the revelation of inadequate capabilities, not disagreement about how to use those capabilities. This suggests that larger ex ante uncertainty over a negotiation participant's capabilities increases the probability of the other participants gaining unfavorable information about those capabilities, creating conditions inhospitable to agreement.

The second competing explanation is reliability concerns, meaning the fear that a prospective ally will defect from providing assistance in a war (Crescenzi et al. 2012; Miller 2012).[24] Reliability concerns range from believing that a counterpart prefers to exploit cooperation (Snyder 1997, 181) to recognizing that a counterpart might prefer cooperation but have limited capacity (Chayes and Chayes 1991). On the one hand, reliability concerns could directly challenge my argument. If a participant enters a negotiation highly concerned about its counterpart's reliability, it will be more difficult for the counterpart to alleviate those concerns during the negotiation.[25] Reliability concerns may induce participants to end negotiations without an agreement, even when they have compatible ideal war plans.[26] On the other hand, reliability concerns might not directly challenge my argument. I am interested in explaining agreement or nonagreement *once the states are in negotiations*. The primary effect of reliability concerns might be to prevent negotiations from occurring. James Fearon (1998, 287) writes, "If we observe states attempting to craft an international agreement, the state's shadow of the future is probably not so short as to make cooperation infeasible due to fears of reneging." Hence, when studying a negotiation, one is likely to "find states failing to cooperate not because of problems arranging credible commitments but rather due to apparent 'deadlock' in bargaining—the failure to find terms acceptable to both sides" (Fearon 1998, 287).[27] In other words, if prospective allies account for reliability concerns prior to entering negotiations, then states in negotiations likely do not have acute reliability concerns: factors other than reliability concerns are needed to explain nonagreement.

The third competing explanation focuses on entrapment concerns. Snyder (1984a, 467) defines entrapment as the fear of "being dragged into a conflict over an ally's interests that one does not share, or shares only partially."[28] Whether the desire to guard sovereignty comes from a monarch's mind or the demands of a democracy's legislators,[29] a participating state could be highly concerned about losing control over if and when its military forces are involved in a crisis or war.[30] In an alliance treaty negotiation, such concerns can manifest themselves as arguments over the text of the treaty. One participant might want the treaty to convey flexibility in its implementation.[31] Indeed, Benson (2012) shows how states seek to write alliance treaties in a manner that renders the provision of support probabilistic: the wording is specific enough to show that a state has made a promise to support its ally but vague enough to leave unclear both the exact nature of the promise and the conditions under which the state will provide support. But another participant might fear that too much flexibility will undermine the protection accorded by the treaty, particularly the treaty's ability to deter a threat.[32] For example, should the treaty contain the phrase "unprovoked aggression" rather than "armed attack"?[33] Or the negotiation participants may agree to include the phrase "support with military means" but with one participant insisting on including the clause "in the manner each member deems appropriate." It is possible that an inability to find words that are mutually satisfactory (what one might call "verbiage disputes") is fundamental to explaining some (or perhaps even most) instances of nonagreement.[34]

Evaluating the Argument

Chapter 1 unpacks the book's argument: that joint war planning provides a use-ful conceptual framework for explaining agreement and nonagreement in alli-ance treaty negotiations. But I will need to evaluate this argument empirically. I start in chapters 2 and 3 by analyzing patterns from data across a large number of alliance treaty negotiations involving European states prior to 1945. Chapter 2 introduces the data used to measure my outcome variable, *agreement*, and the pri-mary explanatory variable, *ideal war plan compatibility*. To code agreement, I use two sources of data: the Alliance Treaty Obligation and Provision (ATOP) data set of Leeds et al. (2002) to identify negotiations that ended in agreement and data originally used in Poast (2012) to identify negotiations that ended in non-agreement. To code ideal war plan compatibility, I need data on both strategic compatibility and operational compatibility. Drawing from well-established data identifying the threats states face, I identify the threats facing each negotiation participant and then code strategic compatibility as the ratio of the participants' shared threats to the total number of threats faced by the participants. The higher this ratio, the more likely the participants are to have compatible views regard-ing which state(s) should be the target of the alliance treaty. Drawing on the idea that the operational component of a state's ideal war plan emanates from its mil-itary doctrine, I use battle-level data from previous wars fought by negotiation participants to code whether the participants shared offensive or defensive mili-tary doctrines. I use these measures of strategic compatibility and operational compatibility to code when the negotiation participants have *only strategic com-patibility*, *only operational compatibility*, or *both strategic and operational compat-ibility*.

After acquiring the necessary data, I turn to analysis in chapter 3. I begin by exploring basic patterns in the data using cross tabulations. While the initial pat-terns are supportive of my theory, I am concerned about potential complications in the data that could undermine my ability to draw inferences about the relation-ships between variables. I discuss two complications: selection bias and omitted variable bias. Selection bias pertains to unobserved negotiation failures (i.e., missing data), the fact that entry into a negotiation is nonrandom (i.e., selection into the sample), and that states could be entering negotiations because they have compatible war plans (i.e., selection into the treatment). Omitted variable bias pertains to the need for my analysis to account for the abovementioned competing explanations (capability concerns, reliability concerns, and entrapment concerns), as well as other factors that could, once accounted for, nullify the relationship between my key explanatory variable and alliance negotiation outcomes.

After describing my plans to address both omitted variable bias and selection bias, I evaluate the direct effect of ideal war plan compatibility on agreement in alliance treaty negotiations using a host of analysis methods. These range from multivariate analyses that account for competing explanations and confounding factors to sensitivity analyses that show how the observed patterns vary if I remove observations, use alternative samples, or apply different estimation approaches. All of these tests point to the same general result: negotiations where the participants have both strategic and operational compatibility have a rate of agreement that is substantially and statistically higher than negotiations where the participants do not have both strategic compatibility and operational compatibility.

I then turn to evaluating the indirect effect of ideal war plan compatibility on agreement in alliance treaty negotiations. This requires operationalizing when participants in negotiations have attractive outside options and then determining whether, as predicted by my theory, the effect of outside options varies according to the war plan compatibility of the participants. Using the possession of an existing alliance treaty as capturing when participants have outside options, I find that the existence of an outside option substantively and statistically reduces the probability of agreement only when the participants do not have both strategic compatibility and operational compatibility.

These large-n statistical analyses offer useful evidence in support of my theory. However, they say little about the process linking the explanatory variables to the outcomes of alliance treaty negotiations. This requires teasing out the mechanisms leading to agreement and nonagreement in alliance treaty negotiations. I do this by conducting two in-depth case studies, both of which I previewed above.

First, I explore the 1901 Anglo-German alliance treaty negotiation, which ended in nonagreement. This case fits the main statistical model used in chapter 3 well, thereby suggesting that it is a useful case for probing the mechanisms linking the key explanatory variables to the outcome variable. This is also a famous instance of nonagreement and one that previous scholars have used to describe a competing explanation: reliability concerns. Drawing from such document collections as *Die Grosse Politik der Europäischen Kabinette* (*Grosse Politik* in the notes), *British Documents on the Origins of the War* (*British Documents* in the notes), and *German Diplomatic Documents, 1871–1914* (*German Documents* in the notes), I instead show how incompatibility in ideal plans, not reliability concerns, led to nonagreement.

Second, I explore the 1948–49 negotiations that produced the North Atlantic Treaty. This case is useful to explore because previous scholarship on these negotiations emphasized the need to overcome entrapment concerns (a key competing explanation). However, by drawing on a host of sources, primarily the U.S. Department of State's *Foreign Relations of the United States* document series, I show that entrapment concerns were not more important (and perhaps less so) than the parties' efforts to overcome incompatibilities in the strategic component of their ideal plans, namely, the geographic scope of the treaty.

The Value of Looking Back

A notable feature of the evidence I use to evaluate the argument is a lack of post-1950 data, either in the large-n analysis or in the case studies. Consequently, readers seeking insights into today's international politics might view this book as having little relevance. This is a mistake. With respect to understanding and forecasting state behavior during the remainder of the twenty-first century, this earlier period is likely more relevant than the majority of the Cold War and immediate post–Cold War period.

From 1815 to 1945, the international system was multipolar, meaning there were more than two great powers at any one time.[35] In contrast, the majority of the post-1945 period was either a bipolar system of U.S.-Soviet rivalry or a unipolar system of U.S. dominance.[36] But for a host of reasons—an assertive Russia coupled with renewed nationalism in Europe, a rising China coupled with a still economically strong Japan, the involvement and intervention by multiple global and regional powers in Syria and Iraq—today's world resembles the multipolar system of major power competition that marked the nineteenth and early twentieth centuries.

Both policy makers and scholars have acknowledged the relevance of the pre–Cold War system for understanding international politics today. In 2013, then U.S. secretary of state John Kerry remarked that "we live in a world that is more like the 18th and 19th centuries" than like the system of superpower competition that marked much of the twentieth century after 1945.[37] Pointing to the behavior of China and Russia, the 2017 U.S. *National Security Strategy* boldly asserted that "after being dismissed as a phenomenon of an earlier century, great power competition returned."[38] These statements echo comments made by scholars since at least the early 1990s. In 1990, Mearsheimer (1990, 5–6) offered a widely cited observation that "the bipolar structure that has characterized Europe since the end of World War II is replaced by a multipolar structure." At the end of the 1990s, George Modelski and William Thompson (1999, 139) concluded that for the next few decades "multipolarity holds some features that resonate with the approaching phase of global politics. . . . Indeed, the closest precedent, the well-known previous locus of balance-of-power behavior, is pre-World War I." In a 2012 essay largely critical of claims that the United States' unipolar moment was ending, Joseph Nye acknowledged that global wealth was returning to Asia and, therefore, the global distribution of economic power (which ultimately underpins military power) would be more reflective of the early nineteenth century, not the second half of the twentieth century.[39]

To further underscore the importance of looking back, consider NATO again. Despite its having played a critical role in European security for decades, NATO's value to the United States has come under intense scrutiny since the turn of the twenty-first century. In 2011, during operations in Libya, the U.S. secretary of defense Robert Gates remarked, "The mightiest military alliance in history is only 11 weeks into an operation against a poorly armed regime in a sparsely populated country—yet many allies are beginning to run short of munitions, requiring the U.S., once more, to make up the difference."[40] While a candidate for president of the United States, Donald Trump expressed a similar sentiment: "NATO was set up at a different time. . . . NATO is costing us a fortune and yes, we're protecting Europe with NATO but we're spending a lot of money . . . I think NATO as a concept is good, but it is not as good as it was when it first evolved."[41] Is NATO still worthwhile for the United States? Do its benefits outweigh the costs? In many ways, NATO perfectly captures why Nordhaus and Tobin (1972, 8) label military expenditures a "regrettable expense." The purchase of weapons and support to allies are not done for their own sake, but for the possibility of "the unfavorable circumstances that prompt these expenditures." This means a society is likely "better off with them than without them." Identifying the possible unfavorable circumstances NATO was designed to stop and whether these circumstances still justify NATO's expense requires reevaluating NATO's creation. Indeed, Trump's own remarks acknowledge this fact, by directly referring to the usefulness of NATO's original purpose. Looking back can offer insight into the relevance of NATO's original purpose for addressing security challenges today and into the future.

A THEORY OF ALLIANCE TREATY NEGOTIATION OUTCOMES

States have a variety of motivations for seeking alliance partners. Some states want a public sign of commitment that could deter a threat.[1] Others want assistance in an ongoing conflict. Still others hope to acquire a means of projecting force abroad, perhaps by stationing troops on an ally's territory.

Regardless of motivation, alliances are ultimately aimed at countering threats by using military means. This requires some degree of planning. Consider the remarks of the Soviet defense minister Kliment Voroshilov at the beginning of the Soviet-British-French alliance treaty negotiations in the summer of 1939:

> Our aim is clear and now it is a matter of *drawing up a plan* to achieve this aim. Our aim is clear-cut: to defend the peace-loving countries headed by Britain, France, and the Soviet Union against the aggressive bloc in Europe. That, I think, is the aim, and we must now discuss the means of achieving it. . . . The aggressive European bloc, if it attacks one of the countries, must be smashed at all costs, and for this we must have an appropriate military plan.[2]

Voroshilov's remarks provide a useful way of conceptualizing what states actually discuss when they sit down to negotiate an alliance treaty: joint war plans. This means the alliance treaty partners, before signing the treaty, must consider in some detail the conditions for fighting together and the means of doing so. This requires addressing a host of questions about the application of force: Against whom are they targeting their efforts? Will they fight jointly anywhere on the globe or only in a specific region? Will they respond by invading the territory of the target? Will they take defensive positions on their own territory? Even if the alliance's goal is to deter a threat in the hope that military force will never be employed, the parties must have general outlines for fighting together in case deterrence fails.

To be clear, joint war planning pertains to the content of the negotiations to form a treaty, not the content of the final text of the treaty produced by those negotiations. Such details can appear in the final treaty text, but they need not. Consider the 1892 Franco-Russian alliance treaty negotiations. The officials argued at length about the proper sequence of actions in case of war with Germany: Should Russia enact a strategic retreat through the Polish territories it controlled? Should French forces advance and hold defensive positions at Verdun?[3] But while these plans were discussed during the negotiations, none of their details appeared in the final text of the treaty.

Conceptualizing alliance treaty negotiations as arguments over joint war plans enables me to explain the conditions leading to negotiations ending in agreement or nonagreement. Drawing on bargaining theory and negotiation analysis, my explanation focuses on two key variables: (1) the compatibility of ideal war plans and (2) the attractiveness of outside options.[4] I will briefly explain each variable here, before elaborating on them later in this chapter.

The first variable is *compatibility of ideal war plans*. This refers to the participants' respective ideal war plans not having contradictory strategic components (i.e., they identify the same or similar threats) or operational components (i.e., they specify similar military action against a threat). Ideal war plan compatibility can be either high or low. Strategic compatibility is high when the participants have similar ideas about the states to be targeted by the alliance. Determining war plan strategic compatibility requires comparing the threats the participants have in common to the ones they do not. Different threats matter because tension can arise if the parties to a negotiation disagree on extending the alliance to cover more than shared threats. Operational compatibility is high when the participants' war plans articulate similar general guidelines for applying military force against the target(s). This entails comparing the participants' military doctrines, because military doctrine determines a war plan's high-level operational component. Tensions can arise from conflicting doctrines, such as one negotiation participant adhering to an offensive doctrine and another following a defensive doctrine.

The key to ideal war plan compatibility is that both participants have similar notions of the threat and similar philosophies about the application of military force against that threat. Suppose participant A unveils an ideal war plan calling for the allies to send troops onto German territory in the event of German aggression. If participant B replies, "That's exactly the same as our ideal war plan," the two ideal war plans have high compatibility. However, if participant B replies,

"We think the alliance should also target Italy, and our plan calls for waiting to engage German forces on our own territory," then the two plans have low compatibility. Agreement in such cases requires compromise between the parties or capitulation by one party. To be clear, "compatibility" need not imply that the plan specifies symmetric action by the prospective allies. If states A and B each have ideal war plans calling for state A to invade the threat's northern border and for state B to hold a defensive position at the threat's southern border, then their plans are still compatible.

The second variable is the *attractiveness of outside options*. Outside options are the policies each participant will pursue if the negotiation ends in nonagreement. Such policies include unilateral action or an alliance treaty with another state. A participant's outside option is attractive when, with respect to achieving its policy goals, the participant perceives the outside option as roughly equivalent to an alliance that adheres to its ideal war plan. When the two policies are perceived as equivalent, the participant is unlikely to agree to a joint war plan that deviates from its ideal. The participant will instead opt for the outside option. For this reason, the number of negotiation participants that perceive themselves as having attractive outside options will have a notable effect on the prospects of reaching agreement. Suppose both participants in a two-party negotiation perceive themselves as having attractive outside options. In this case, neither party will wish to deviate from its ideal war plan, and neither party is likely to make substantial compromises for the sake of agreement. Nonagreement is possible.

Whether compromises are necessary to avoid nonagreement depends on how the two variables—*compatibility of ideal war plans* and *attractiveness of outside options*—interact. This is illustrated in figure 1.1. The rows of figure 1.1 capture the compatibility of the participants' ideal war plans. Ideal war plan compatibility can be either high (the top row) or low (the bottom row). The columns of figure 1.1 report the number of participants that perceive their outside options as attractive. Either all (right-hand column) or not all (left-hand column) participants have an attractive outside option. Though both variables can take on more than two values, I explain later in the chapter why dichotomizing the variables is useful for focusing on core elements of my theory.

These two variables interact to create four types of alliance treaty negotiations: Same Page, Pleasant Surprise, Revealed Deadlock, and Standard Bargaining. The *expected outcome* listed in each cell of figure 1.1 reports whether the conditions in a particular negotiation type are conducive to agreement or nonagreement. Though it is difficult in any specific bargaining situation to predict nonagreement ex ante (Gartzke 1999), figure 1.1 illustrates how some conditions are more likely than others to lead to agreement.[5]

Number of Participants with Attractive Outside Options

		Not All	All
Compatibility of Ideal War Plans	**High**	**"Same Page" Negotiations** *Expected Outcome: Agreement*	**"Pleasant Surprise" Negotiations** *Expected Outcome: Agreement*
	Low	**"Standard Bargaining" Negotiations** *Expected Outcome: Mixed*	**"Revealed Deadlock" Negotiations** *Expected Outcome: Nonagreement*

FIGURE 1.1. Negotiation Types and Expected Negotiation Outcomes

Ideal war plan compatibility is high in Same Page and Pleasant Surprise negotiations. When ideal war plan compatibility is high, no participant is asked to consider major deviations (or, perhaps, any deviation) from its ideal plan. In this sense, Same Page and Pleasant Surprise negotiations represent the world described by Downs, Rocke, and Barsoom (1996) and Mearsheimer (1994/95): states are signing agreements that require, at most, small deviations from their desired policies.[6] Both negotiation types are expected to end in agreement.

In contrast, ideal war plan compatibility is low in Revealed Deadlock and Standard Bargaining negotiations. When ideal war plan compatibility is low, the second variable, the *attractiveness of outside options*, comes into play. In Revealed Deadlock negotiations, all participants have attractive outside options, meaning they are all content to walk away and pursue their outside options. Since the participants' ideal war plans have low compatibility and none of them are willing to consider deviations from their ideal war plans, nonagreement is the likely outcome.

In Standard Bargaining negotiations, only some of the participants have an attractive outside option. The prospects for agreement in Standard Bargaining negotiations are mixed; some negotiations of this type could end in agreement, but others will end in nonagreement. This is because the attractiveness of a given participant's outside option is not perfectly observable to the other participants (since attractiveness is a matter of perception) and the parties have incentives to bluff about the attractiveness of those options (to secure a treaty closer to their ideal war plans). Consider a Standard Bargaining negotiation from the perspective of a participant that lacks an attractive outside option. On the one hand, this participant could capitulate to the ideal war plan of the other participants. On the other hand, this participant has an incentive to misrepresent the attractiveness of its outside option in order to induce concessions from the other participants. Moreover, the participant might believe that the other participants are also bluffing about the attractiveness of their outside options. In this case, the participant without an attractive outside option could refuse to capitulate to the other ideal war plans. But if the other participants do have attractive outside options, then the first participant's belief in mutual bluffing may be a recipe for nonagreement. Overall, the likelihood of agreement in Standard Bargaining negotiations is higher than in Revealed Deadlock negotiations but lower than in Same Page and Pleasant Surprise negotiations.

The remainder of this chapter unpacks the above summary of my theory. The chapter begins by detailing the three components of a war plan: strategic, operational, and tactical. This makes it possible to describe when ideal war plans are compatible. Next, I detail the variables influencing when negotiations are likely to end in agreement: *compatibility of ideal war plans* and *attractiveness of outside options*. The latter half of the chapter explains how these two variables lead to four types of alliance treaty negotiations (Same Page, Pleasant Surprise, Revealed Deadlock, and Standard Bargaining) and how this classification represents when conditions are amendable to agreement or to nonagreement. I illustrate each negotiation type with examples of alliance treaty negotiations involving the British prior to 1945. By having the British in each example, I show that, depending on the circumstances, the same country can be involved in different negotiation types.

Conceptual Foundation: War Plans

If joint war planning is a useful way to conceptualize alliance treaty negotiations, what exactly is a war plan? Within a government, a war plan is devised through discussions between the military and diplomatic staffs.[7] A war plan could be written in a single official document or be expressed in the views (some written, some unwritten) of a state's key military and diplomatic officials. Regardless of its form, a war plan has three broad components: (1) the strategic component, which identifies against whom the plan is directed and where; (2) the operational component, which specifies the general guidelines for and logistical aspects of engaging the target militarily; and (3) the tactical component, which delineates exactly how to engage the target's forces in battle. This general structure of a war plan is summarized in table 1.1. The distinction between the three levels—strategic, operational, and tactical—is described well by Clayton R. Newell (1991, 20), the former director of Joint Operations Concepts at the U.S. Army War College: "military commanders who have a tactical perspective fight, military commanders with an operational perspective define where and how to fight, and national political leaders and military commanders with their strategic perspective decide whether or not to fight."

The goal of this section is to describe the details of each component of a war plan. I will make regular use of Germany's famous 1914 war plan, traditionally referred to as the Schlieffen plan, to illustrate these components.[8] Before starting this description, a point of clarification is in order. Having a plan about how to fight a future war does not mean accurately knowing the course of that war. For example, all the major powers had detailed war plans prior to World War I (Kennedy 1979; Hamilton and Herwig 2010), but decision makers in all of those states did not foresee the war's length (over four years) and magnitude (millions of deaths). In other words, a lack of foresight about the course of an actual war is not the same as lacking a plan about how to fight if a war takes place.

The Strategic Component

The strategic component determines against whom and where to use military force.[9] It requires identifying the threat to be targeted. Threats are states that a government's decision makers perceive as likely to intentionally use physical violence to impair the well-being of its citizens.[10] Consider the Schlieffen plan. The plan's strategic component focused on Germany's geographically contiguous rivals: France and Russia. General Helmuth von Moltke (Moltke the Younger), who was the chief of the German general staff in 1914 and was responsible for the drafting of the German war plans, remarked in 1911: "The [French] Republic is our most dangerous enemy, but we can hope to achieve an early decision here."[11]

This raises a question: When do decision makers in one state deem another state a threat? Though written a few decades ago, Walt (1987) continues to provide a useful starting point for answering this question.[12] Total resources (total population, industrial capacity, and technological prowess) and geographic proximity are not irrelevant to determining the level of threat posed by a state: a small state is likely to be more concerned about invasion from a large neighbor than by a tiny distant country.[13] But beliefs about the intentions of a state's decision makers, particularly whether those decision makers harbor aggressive intentions toward its neighbors, are key to designating it a threat. Walt (1987, 25)

TABLE 1.1.   The components of a war plan

COMPONENT		BRIEF DESCRIPTION
Strategic		Identifies *where* and against *whom* to use military force. Determined by *threat perceptions*.
Operational		Specifies the general guidelines and logistical aspects of *how* to engage the target militarily.
	High-level	The guidelines for the use of force. Determined by *doctrine*: *Offensive*: take the fight to the target. *Defensive*: impede an attacker's advance.
	Low-level	The logistics of force placement and supply.
Tactical		Details the exact application of military force to destroy target forces and seize specific objectives.

writes, "Indeed, even states with rather modest capabilities may prompt others to balance if they are perceived as especially aggressive." Key to Walt's discussion of aggressive intentions is *perception*. Whether a state's decision makers actually harbor aggressive intentions is less important than how others perceive those intentions: state *A* is a threat to state *B* if key decision makers in *B* perceive *A* as having aggressive intentions. States can be perceived as threats for a host of reasons: disputed territory, a history of conflict, ideological differences, or a combination of these and other factors. What ultimately matters for my purpose is the existence of such perceptions, not the reason(s) underlying them.[14]

Consider the 1907 statements by the senior British diplomat Sir Eyre Crowe about British policy toward Germany.[15] Crowe made clear that German material power, in and of itself, did not constitute a threat to Britain. Indeed, he explicitly acknowledged that a powerful Germany could be good for both Britain and Europe: "It cannot for a moment be questioned that the mere existence and healthy activity of a powerful Germany is an undoubted blessing to the world."[16] But Crowe added an important caveat: German power is acceptable, even desirable, so long as England does not perceive Germany as disrespecting the territorial integrity and economic resources of other nations. Crowe writes, "For England particularly, intellectual and moral kinship creates a sympathy and appreciation of what is best in the German mind . . . on one condition: there must be respect for the individualities of other nations, equally valuable coadjutors, in their way, in the work of human progress, equally entitled to full elbow-room in which to contribute, in freedom, to the evolution of a higher civilization."[17]

This is not to say that intentions are always perceived correctly. Cognitive biases can influence perceptions. Jack S. Levy (2013, 308) highlights how, according to cognitive approaches to understanding decision making by leaders, perceptions of another state's intentions are "more theory driven than data driven."[18] Leaders and other key decision makers have "a general tendency to selective attention to information, to premature cognitive closure, for people to see what they expect to see based on prior belief and world views, and consequently to the perseverance of beliefs" (Levy 2013, 308). Keren Yarhi-Milo (2014, 22) echoes this assessment: "decision makers' expectations influence what information they attend to and ignore, and both preexisting beliefs and individual theories shape these expectations."

For example, in 1891 the Russian foreign minister Nicholas de Giers informed the French foreign minister Alexander Ribot that Russia was perceived by other nations as a threat because "some people imagine that we have designs upon Constantinople."[19] Giers assured Ribot that this view was mistaken. In reality, asserted Giers, "nothing would be more embarrassing for Russia" because conquering Constantinople would shift Russia's "center of gravity" away from St. Petersburg.[20] Whether Russia truly posed a threat to Turkey is moot: Russia was perceived by other European powers as having aggressive intentions and, therefore, was deemed a threat by these powers.

The Operational and Tactical Components

To understand a war plan's operational component, it is best to first describe the tactical component. In many ways, the tactical component is the opposite of the strategic component. A high-level perspective is required to assess the extent to which another country poses a threat to national interests. In contrast, the tactical component delves into the minutiae of applying military force to destroy a threat's military assets and seize specific objectives: "the situation viewed tactically might be as simple as an infantry squad leader telling his soldiers that they will be facing a similar sized enemy force dug in around a farmhouse in front of them" (Newell 1991, 39). "Success" in the tactical component "simply equates to survival on the battlefield" (Newell 1991, 18).

For example, the strategic component in nuclear war planning entails political leaders determining whether nuclear weapons should be used and against whom, while the tactical component in nuclear war planning involves selecting specific targets for individual weapons (Newell 1991, 49–50).[21] The strategic-tactical distinction is also illustrated by German war plans in 1914. As mentioned above, the strategic component of the German plans identified France as the primary threat. Applying military force against France in a war required tactics for defeating French military units on the battlefield. The most notable tactic was the envelopment maneuver designed to take German forces deep into France, via Belgium, in order to destroy the French army.[22] This required moving a large contingent of German forces along a 450-kilometer-long path in forty-two days, while a smaller portion of German forces remained in Lorraine (Herwig 2003, 153).

Between the strategic and tactical components lies the operational component of a war plan. The operational component specifies the general guidelines and logistical aspects of how to engage the threat militarily. At its core, the operational component specifies the "ends, ways, and means of applying military force ... [by linking] the national goals set by the strategic perspective with the tactical military forces which actually use force to attain the desired order" (Newell 1991, 77–79). This echoes Millett, Murray, and Watman (1986, 50): "The operational level of military activity refers to the analysis, selection, and development of institutional concepts or doctrines for employing major forces to achieve strategic objectives within a theater of war."[23]

The operational component can exhibit high-level and/or low-level planning.[24] Low-level operational planning links closely to the tactical component. It specifies exact procedures (and perhaps even numbers) for achieving tactical objectives. As such, low-level operational planning is driven by considerations of military logistics, including mobilization timetables, troop placements, and equipment supply.[25] This includes specifying how many forces will be moved into a particular theater of war and how. The Schlieffen plan epitomized detailed low-level operational planning. German planners devised precise deployment schedules, expressed by exacting train timetables.[26] As described by Barbara Tuchman (1962, 89): "From the moment the order was given, everything was to move at fixed times according to a schedule precise down to the number of train axles that would pass over a given bridge within a given time." For instance, it was specified that for seventeen days a bridge over the Rhine at Cologne would carry 2,150 trains of fifty-four cars each at ten-minute intervals (Mauer 1995, 12). German war planners also constantly tweaked the number of troops to be moved and their locations. According to Mombauer (2014, 56):

> From [1906] onward the plan was to deploy the Seventh Army (three army corps and one reserve corps) on the Rhine to defend Alsace, as well as the Sixth Army (four corps) in southern Lorraine. From 1910–1911 on, the plan no longer included committing troops of the Seventh Army elsewhere. The final deployment plan before the outbreak of war envisioned the deployment of both armies in Lorraine. In other words, a total of eight army corps were to deploy on the left wing.

While low-level operational planning links closely to a war plan's tactical component, high-level operational planning links closely to a war plan's strategic component. High-level operational planning is not consumed with the minutiae of executing military maneuvers against an opponent's forces. Nor is it focused on logistics. Instead, high-level operational planning sets out general guidelines and objectives for how military force will be used to achieve strategic aims: Is the application of military force predicated on a first or second strike? Is the objective to take the fight to the enemy's territory or to hold the line on one's own territory?

While low-level operational planning is driven by military logistics, high-level operational planning is driven by *military doctrine*. Military doctrine is the general principle (or principles) guiding a state's use of military force.[27] As expressed by Posen (1984, 13), military doctrine deals with two questions: "*What* means shall be employed? and *How* shall they be employed?"[28] Doctrine sets the general approach guiding low-level operational and tactical planning.[29] As Deborah Avant (1993, 410) writes, "doctrine falls between the technical details of tactics and the broad outline of grand strategy. Whereas tactics deal with issues about how battles are fought, doctrine encompasses the broader set of issues about how one wages war." For Newell (1991, 94), the word "guides" is key to understanding the role of doctrine: "some sort of doctrinal framework which guides all military commanders in the planning and conduct of war is essential to ensure that operations plans and orders are clearly understood at all levels of command."[30]

Just as the operational component can be divided into two categories, military doctrine can be further divided into two categories: offensive and defensive. Offensive doctrines call for taking the fight to the target. The aim of an offensive doctrine is to disarm the enemy by destroying their armed forces with an early and intense attack, typically via a first strike.[31] The idea is aptly captured by the Confederate general Nathan Bedford Forrest's quip "got there first, with the most."[32] Defensive doctrines are, relative to offensive doctrines, passive. Rather than launching a first strike and taking the fight to the enemy, defensive doctrines aim to deny or impede an attacking enemy's advance.[33] Posen (1984, 23–24) makes the distinction between offensive and defensive doctrine clear by comparing French doctrine in 1914 to French doctrine in 1939: "In 1914 the French rushed into Germany, believing that the war could be ended quickly and cheaply if she did so, and that it would be lost quickly if she did not. In 1939 the French ran for their trenches and fortifications."[34] Adherence to an offensive doctrine was evident in Germany's 1914 war plan. As explained by Moltke in a 1909 letter to Franz Conrad von Hötzendorf, the chief of the Austro-Hungarian general staff: "In order to be successful against one of the two opponents we have to restrict ourselves with the minimum amount of defence against the other. Our foremost intention must be to achieve a speedy decision."[35]

Before concluding this section, I should make clear that a state's military doctrine is not the same as its war aims, meaning the policy motivating the war.

Consider Israel during the 1956 Suez War and the 1967 Six-Day War. In the Suez War, Israel, along with France and Britain, took the initiative to attack Egypt in order to acquire control of the Suez Canal Zone and shift the region's territorial status quo (Sarkees and Wayman 2010, 150).[36] In contrast, in the Six-Day War Israel launched a preemptive strike in response to mobilizations by Egypt and Jordan and Israeli perception that an attack was imminent (Sarkees and Wayman 2010, 158).[37] Israel's military followed an offensive doctrine in both wars,[38] but the motivation for using force was different in the two cases: one was to alter the status quo; the other was to preserve it. Thus, states with different goals regarding the regional status quo can have their military actions guided by the same military doctrine.

The Explanatory Variables

Given the composition of war plans, how can we know if a group of states will reach agreement on a joint war plan and, therefore, sign an alliance treaty? We must first know if one participant will demand that another deviate from its ideal war plan. This requires knowing the compatibility of the participants' ideal war plans. If the participants find that their ideal war plans have high compatibility, no participant will be asked to make meaningful changes to its plan. Agreement is the likely outcome of the negotiation. If the participants' ideal war plans have low compatibility, some parties would have to make concessions in order to reach agreement. But a participant will make concessions only if its outside options are unattractive. Outside options are policies that negotiation participants will pursue if the negotiation ends in nonagreement. An outside option is unattractive to a participant if the policy is unlikely to achieve that participant's policy goals. Such a participant will be more willing to make concessions for the sake of concluding an alliance.[39]

Ideal war plan compatibility and outside option attractiveness set the conditions for a negotiation to end in agreement. But each concept has elements that must be unpacked to fully understand how they influence negotiation outcomes. Therefore, the remainder of this section describes each concept, starting with compatibility of ideal war plans.

Compatibility of Ideal War Plans

Each participant enters the alliance treaty negotiation with war plan preferences. Specifically, each participant enters with an ideal war plan. Given the above description of war plans, a participant's ideal war plan reflects its threat perceptions and military doctrine. This plan is considered ideal because it is the plan that a participant deems best suited for achieving security. Each participant also wishes to avoid the adjustment costs associated with having to carry out an alternative war plan.[40] States develop their war plans based on threat assessments, presently available physical resources (e.g., available active duty forces and trained reservists), technology (e.g., the type of battleships used by the state's navy), and military knowledge (e.g., intelligence and conceptions of best practices in military training). Many of these factors are fixed in the short term: it takes time to substantially increase the number of personnel in uniform, adequately train reservists to fight, increase the number of rail lines that can move troops, or alter training practices.[41]

To understand how participants having ideal war plans influences the outcome of negotiations, we must consider public knowledge about each participant's ideal war plans. Stated as a question: What does each participant know about the other participants' ideal war plans? The answer depends on time: knowledge is different before negotiations than once the negotiations begin.

Prior to entering an alliance treaty negotiation, a participant will not perfectly know another participant's ideal war plan. Decision makers in state J will likely have beliefs, perhaps even well-informed beliefs, about state I's ideal war plan. But they will not fully and accurately know state I's ideal war plan.[42] This seems obvious about the strategic component of an ideal war plan, as it is determined by threat perceptions in the heads of a state's key decision makers. Yet the operational component of an ideal war plan is also private information. For instance, an outsider is not privy to the internal planning sessions that determine the state's military doctrine. While an outsider can gain some insight into a state's internal military plans by observing its military exercises or wars,[43] cognitive bias can cloud assessments, or misapplied heuristics can lead to systematic errors in interpreting information.[44] For example, upon observing the speed with which German forces executed maneuvers during military exercises in the 1930s, French military planners thought it impossible for Germany to execute such rapid maneuvers during actual war. As remarked by Mark Bloch, the French historian and captain in the French army during the 1940 Battle of France, "faced by the undisputed evidence of Germany's new tactics, we ignored, or wholly failed to understand, the quickened rhythm of the times" (Bloch 1968 [1946], 37).

Once a participant enters the negotiations, however, it has an incentive to reveal its ideal war plan to the other participants. After all, state J is unlikely to adopt state I's ideal plan without knowing what it is. A participant could reveal its ideal plan at the very beginning of negotiations or could unveil portions of its ideal plan over the course of a negotiation. The exact timing of when a participant fully reveals its ideal plan is not important, only that it does reveal its ideal plan during negotiations. To be clear, while a participant has an incentive to inform the other participants of its ideal war plan, the participant will conceal its willingness to deviate from that plan. A participant might be open to accepting a joint war plan that in no way reflects its ideal war plan. However, all things being equal, the participant would prefer that the other participants adopt its ideal war plan. Since a participant's willingness to deviate from its ideal war plan is intimately tied to the attractiveness of outside options, it will be further discussed below.

Once the participants reveal their ideal war plans, they must determine the compatibility of those plans. "Compatibility" refers to the extent that the plans are not difficult to rectify. For example, during the meetings between British and French military officials in the spring of 1939, General Henry Pownall, the chief of staff of the British Expeditionary Force, noted the remarkable overlap in the British and French ideal war plans: "It's very interesting to note how French Staff officers in discussing these problems of strategy, tactics, and staff duties talk and think on exactly the same lines as we do. There is an 'Esperanto' between us in these sort of things."[45] This was echoed by General John Slessor, one of Britain's three principal representatives at the Anglo-French military staff talks: "we found no difficulty in agreeing on the outline of the strategy to be followed."[46] Specifically, both parties wanted to adopt a defensive approach to engaging Germany militarily.

Though war plans can vary along a host of dimensions, it is useful to conceptualize ideal war plan compatibility as binary: the plans either have high compatibility, meaning they are not difficult to rectify, or low compatibility, meaning they would be difficult to rectify. This focuses on an essential idea: there are negotiations where each participant has largely (perhaps even exactly) the same view regarding the threat(s) and manner of approaching the threat(s).[47] Determining when the participants have the same view about the threats and the best way of approaching them requires evaluating the strategic and operational compatibility of their ideal war plans.

Strategic compatibility pertains to the participants' views about the target of military force. Strategic compatibility is the central issue in alliance treaty negotiations: if the parties have diametrically opposed views about the target of military force, there is virtually no basis for agreement. Strategic compatibility is high when the participants have similar views regarding against whom and where to use military force. A shared threat is an important determinant of strategic compatibility. But high strategic compatibility requires more than a shared threat. Strategic compatibility also depends on the differences in the threat perceptions of the participants. While the participants may have a shared threat, they can have different perceptions regarding other threats. They might agree about targeting the shared threat, but disagree about whether the alliance should address other threats. Such differences could drive a wedge between the negotiation participants. Moreover, even if the participants perceive the same state(s) as the alliance's target, they may have different views about the geographic area in which a target's actions can trigger a military response. For instance, one participant might want the alliance to oppose the target's actions in Europe, while another wants the alliance's scope limited to Asia. Such differences in threat perceptions could be difficult to rectify, creating conditions for nonagreement.

To make strategic compatibility concrete, consider the negotiations culminating in the 1892 Franco-Russian alliance treaty. The French and Russians agreed that Germany was a threat but disagreed about Austria.[48] Russia perceived both Austria and Germany as threats, with Austria more likely to initiate hostilities.[49] As the Russian war minister Pyotr Vannovski remarked to Raoul Boisdeffre, the chief of the French general staff, "Our absolute conviction is that we will be attacked first by Austria helped by Italy and possibly Romania. Germany will stand ready to intervene at the moment chosen by her, but she will never attack first."[50] Boisdeffre opposed this "Austria first" formula. France did not want to become involved in a war between Russia and Austria when France's primary threat was Germany.[51] Debate over this issue consumed the negotiations (though agreement was reached).

Operational compatibility pertains to the high-level operational component of war plans. Recall that a war plan's high-level operational component is determined by the state's military doctrine, which can be either offensive or defensive. This means operational compatibility is high when the participants have similar general principles guiding how military force will be used to achieve strategic aims. More precisely, operational compatibility has three characteristics: (1) noncontradictory military doctrines, (2) irrelevance of logistical and tactical details, and (3) nonnecessity of symmetrical tactical actions.

First, operational compatibility is high when the participants do not have contradictory military doctrines. There are two scenarios under which participants will not have contradictory military doctrines. In one scenario, all participants have the same doctrine, such as all having offensive doctrines. In a second scenario, some of the participants follow a particular doctrine (say, an offensive doctrine), while the other participants, perhaps due to being newly independent states, have not yet devised a military doctrine. In contrast to these two scenarios, the compatibility of military doctrines is low if the participants have a mix of military doctrines. For instance, one participant could have a defensive doctrine while the other has an offensive doctrine. Under such circumstances, engaging in joint military operations will be extremely difficult at best and, at worst, contrary to the goal of countering a threat. Bensahel (2007, 197) writes of how "differing command styles, doctrine, and training," all of which are high-level components of war planning, "would make it very difficult for personnel from two such militaries to operate as effectively together as each one would on its own."

Second, differences in low-level operational components of war plans are not considered when evaluating operational compatibility. This is not to say that the low-level operational and tactical components of war plans are unimportant. A joint war plan's logistical and tactical details will need to be addressed at some point by the alliance members. But final agreement on such details is more likely when the parties already agree on underlying principles guiding the application of force (i.e., they have similar doctrines). Though discussions over logistical and tactical details could delay finalizing text of the alliance treaty, sorting out such details should not pose a danger to the alliance treaty negotiation ending in agreement. Discussions over these details can be (and have been) relegated to subsequent talks between lower-level officials. For example, in the case of the North Atlantic Treaty negotiations, logistical and tactical details were delegated to an international organization to be created later (see chapter 5).

Third, and directly related to the second characteristic, high operational compatibility does not require that each participant's ideal war plan specify symmetric tactical actions. For instance, the low-level operational and tactical components of state I's ideal war plan might call for state J to conduct all the ground fighting on the territory of a threat. While this places a large burden on state J, that might also be state J's ideal plan: state J might want to do all of the ground fighting.[52] What matters is that the participants do not have contradictory views on the general principles underlying the application of military force: in this case, both participants view taking the fight to the territory of the target as ideal.

As with strategic compatibility, operational compatibility can be illustrated using the 1892 Franco-Russian alliance treaty negotiations. It is clear from the negotiations that both parties adhered to offensive doctrines and that this facilitated agreement. In an August 1892 meeting, Boisdeffre told Russia's Tsar Alexander, "Mobilization was the declaration of war; that it compelled one's neighbor to do the same; that mobilization entailed the implementation of strategic transport and concentration."[53] Boisdeffre then remarked that "to leave a million men mobilized along one's border without simultaneously doing otherwise . . . [would be like a man who] left a gun in his pocket and allowed his neighbor to put a gun to his forehead."[54] Alexander replied, "That's how I understand it." In other words, Boisdeffre and Alexander agreed that mobilization meant war, and, hence, quick mobilization followed by offensive action was essential for the Franco-Russian alliance to be militarily effective.[55]

Attractiveness of Outside Options

The compatibility of ideal war plans goes a long way toward detailing the conditions conducive to agreement in alliance treaty negotiations. But it is not the whole story. While low compatibility in ideal war plans increases the difficulty of reaching agreement, agreement is still possible. But this possibility depends on outside options, meaning alternative policies a participant will pursue if the negotiation ends in nonagreement.[56]

There are a wide variety of policies that can constitute an outside option. Indeed, a given state might have a different outside option from negotiation to negotiation. But the outside options available to participants in alliance treaty negotiations generally fall into one of three broad categories: (1) unilateral action, (2) buck-passing, or (3) an alternative alliance treaty.[57]

First, states could take unilateral action. In this case, a state does not need allies in order to act against a threat. This outside option can embolden a diplomat to assert to the other negotiation participants, "We would love for you to participate in an attack on the target, but we are fully prepared and capable of taking action on our own." I will describe below how the French, during their 1848 negotiations with Britain, were prepared to take unilateral military action against Austria. French officials valued British assistance, but the absence of British assistance was not going to prevent French action.

Second, states could pass the buck. In this case, a state is not desperate to take action against the threat. It is unconcerned with the immediate consequences of the threat committing aggression, at least compared to the cost of taking action against the threat. Unless the state can act under the terms that it deems ideal, it is more than willing to sit back and allow others to take the initiative in countering the threat. As Thomas Christensen and Jack Snyder (1991, 141) explain, the free-riding state wants to avoid the costs of action or expects its "relative position to be strengthened by standing aloof from the mutual bloodletting of the other powers."[58] In other words, buck-passing is acquiring security "on the cheap" (Mearsheimer 2001, 160). There were times when the British were reluctant to make concessions because they viewed the English Channel as according Britain "splendid isolation," meaning they believed Britain could stay above the fray unfolding on the European continent.[59]

Third, states could pursue an alliance treaty with a nonparticipant.[60] Similar to unilateral action, the participant is prepared to take action without the help of the negotiation participants. Unlike unilateral action, the state still needs allies, but the allies can be found elsewhere. This outside option creates the possibility that a state could enter simultaneous negotiations in order to use one negotiation as leverage to induce concessions in the other. At the extreme, one of the negotiations might be "insincere," meaning state I never intended to agree with state J but only wanted to use the negotiation to reach an agreement with state K.[61] But one negotiation being used purely and solely as leverage in another is probably rare. It is always possible for state J to reach agreement with state I if state J is willing to offer a sufficiently attractive alliance—perhaps by offering a host of autonomy-enhancing concessions (Morrow 1991; Poast 2012). Moreover, initiating and engaging in alliance treaty negotiations is not without cost. There are opportunity costs, which arise from spending time negotiating with one country (or set of countries) rather than another potential ally or allocating those resources to any of a host of other diplomatic activities. There are also revelation costs, which arise because negotiating an alliance can entail revealing militarily sensitive information, such as procurement schedules, troop levels, and mobilization capacity. States are not casual about providing such information.[62] Even if the proposal is rejected straightaway, the proposer could fear giving the impression that it is unable, with its present capabilities, to counter the identified threat.[63]

Each negotiation participant has at least one outside option, and some states might have two or more. In the latter case, a state may not consider all its outside options to be equal with respect to its security goals. One of the options could stand out as a participant's "best available" outside option. Of course, having an outside option says nothing about whether the participant finds the outside option to be a suitable alternative to an alliance treaty. This is where the concept of attractiveness comes into play.

The attractiveness of an outside option pertains to how a state's decision makers perceive, relative to their ideal war plan, an outside option's ability to achieve the state's security goals.[64] Do the state's diplomatic and military officials perceive the two policies—the ideal war plan and the best available outside option—as roughly equivalent in their ability to enhance the state's security?[65] If so, that participant will consider its outside option attractive.[66] A participant with an attractive outside option has little willingness to accept a jointly negotiated war plan that deviates greatly from its ideal war plan. Stated differently, having an attractive outside option means a participant's minimally acceptable war plan will be very similar to its ideal plan. Alternatively, do the state's diplomatic and military officials perceive their ideal war plan as far superior to the best available outside option? If so, the outside option is considered unattractive. A participant with an unattractive outside option has an incentive to accept a wide range of jointly negotiated war plans, even ones that deviate greatly from its ideal. Stated differently, having an unattractive outside option means a participant's minimally acceptable war plan can be substantially different from its ideal war plan.

Attractiveness is subjective. This necessarily means that the attractiveness of a participant's outside option is private information to that participant: a participant cannot know exactly how its counterparts perceive their own outside options.[67] Since the attractiveness of an outside option determines the extent to which a state is willing to deviate from its ideal war plan, this means that a party's willingness to deviate from its ideal war plan is also private information. This point is critical to the potential success of a negotiation, because attractiveness as private information can lead a party with an unattractive outside option to nevertheless not make concessions. This is for two reasons: (1) the incentive to misrepresent the attractiveness of an outside option and (2) that this incentive to misrepresent is common knowledge.

First, a party has an incentive to misrepresent the attractiveness of its outside option. Each participant has an incentive to make the other participants believe it holds an attractive outside option in order to induce them to make concessions.[68] For each participant, obtaining the best possible deal means having the final joint war plan be as close as possible to its own ideal war plan. Achieving this objective can be facilitated by the participant not fully divulging the extent to which it is willing to deviate from its ideal plan. If a participant reveals that its outside option is unattractive, its counterparts know that the participant will accept large deviations from its ideal plan. This is a well-recognized feature of international bargaining in general (Fearon 1995, 395). Military alliance negotiations are no exception.[69]

Second, each participant knows that its counterparts have an incentive to misrepresent the attractiveness of their outside options. Everyone knows that everyone else can benefit from claiming to have a highly attractive outside option (even when they do not). Consequently, negotiators are unlikely to believe such verbal statements as "You do realize that I have an attractive outside option and, therefore, am more than willing to leave without a signed treaty?"[70] A participant with an unattractive outside option might therefore mistakenly think that its counterpart also has an unattractive outside option and, therefore, hold out for the counterpart to concede.[71] Nonagreement could ensue. This is why Johannes Urpelainen (2012, 134) writes that when states have incentives to exploit private information to improve the terms of an agreement, "the resulting bargaining may restrain the scope of admissible solutions or even produce a cooperation failure."

All of this suggests that the number of participants with an attractive outside option can be key to whether a negotiation ends in agreement. In general, either all participants perceive themselves as having an attractive outside option, or not all participants do. When all participants in a negotiation perceive themselves as having an attractive outside option, none of them are likely to consider deviating from their ideal plan. Instead, they are all willing to say, "I either receive my ideal war plan, or I walk!" This is a recipe for nonagreement. When not all participants have attractive outside options, the negotiation dynamics become complicated. On the one hand, a party with an unattractive outside option may make concessions in order to ensure agreement. On the other hand, a party lacking an attractive outside option might still refrain from making concessions.[72]

Alliance Treaty Negotiation Types and Expected Outcomes

The two variables discussed above, *compatibility of ideal war plans* and *attractiveness of outside options*, can identify the conditions in which negotiations are likely to end in agreement. Recall figure 1.1. The rows of figure 1.1 capture ideal war plan compatibility, which is either high (top row) or low (bottom row). As discussed above, dichotomizing ideal war plan compatibility is useful for focusing on the idea that there are negotiations where each participant has approximately the same view of the threat(s) and how to approach them. The columns of figure 1.1 report whether all participants have an attractive outside option (the right-hand column) or not all participants do (the left-hand column). Building on the above discussion of how attractive outside options influence a negotiation, one can think of the columns as splitting negotiations into those with zero probability of concessions (i.e., negotiations where all participants have attractive outside options) and those with a positive probability of concessions (i.e., negotiations where not all participants have attractive outside options). As with the compatibility of ideal war plans, the number of participants with attractive outside options technically has more than two values. For example, in a negotiation between two participants, there could be zero, one, or two participants with attractive outside options. But there is a possibility that concessions will be made for two of the values (no participant or one participant has an attractive outside option), while no concessions are to be expected for the third value (two participants have an attractive outside option).

These two variables interact to produce four types of alliance treaty negotiations, as captured in the four cells of figure 1.1. I refer to these negotiation types as Same Page negotiations, Pleasant Surprise negotiations, Standard Bargaining negotiations, and Revealed Deadlock negotiations. Each negotiation type has conditions that make either agreement or nonagreement the expected outcome. I expect both Same Page and Pleasant Surprise negotiations to end in agreement. The participants in these types of negotiations have no reason not to agree: they have very similar views about the parameters of a war plan. In contrast, I expect Revealed Deadlock negotiations to be rife with nonagreement: the participants have highly dissimilar views about the parameters of a war plan and have little

Number of Participants with Attractive Outside Options

		Not All	**All**
Compatibility of Ideal War Plans	**High**	"Same Page" Negotiations E.g.: 1941 Anglo-American	"Pleasant Surprise" Negotiations E.g.: 1826 Anglo-Russian
	Low	"Standard Bargaining" Negotiations Capitulation E.g.: 1878 Anglo-Turkish Compromise E.g.: 1887 Anglo-Italian Collapse E.g.: 1939 Anglo/French-Soviet	"Revealed Deadlock" Negotiations E.g.: 1848 Anglo-French

FIGURE 1.2.   Examples of Each Alliance Treaty Negotiation Type

incentive to change their views. Standard Bargaining negotiations produces a mix of outcomes, which I label *capitulation* (i.e., one party holds firm to its ideal plan and the other party or parties concede by deviating from their ideal plans), *compromise* (i.e., all parties make concessions by deviating from their ideal plans), and *collapse* (i.e., one or more parties walk away). This mixture of outcomes is due to the participants having private information about the attractiveness of their outside options (along with the known incentive to misrepresent the attractiveness of those option).

I will now offer more complete descriptions of each type of alliance treaty negotiation and will illustrate each type with historical examples. These examples are summarized in figure 1.2. They all involve the British and are from before 1945. This is useful, as it shows how the same country can be involved in different negotiation types.

Same Page Negotiations

Same Page negotiations have two key features: not all participants have attractive outside options, and the participants have highly compatible ideal plans. The former is largely irrelevant since the participants are essentially already on the same page with respect to a war plan. Given that the parties have highly compatible ideal war plans, agreement should be reached easily. There might be some discussions over secondary issues, but the joint war plan's overall blueprint should fall into place with little difficulty.

A prime example of a Same Page negotiation is the Anglo-American negotiation that produced signed treaties in mid-1941 and early 1942. Of critical importance are the meetings of January through March 1941. The resulting document, titled simply "ABC-1,"[73] provided the basis for the Anglo-American Atlantic Charter signed in August and then the January 1, 1942, Declaration of the United Nations.[74] Indeed, when British and American officials gathered in Washington after the attack on Pearl Harbor, the eventual plans were explicit modifications of the ABC report.[75]

Entering the negotiation, neither party saw itself as having a very attractive outside option. The United States was not yet positioned to enter the war, as it lacked both the material and the domestic political support for fighting a war. But a German defeat of Britain would be strategically cataclysmic. Days before the meeting, a joint U.S. Army-Navy planning report concluded, "Great Britain cannot encompass the defeat of Germany unless the United States provides that nation with direct military assistance, plus a far greater degree of material aid than is being given now; and that, even then, success against the Axis is not assured."[76] Britain was losing between 4 and 5 million ship tons a year, against a British shipbuilding rate of only 1.5 million ship tons (Watson 1950, 368). The British were well aware of their precarious state. They continually requested arms and aid from the United States,[77] and as Churchill famously remarked in June 1940 to Hasting Ismay, the secretary of the Committee of Imperial Defence, "You and I will be dead in three months' time."[78] Britain was still alive in November 1940. The RAF had defeated the German Luftwaffe in the Battle of Britain and the English Channel proved an effective deterrent to a land invasion. But the aforementioned shipping loses posed an existential threat. British splendid isolation was contingent on control of the seas, which it lacked. As Churchill wrote to Roosevelt in December 1940,

> The danger of Great Britain being destroyed by a swift, overwhelming blow, has for the time being very greatly receded. In its place, there is a long, gradually maturing danger, less sudden and less spectacular, but equally deadly. This mortal danger is the steady and increasing diminution of sea tonnage. . . . It is therefore in shipping and the power to transport across the oceans, particularly the Atlantic Ocean, that in 1941 the crunch of the whole war will be found.[79]

When British and American officials began formal talks on January 29, 1941,[80] the parties found their initial ideal war plans to be highly compatible.[81] The two core propositions of the British plan were (1) the European theater is the vital theater where a decision must first be sought, and (2) the general policy should therefore be to defeat Germany and Italy first, and then deal with Japan.[82] To accomplish these aims, the British proposed that the U.S. naval forces should first make necessary provisions for defending the Western Hemisphere and only then make their main effort "the Atlantic and European theaters."[83] This corresponded well with the initial U.S. war plans. The U.S. plans stated that "if the U.S. Government decides to make war in common with the British Commonwealth," then its broad military objectives should be:

1. The defeat of Germany and her allies.
2. Maintaining dispositions which under all eventualities will prevent the extensions in the Western Hemisphere of European or Asiatic political and military power.
3. Exerting its principal military effort in the Atlantic or navally in the Mediterranean regions.
4. Keeping Japan from entering the war or attacking the Dutch.
5. If Japan enters the war, conducting operations in the mid-Pacific and the Far East in such a manner as to facilitate the exertion of its principal military effort in the Atlantic or navally in the Mediterranean.[84]

In short, the Americans and British agreed on the need for the United States to secure the Western Hemisphere, to then focus on defeating Germany, and only then to turn to defeating Japan (if Japan entered the war). Based on this commonality in their views about the Atlantic theater, by March 5 the talks produced a two-part proposal for the initial steps in a joint war effort:

1. The primary role of the land forces of the Associated Powers will be to hold the British Isles against invasion; to defend the western hemisphere, and to protect naval bases and islands of strategic importance against land, air, or sea-borne attack. Forces will be built up for an eventual offensive in a manner to be agreed upon at a later date.
2. The primary objective of the air forces, subject to the requirements of the security of the United States and an unimpaired pursuit cover in the British Isles, will be to reduce as quickly as possible the disparity between the Associated and enemy air strength particularly with respect to long-range striking forces operating from and against the British Isles.[85]

The talks concluded on March 29, 1940, with the production of the ABC report.[86] The report is an impressive document: sixty-seven pages covering the interests of both parties, the threats against which the actions are targeted, a general description of the actions to be taken by either party, and the establishment of military missions "to ensure the coordination of administrative action and command."[87]

Pleasant Surprise Negotiations

As with Same Page negotiations, the participants in Pleasant Surprise negotiations have highly compatible ideal war plans. The difference is that all participants also have attractive outside options, which implies that none of them are desperate to form an alliance. This negotiation type is labeled Pleasant Surprise because each participant enters the negotiation strongly opposed to considering plans that deviate from its ideal war plan and is then pleased to find such deviations unnecessary (since the participants have highly compatible ideal war plans). Agreement is the likely outcome.

Negotiations of this type are illustrated well by the 1826 Anglo-Russian talks leading to the St. Petersburg Protocol.[88] Both parties entered the negotiation with attractive outside options. Since 1825, the British minister of foreign affairs, George Canning, was willing to mediate the ongoing dispute between the Ottoman Porte and Greek revolutionaries on his own.[89] Russia was interested in an alliance with England to target the Ottoman Empire but not desperate. In a message to Canning and other members of the British cabinet,[90] Tsar Alexander I confided, "We cannot make the least advances to England . . . but we can make the Cabinet of England understand that, if it takes a step, it will not be repulsed, that we shall always be ready to welcome ideas."[91] Alexander died shortly after the message was delivered.[92] His successor, Nicholas I, favored an aggressive policy toward the Ottoman Empire, even to the extent of unilaterally waging war (Schroder 1994, 645–46).

The major components of the two states' war plans were highly compatible. Both participants viewed the target as the Ottomans and the triggering event as a failure to resolve the Greek revolt. Additionally, both wanted to first pursue a peaceful solution and only then use limited offensive force. British plans are found in the January 1826 instructions from Canning to the Duke of Wellington (Temperley 1925, 352).[93] Wellington was to make clear that while Britain could not prevent Russia from unilaterally going to war with Turkey, it would not tolerate the destruction of Turkey.[94] Canning then outlined the conditions under which the British would find force acceptable, namely, that the war must focus only on the Greek issue since a war "by Russia against the Porte on any other account than that of the Greeks . . . [would result in] wide and disastrous consequences."[95] Russian plans are conveyed in a February 1826 memorandum by the Russian foreign minister, Count Karl Nesselrode, to Tsar Nicholas. The memorandum called for

Russia to consider unilateral action so long as the aims were limited and the destruction of the Ottoman Empire was not pursued (Jelavich 2004, 79). Additionally, the memorandum called on Tsar Nicholas to provide "irrefutable proof of his pacific intention" by giving the Ottomans one last opportunity to meet Russia's terms.[96] One of Russia's terms was "to assure Greece of a prosperous existence and a perfect commercial liberty."[97]

High compatibility in the ideal war plans enabled quick agreement on the protocol. Wellington describes how agreement was reached in an April 4, 1826, communication to Canning.[98] Following verbal assurances from Nicholas to Wellington, Wellington requested the assurances in writing.[99] Nesselrode gave Wellington a draft protocol on March 25, with Wellington offering revisions the following day.[100] Over the next several days the parties debated the content and wording of the document.[101] They signed the document on April 4. It called for full Greek autonomy (Article 1) and for Britain and Russia to intervene "in concert or separately" if the Porte rejected an offer of mediation (Article 3).[102]

Revealed Deadlock Negotiations

Like Pleasant Surprise negotiations, all participants in Revealed Deadlock negotiations have attractive outside options. But in contrast to Same Page and Pleasant Surprise negotiations, Revealed Deadlock negotiations are characterized by low compatibility in the participants' ideal war plans. Agreement would require compromises, but all participants enter the negotiations strongly opposed to deviating from their ideal war plans. This combination—the participants having profound differences about key elements of a joint war plan and having attractive outside options—is a recipe for nonagreement.

The Anglo-French negotiation of August 1848 offers a straightforward example of Revealed Deadlock. An armistice between Sardinia and Austria had stipulated that Venice be returned to Austrian rule. Venice instead declared its independence and then appealed to the French for assistance against Austrian aggression. In August 1848, Gustave de Beaumont, the French minister to London, initiated negotiations with British foreign minister Lord Palmerston about an alliance aimed at using armed intervention to secure Venetian independence.

There was little overlap in the two ideal war plans. The French offered a detailed plan for offensive action. The plan called for (1) occupation of Venice by either an Anglo-French garrison or a French garrison and an English naval division, (2) the French army of the Alps to be placed on the frontier, and (3) a joint declaration by England and France calling for Austria to accept mediation.[103] Britain saw no need to devise offensive military arrangements. The British wanted nothing more than to continue pursuing an offer (with France) of mediation. As

Palmerston remarked to Beaumont, "I feel confident that means will be found of settling these Italian affairs without recourse to arms."[104] Palmerston did inform Beaumont that the English position might well change if war erupted: "while England refused to act when the time did not seem to her to have come it would be wrong to conclude that she would not act if the time did come."[105]

Both parties had attractive outside options. The English Channel and the Royal Navy gave the British cabinet (and, by extension, Parliament) the luxury of buck-passing.[106] French officials viewed unilateral action as a viable alternative to an agreement with England. France preferred cooperation but was prepared to go it alone. The French minister of foreign affairs, Jules Bastide, wrote to Beaumont, "Insist with all your power on the English Government's adopting this resolution; if unfortunately, it does not, it would only mean for us to ask the National Assembly to authorise us to recall our Minister from Vienna and to march our army into Lombardy."[107] Beaumont made this point clear to Palmerston: "France wants peace, but she is resolved to intervene in Italy if the terms of mediation offered by England and France are refused by Austria . . . France will never consent to abandon the Italian cause."[108] This led Palmerston to inform British prime minister John Russell, "France now says that [if mediation is declined] she must send a garrison to hold Venice, that she will do it without us if we prefer, but that she prefers doing it with our concurrence. . . . If we believe she will go on, and that is my belief, we must say something about it."[109] But since French officials felt that an agreement with England was not necessary for intervention, they were willing to allow the negotiations to end without an agreement.[110]

Standard Bargaining Negotiations

Of the four negotiation types, Standard Bargaining negotiations are perhaps the most interesting. Unlike Pleasant Surprise and Same Page negotiations, participants in Standard Bargaining negotiations have low compatibility in their ideal war plans. But unlike Revealed Deadlock negotiations, they do not all have attractive outside options. This means that agreement is still possible but not as likely as in Same Page and Pleasant Surprise negotiations.

More precisely, I expect Standard Bargaining negotiations to end in one of three ways: capitulation, compromise, or collapse. Capitulation occurs when one party accepts the ideal war plan of the other. In this outcome, the alliance treaty fully reflects the ideal war plan of one party (e.g., in a bilateral negotiation, participant A agrees to fully adopt participant B's ideal plan). Compromise takes place when both participants choose to concede. In this outcome, the agreed-upon joint war plan is a mixture of the two plans (e.g., in a bilateral negotiation, the agreed-upon plan might use the strategic component of participant A's ideal plan and the operational component of B's).[111] Collapse is when a participant chooses to walk away, thereby ending the negotiation in nonagreement.

My theoretical framework is too sparse to predict which outcome—capitulation, compromise, or collapse—will result from a particular Standard Bargaining negotiation. But my theory does point to how private information about the attractiveness of outside options, coupled with an incentive to misrepresent their attractiveness, makes it possible for negotiations to end in nonagreement. One could add features to my theory that enabled a participant to credibly reveal the existence of an attractive outside option.[112] For instance, if unilateral action is a participant's attractive outside option, that participant could begin mobilizing its forces in order to attack the target.[113] If a participant can credibly show the attractiveness of its outside option, its counterparts might immediately concede or might compensate the participant using a side payment or issue linkage (e.g., offering to sign a trade deal if the reluctant party signs the alliance treaty).[114] While such features could improve the prospects for Standard Bargaining negotiations to end in agreement, adding them to my theory will not alter my main point regarding such negotiations: even when participants lack attractive outside options, low ideal war plan compatibility increases the difficulty of reaching agreement.

To make this discussion concrete, I will provide an example of each Standard Bargaining negotiation outcome. I will use the 1878 Anglo-Turkish negotiations to illustrate capitulation, the 1887 Anglo-Italian negotiations to illustrate compromise, and the 1939 Anglo-French-Soviet negotiations to illustrate collapse.

The 1878 Anglo-Turkish negotiations exemplify capitulation. Incompatibilities arose over the operational elements of the respective plans. British officials thought that maintaining a military and naval presence on Ottoman territory would prevent further Russian incursions into the Ottoman Empire. They identified Cyprus as a suitable location for a British base.[115] British foreign minister Salisbury authorized Sir Henry Layard, the British ambassador to the Ottoman Empire, to negotiate an alliance with Turkey in which a core provision would grant Cyprus to Britain: "We shall instruct you to offer a formal engagement on our part to defend her territory in Asia from any further encroachment by Russia. . . . But the Porte should concede to us the occupation of Cyprus."[116] Rather than requesting British troops on Ottoman territory as a defensive deterrent, Ottoman negotiators wanted a British promise of direct assistance in case Russia attempted to occupy Constantinople and British financial assistance with constructing fortifications around Constantinople.[117] The sultan "was in the greatest lack of money" and desired a £4,000,000 loan from Britain.[118] Britain refused the loan and instead made its demand for Cyprus.[119] According to Salisbury's instructions to Layard, the sultan was to be given forty-eight hours to agree to Britain's terms, or "it will not be in the power of England to pursue negotiations any further, the capture of Constantinople [by Russia] and the partition of the Empire will be the immediate result."[120] Ottoman officials, lacking attractive alternatives to an alliance with Britain, quickly accepted Britain's terms.[121]

The February 1887 Anglo-Italian negotiations exemplify compromise.[122] Incompatibilities arose over the strategic component of the participants' plans. According to the draft treaty the Italian ambassador in London, Count Corti Lodovico, handed to Salisbury, Italy wanted the parties to support one another "in every war against France in the Mediterranean."[123] Salisbury had grave reservations about explicitly mentioning France and implying direct material assistance from Britain,[124] but neither party had an attractive outside option. For Italy, the historian Jan Buben observes that its two Triple Alliance partners, Germany and Austria-Hungary, lacked the naval prowess to offer support in the Mediterranean against France or Russia: "To be honest, Italy had no other choice [but an agreement with London]" (Buben 1999, 133).[125] As for Britain, Salisbury, who had just been reappointed foreign minister in January 1887, saw the option of "splendid isolation" as fiction: the acquisition of Egypt in 1882 meant a key piece of British territory—the canal zone in Suez—was not "isolated."[126] Maintaining free passage through the eastern Mediterranean required checking possible French and Russia influence (Goodlad 2000, 56–60).

After negotiating for a little more than ten days, Britain and Italy reached a compromise agreement.[127] Explicit mention of France and the phrase "in every war" were stricken from the written document.[128] This satisfied Britain. But the treaty also outlined concrete principles of cooperation in response to instability in the Mediterranean.[129] This satisfied Italy.

The 1939 Anglo-French-Soviet negotiation is a famous example of collapse. The major ideal war plan incompatibility pertained to whether Russia's response to German aggression should be offensive or defensive. Complicating the matter was the lack of a common border between the Soviet Union and Germany: Poland and Romania separated the two powers. The Anglo-French plan called for Russia to adopt a defensive approach: provide indirect assistance to Romania in the event of German aggression and direct military assistance only if German troops invaded Poland (and, even then, only with Polish consent) (Manne 1974, 10).[130] The Soviets wanted an offensive approach: they wanted to engage Germany on German soil. This required Britain and France to consent to the passage of Soviet troops through Poland (even if Poland itself did not consent).[131] This was problematic for Britain and France. Polish officials had made clear for months that they would oppose any policy that facilitated Soviet territorial access.[132]

The British and French thought the Soviets might concede on their requirement of explicit pass-through rights as necessary for agreement. But the Soviets
perceived themselves as having two attractive outside options. First, they could
sign a treaty with Germany itself, as Germany had approached the Soviets before
the beginning of the August British-French-Soviet talks. Second, the Soviet
Union, unlike France, had a buffer state between Germany and the Russian
homeland: Poland.[133] These attractive outside options made it easier for the
Soviets to end the negotiations in nonagreement rather than concede. By the
August 21 meeting between the delegates, the Soviets had made the decision to
walk away. They planned to hold a few more minutes of discussion and then
adjourn without scheduling further talks. To this end, Voroshilov opened the final
meeting by chastising the British and French delegations for wasting his time:

> The Soviet Military Mission considers that the U.S.S.R., not having a
> common frontier with Germany, can give help to France, Britain, Po-
> land, and Roumania only on condition that her troops are given rights
> of passage across Polish and Roumanian territory. . . . The Soviet Mili-
> tary Delegation cannot picture to itself how the Governments and Gen-
> eral Staffs of Britain and France, in sending their missions to the U.S.S.R.
> for discussions to arrange a military convention, could not have given
> them some directives on such elementary matters as the passage and ac-
> tion of Soviet armed forces against the troops of the aggressor, on the
> territory of Poland and Roumania, with which countries France and Brit-
> ain have corresponding military and political agreements.[134]

Crafting joint war plans is a major focus of alliance treaty negotiations. Building
on this premise, I offered a theory of alliance treaty negotiation outcomes. The
chapter shows how the compatibility of ideal war plans and the attractiveness of
outside options interact to create conditions conducive to agreement or nonagreement. I describe these conditions using four negotiation types: Same Page, Pleasant Surprise, Standard Bargaining, and Revealed Deadlock. The negotiation types
vary by the compatibility of the participants' ideal war plans and by the number
of participants with attractive outside options.

The theory shows that agreement is likely if the participants' ideal war plans
have high compatibility. When ideal war plan compatibility is low, the presence
of attractive outside options can influence the prospects for agreement. If all participants have attractive outside options and ideal war plan compatibility is low,
deadlock (and, hence, nonagreement) is likely. If ideal war plan compatibility is
low and not all participants have attractive outside options, the outcomes are

Number of Participants with Attractive Outside Options

Not All   **All**

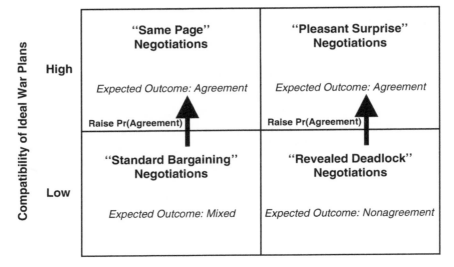

Number of Participants with Attractive Outside Options

Not All   **All**

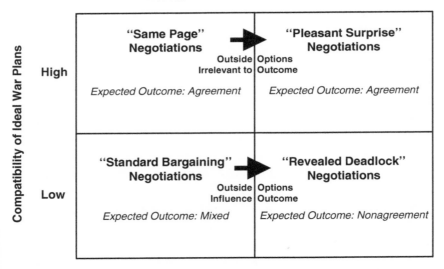

FIGURE 1.3. Empirical Implications of War Plans and Negotiation Outcomes

mixed. Agreement via compromise or capitulation is possible, but so is collapse. This mixture of outcomes is due to the attractiveness of outside options being private information and to the known incentive of participants to misrepresent the attractiveness of their outside options.

I illustrated the theory's components and claims with a host of examples. But testing the usefulness of my theory requires that I subject it to systematic empirical evaluation. More precisely, the theory suggests empirical implications that, if supported by data, will lend credence to my claim that war planning is a central component of alliance treaty negotiations and key for understanding their outcomes. These implications are illustrated in figure 1.3.

Panel (a) of figure 1.3 shows the expected direct influence of ideal war plan compatibility on the outcome of alliance treaty negotiations. Regardless of the number of participants with attractive outside options, negotiations with highly compatible ideal war plans will have a higher likelihood of agreement than negotiations with less-compatible ideal war plans. Negotiations with low *compatibility of ideal war plans* (the bottom row of panel [a] of figure 1.3) are expected to end in either nonagreement (in Revealed Deadlock negotiations) or, at best, mixed outcomes (in Standard Bargaining negotiations). In contrast, all negotiations with high *compatibility of ideal war plans* are expected to end in agreement. This expectation holds regardless of the number of participants with attractive outside options. This expectation can be expressed as an explicit hypothesis:

Hypothesis 1.1—Direct Relationship between Ideal War Plan Compatibility and Negotiation Outcomes: *Negotiations where the participants have high compatibility in their ideal war plans are more likely to end in agreement than negotiations where the participants have low compatibility in their ideal war plans.*

Panel (b) of figure 1.3 shows that war plan compatibility is also expected to have an indirect influence on alliance negotiation outcomes. Specifically, ideal war plan compatibility should determine when the existence of attractive outside options influences the outcome. When the ideal war plans are highly compatible, agreement is reached because the treaty is consistent with the preferred policy of each participant. But when the compatibility of the ideal war plans is low, some (or perhaps all) parties must decide how much they value a treaty relative to the next best alternative policy. This expectation can be expressed as an explicit hypothesis:

Hypothesis 1.2—Indirect Relationship between Ideal War Plan Compatibility and Negotiation Outcomes: *A negotiation reaching agreement is influenced by the* *participants having attractive outside options only when the compatibility of the participants' ideal war plans is low.*

Given the centrality of ideal war plan compatibility to my theory—it is the key explanatory variable in hypothesis 1.1 and the core modifying variable in hypothesis 1.2—the next chapter, after explaining how I identify when alliance treaty negotiations end in agreement or nonagreement, will explain how I measure ideal war plan compatibility.

MEASURING WAR PLANNING AND NEGOTIATION OUTCOMES

War planning lies at the heart of alliance treaty negotiations. While the final text of the treaty may not convey details of a war plan, war planning is a key point of discussion during the negotiations leading to the treaty. The previous chapter put forward the logic for how the compatibility of the participants' ideal war plans directly and indirectly shapes whether the negotiations will end in agreement.

However, the usefulness of my theoretical claims linking war plan compatibility to alliance treaty negotiation outcomes depends on systematic empirical evidence. This is why the previous chapter concluded with two hypotheses that I can evaluate empirically. The first hypothesis holds that, all else being equal, negotiations are more likely to end in agreement when the participants' ideal war plans are highly compatible. The second hypothesis holds that, all else being equal, the compatibility of the participants' ideal war plans will determine when the existence of attractive outside options influences the outcome of negotiations. To test either hypothesis, I must measure when states are involved in alliance treaty negotiations, the outcomes of those negotiations, and when the participants had compatible ideal war plans. Therefore, this chapter will focus on how I capture these concepts empirically.

Offering reasonable measures of the explanatory and outcome variables is crucial for testing any hypothesis, but measurement of concepts can be difficult. It requires making complex choices about how to "connect ideas with facts" (Adcock and Collier 2001, 529). This is why I will carefully describe the data collection and data manipulation required to measure alliance treaty negotiation outcomes (agreement or nonagreement) and ideal war plan compatibility.

I begin by discussing how I code when states are involved in alliance treaty negotiations and the outcome, agreement or nonagreement, of those negotiations. Such coding is necessary to create a set of observations and to operationalize the dependent variable of my analysis. Next, I explain how I operationalize the strategic component of an ideal war plan. I do this by coding the proportion of all threats faced by at least one participant in the negotiation that are shared by all the participants. Participants that have a high ratio of shared-to-nonshared threats are more likely to have compatible views regarding which state or states should be the target of the alliance treaty. I then detail my coding of the high-level operational component of a state's ideal war plan. Drawing from my conceptual claim that the high-level operational component of a state's ideal war plan emanates from its military doctrine, I code whether the negotiation participants share offensive or defensive military doctrines.

Coding Negotiation and Negotiation Outcomes

My analysis focuses on European alliance relations from 1815 to 1945. I discussed in the introductory chapter my reason for focusing on this time period, namely that it is highly relevant for understanding contemporary international politics. As for focusing on European states, this is sensible given the composition of membership in known alliances for the pre-1945 period. Specifically, I use the Alliance Treaty Obligation and Provision (ATOP) data set to code when states formed alliances. According to the ATOP data, nearly 76 percent of the alliances formed between 1815 and 1945 involved only European powers. So while there were some alliance negotiations exclusively between non-European states, focusing on negotiations involving at least one European state should still capture a sample representative of the true nature of alliance negotiations.

As I have maintained throughout the text, I consider agreement to be when the parties leave the negotiations with a signed treaty. This makes the identification of negotiations ending in agreement relatively straightforward. The ATOP data set codes when states have signed an offensive pact, a defensive pact, a nonaggression pact, a neutrality pact, or a consultative pact between 1815 and 2003. According to ATOP, 184 pacts involving at least one European country were formed between 1815 and 1945. I assume that these 184 pacts represent 184 negotiations that ended in agreement. Of course, as emphasized in the introductory chapter and as will be mentioned again below, I consider only offensive and defensive pacts to be true alliance treaties. According to the ATOP data, 106 such pacts involving at least one European state were signed between 1815 and 1945. Hence, my analysis will only treat these 106 pacts as representing negotiations that ended in agreement.

Before describing how I identify cases of nonagreement, I should address a concern about using the signing of treaties to indicate agreement. Could states sometimes sign watered-down agreements (with extremely vague commitments) simply to avoid nonagreement? The short answer is yes. But this leads to another question: What conditions make signing a watered-down agreement more attractive than no agreement at all? Moreover, such behavior would bias against finding results that support my hypotheses. Specifically, it could mean that some negotiations ending in agreement have characteristics very similar to those that end in nonagreement. This would make it more difficult to find systematic differences between negotiations that ended in agreement and those that ended in nonagreement.

Identifying when negotiations end in nonagreement is not as straightforward as identifying when negotiations end in agreement. To put the challenge simply, it requires identifying, to borrow from Sherlock Holmes, the dogs that didn't bark. Perhaps more accurately, it requires identifying the dogs that thought about barking but decided not to.

The ATOP project highlights exactly why it is difficult to code when negotiations fail to reach agreement. The sources underlying ATOP are signed and deposited alliance treaties. But when an alliance negotiation fails, it does not produce a signed document—such as an alliance treaty—that is then archived. Hence, identifying failed negotiations requires identifying historical events for which a culminating document does not exist. How can I overcome this challenge?

A logical starting point is foreign ministry archives or collections of foreign diplomatic documents, such as the *British Foreign and State Papers* or the *Foreign Relations of the United States*. However, this amounts to looking for a needle in a hay barn (not even a haystack!) and is costly in terms of money and time. For instance, if one focused only on British foreign ministry documents, failed attempts could be identified (assuming the ministry kept documents of the failure), but after extensive time spent reading these documents, one would only have coded the failed negotiations of a single country.

An alternative approach is to draw upon the decades of archival research already conducted by historians.[1] This can be done by using published diplomatic histories.[2] Other, highly prominent and widely used international relations data sets were created through similar sources. For instance, Brett Ashley Leeds and her coauthors used diplomatic histories to initiate the process of identifying cases of alliance formation when constructing the ATOP data set. Melvin Small and J. D.

Singer (1966) drew on diplomatic histories when constructing the original Correlates of War (COW) listing of military alliances and wars.[3] Michael Colaresi, Karen A. Rasler, and William R. Thompson (2007) drew from a voluminous number of diplomatic histories to identify when states considered one another to be strategic rivals. I adopt this approach to create my data set of failed alliance negotiations.

In Poast (2012), I overcame these difficulties by drawing on a number of prominent diplomatic historical sources, such as *European Alliances and Alignments* by William Langer, *A Diplomatic History of Europe since the Congress of Vienna* by René Albrecht-Carrie, *The Transformation of European Politics* by Paul Schroeder, *The Struggle for Mastery in Europe* by A. J. P. Taylor, and *The Lights That Failed: European International History* by Zara Steiner.[4] Using diplomatic histories as my source material is not without problems. In chapter 3 (see the "Data Complications" section) I explain these limits, how they open the possibility of selection bias, and how I attempt to account for them.

Having identified sources, using them to identify alliance treaty negotiations that ended in nonagreement requires a coding rule. I develop and apply the following coding rule to identify alliance treaty negotiations that end in nonagreement: *There must exist evidence of a meeting at the diplomatic level where a proposal of a formal alliance is made and then evidence of a rejection or refusal.* To understand how I applied this coding rule, it is useful to briefly unpack each component of the rule.

First, there must exist evidence of a meeting. I am catholic regarding the concept of "meeting." Alliance negotiations can take the form of a physical meeting or a written correspondence. Second, this meeting must be at the diplomatic level. This means the meeting must be between ambassadors, heads of state, or foreign ministers. Again, evidence of a meeting need not entail the two diplomats or heads of state being physically present in the same location. Instead, a meeting could entail an exchange of letters. Third, there must be a proposal of a formal alliance treaty. By "formal," I mean written. This is in contrast to attempts to create an informal coalition of states operating together without a codified document.

Fourth, there must be evidence that this proposal was rejected/refused. This means one side must decline to form an alliance. This fourth component of my coding rule has a couple complications. First, declining to form an alliance may not take the form of a simple no. These are, after all, diplomats (and, hence, their response could be quite diplomatic)! For example, when rejecting a proposal from France, the Russian chancellor Alexander Gorchakov said, "We shall occupy ourselves later with uniting France to Russia" (quoted in Taylor 1954, 214–15). Second, Underdal (1983, 184) claims that failure to reach agreement need not mean that the negotiation failed. Specifically, the negotiation might have made progress on a "particularly knotty issue," which the states can use as a basis for future negotiations. While this may be true, I view the inability of the states to achieve the core objective of an alliance negotiation—a signed treaty—as a clear indicator of failure. If this occurs, then even if the same group of states try again a year later to reach an agreement, I consider this a new negotiation (with the previous negotiation having failed).

In summary, alliance negotiations end in nonagreement when states end the negotiations without signing a treaty or setting an explicit date for resuming the negotiations. More precisely, in a failed negotiation there was contact (correspondence or physical meetings) at the diplomatic level (between ambassadors, heads of state, or foreign ministers) where a proposal of a formal (i.e., written) alliance (mutual defense pact or offensive pact) was made, but that proposal was rejected/refused with no counterproposal.

Inevitably, applying my coding rule to diplomatic histories will involve making subjective judgments. Interpreting diplomatic histories lacks the strict objectivity associated with, for example, counting treaty texts. However, as Colaresi, Rasler, and Thompson (2007, 29) state, "No phenomenon is so clearcut that counting it does not require some level of interpretation. . . . The point remains that measurement choices rarely boil down to interpreting the raw information versus allowing the facts to speak for themselves. Some interpretation of the raw information is inevitable." As an example of the judgment calls I had to make, I count as a failed negotiation an outright refusal of an initial proposal for an alliance treaty (such as ignoring a letter that broaches the subject). I do so precisely because a number of agreements were reached between states immediately following or just a few weeks after the initial offer. For instance, a simple exchange of letters between two ambassadors can constitute an official agreement. In Michael Hurst's two-volume collection, *Key Treaties for the Great Powers, 1814–1914,* the 1902 "treaty" between France and Italy about coordinating their policies in the Mediterranean was a simple exchange of letters between the French and Italian ambassadors (Hurst 1972, 735–38).[5] Another prominent example is the "Andrassy Note" of 1875, named after the Hungarian prime minister at that time. This was a single note unilaterally sent out by Gyula Andrassy and immediately accepted by the governments it was sent to.[6]

Being mindful of the need to make judgement calls, I then read these histories looking for evidence meeting my coding rule.[7] Consider an example. I interpreted the following account by the historian A. J. P. Taylor as a failed attempt to form an alliance treaty: "[The Russian chancellor] Gorchakov said to [the French president] Thiers: 'We shall occupy ourselves later with uniting France to Russia', and [Tsar] Alexander II added: 'I should much like to gain an alliance like that of France, an alliance of peace, and not of war and conquest.' These words, uttered on 29 September 1870, defined the Franco-Russian alliance as it was achieved twenty years later; they were of no use to Thiers in the circumstances of the moment. He returned to Paris empty-handed; and the French had to try to reverse the Prussian victories by their own efforts."[8] This excerpt shows that the Russian chancellor and the French president met, that there was discussion of creating an alliance between the two nations ("I should much like to gain an alliance like that of France, an alliance of peace, and not of war and conquest"), and that this attempt failed (Thiers "returned to Paris empty-handed").

A second example comes from a passage by the historian Paul Schroeder. Schroeder writes, "Russian policy was not hostile to Britain, nor was it opposed to all reform of the Ottoman Empire. . . . In 1836 [the Russian diplomat and foreign minister] Nesselrode began seeking an entente with Britain, for the sake of general peace and Russia's economic development. His feelers were ignored at London. Instead, from 1834 to 1838 [the British foreign secretary] Palmerston considered various ideas for shoring up the Ottoman Empire against Russia."[9] Again, there is evidence that the Russian diplomat broached the idea of an alliance to the British diplomat ("his feelers"), but this idea was rejected ("were ignored at London").

Using this approach, I identify 91 failed negotiations. For each negotiation, I code the following: year of negotiation, states involved, and whether the negotiation is over a defensive pact or an offensive pact. I combine these 91 alliance treaty negotiations ending in nonagreement with the 106 alliance negotiations ending in agreement, for a combined data set of 197 alliance treaty negotiations. The 197 negotiations include 145 bilateral negotiations, 38 trilateral negotiations, 8 quadrilateral negotiations, and 6 pentalateral negotiations.[10]

Figure 2.1 shows the number of alliance negotiations by year from 1815 to 1945. Besides the variation over time, one should notice the spikes in alliance negotiations around the Crimean War (1853 to 1856), the Franco-Prussian War (1870 to 1871), the start of World War I (1914), and the start of World War II (1939). These spikes reveal the tendency of states to seek out alliance partners during the lead-up to major international crises and confrontations. As Langer (1966, 5) observes, "leaving aside such vague international connexions as the Family Compact of the 18th century or the Holy Alliance of the 19th, the great coalitions of modern history were almost always made just before the outbreak of war or during the course of the conflict itself."[11] While many notable alliances (though perhaps not the grand coalitions referenced by Langer) formed during peacetime (e.g., the Franco-Russian pact of 1892), the point still stands: alliances are about guarding against a threat.[12]

With respect to the participants, the negotiations were dominated by the major powers: Prussia/Germany (seventy-one negotiations), Russia/USSR (sixty-seven), Britain (sixty-six), France (sixty), and Austria-Hungary/Austria (fifty). A large gap separates these five states from the other negotiation participants. Specifically, the country with the fifth most negotiations—Austria, with fifty—has over twice as many negotiations as the country with the sixth most negotiations: Italy, with twenty-four. The dominance of major power participation should be unsurprising—after all, a highly active foreign policy is a characteristic of a major power (see below). One might be concerned that this is partially due to my use of diplomatic histories as a source of data for identifying failed negotiations. But it should be noted that the same five states are the dominant participants in both my diplomatic history–based nonagreement negotiations—Prussia/Germany (forty-three), Russia (thirty-seven), France (thirty-five), Britain (thirty-five), and Austria (twenty-five)—and the ATOP-based agreement negotiations: Britain (thirty-one), Russia (thirty), Prussia/Germany (twenty-eight), Austria (twenty-five), and France (twenty-five).

I use these data to create my outcome variable, *agreement*. This is a dichotomous variable, equal to 1 if a negotiation ends in agreement or 0 if it does not. I am interested only in whether agreement is reached. This variable does not indicate whether the negotiations were "successful" in the sense that they resulted in a treaty that can be considered just, fair, or equitable. Also, the outcome variable

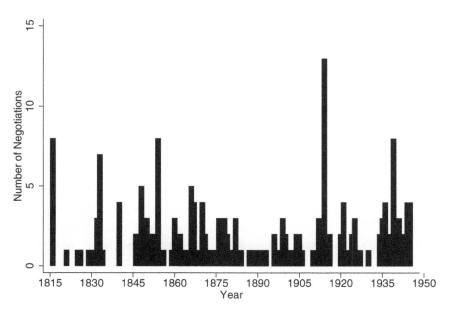

FIGURE 2.1. Number of Military Alliance Treaty Negotiations Involving European Countries, 1815 to 1945

does not code whether states remain committed to the treaty. Instead, the outcome variable captures only whether the parties formed a treaty.

With 91 of 197 negotiations ending in nonagreement, the overall nonagreement rate in my data set is 46 percent. This rate shows that nonagreement is far from rare. Indeed, for the reasons that I will discuss in chapter 3 regarding the possible bias in the data reported by diplomatic historians (namely, that they may overlook failed events); this percentage might understate the actual nonagreement rate. But even a rate of just under half of the reported cases shows that nonagreement is sufficiently common (let alone consequential) to be worthy of investigation.

Coding "Strategic Compatibility"

Having described the unit of analysis and my dependent variable, I now describe how I measure my key independent variable: *compatibility of ideal war plans*. The first component of a state's ideal war plan relevant to alliance treaty negotiations is the strategic component. Coding the strategic component requires identifying a threat, meaning a state that is perceived as having aggressive intentions. Strategic compatibility is high when the negotiation participants have similar threat perceptions. But how should I empirically capture the threat perceptions of states or, more precisely, of their key foreign policy decision makers? There are presently three ways of capturing, across a large number of cases, when a state is perceived as a threat: (1) "dispute density," (2) political relevance, and (3) strategic rivalry.[13] I will now describe each of these before explaining why I will primarily use the third approach, strategic rivalry, to code strategic compatibility between negotiation participants.

Data Sources and Limits

The first approach is a "dispute density" approach.[14] As employed by Klein, Goertz, and Diehl (2006, 337), this approach begins by identifying potential rivalries: all state-to-state pairs that engaged in three or more militarized interstate disputes (MID) between 1816 and 2001. An MID is coded by Ghosn, Palmer, and Bremer (2004) as an event where one state threatens to use force, makes a display of force, uses force, or initiates a war against another state. The list of potential rivalries includes state-to-state pairs ranging from the United States–Cambodia to China-Japan and France-Germany. Next, the list of "potential rivalries" is adjusted by removing state-to-state pairs with MIDs related to a single war, with fewer than three MIDs linked with respect to a particular issue, or where sufficient time elapsed (generally forty to fifty years) between MIDs.[15] Removing these state-to-state pairs produces the list of actual rivalries. Although a dispute density coding of rivals is straightforward and objective, it misses rivalries that do not generate militarized disputes (Thompson 2001, 577).[16] Indeed, the absence of militarized disputes does not necessarily mean the underlying disagreements have been resolved (Thompson 2001, 574). For example, a strategic rivalry existed between Egypt and Iran from 1955 to 1971 even though neither state engaged in an MID against the other. We require an approach that is able to capture when a state perceives another state as a threat even if that other state has not recently—or at all—and actively attacked the state.

A second approach is to identify the "politically relevant international environment" (PRIE) (Maoz 1996).[17] Members of a given state's PRIE are those states "whose behavior and internal processes are deemed by decision makers to be relevant to their own strategic calculations" (Maoz 1996, 168). More precisely, a state's PRIE members have "a high probability a priori of engaging in conflict" with the state because they have the means (and perhaps incentive) to use military force against it (Maoz 1996, 63). A PRIE member has at least one of two characteristics: being contiguous with the given state or being a major power.[18] The COW project identifies all state-to-state dyads that are directly contiguous from 1816 through 2006 (Stinnett et al. 2002).[19] Contiguity includes countries sharing a land border (e.g., the majority of the U.S.-Canada border) and boundaries defined by rivers (the Rio Grande part of the U.S.-Mexico border).[20] Major powers are large states with the means to project power over large distances and the desire to do so.[21] COW identifies the states with these characteristics by drawing on the consensus results from surveying diplomatic historians (Small and Singer 1982).[22] COW identifies a total of eight countries as major powers for some portion of the time from 1816 to 1945. Only Britain is identified as a major power for the entire period. Austria/Austria-Hungary (1816 to 1918) and Italy (1860 to 1943) were major powers for a portion of the period but were no longer major powers by 1945. Prussia/Germany (1816 to 1918 and 1925 to 1945), France (1816 to 1940 and 1945), and Russia/USSR (1816 to 1917 and 1922 to 1945) had interruptions in the years they were classified as major powers.[23] The PRIE approach has the advantage of using clear markers to identify threats. Yet, a major disadvantage of the PRIE approach is that it can overstate the threats perceived by states. For instance, a neighboring major power "might" be a threat, but not always. We require an approach that is better able to capture how a state perceives the intentions of another state; be it a neighbor, major power, or otherwise.

A third approach to coding threats is identifying "strategic rivals."[24] According to Thompson (2001) and Colaresi, Rasler, and Thompson (2007), strategic rivalries are "instances in which decision makers in one state perceive another state of relatively equal status as a competitor for the same resources against whom it is likely to become militarily engaged" (Colaresi, Rasler, and Thompson 2007, 15). To identify when decision makers in one state perceived another as a rival, Thompson (2001) and Colaresi, Rasler, and Thompson (2007) draw upon diplomatic and political histories of individual states' foreign policy activities. Why the state is perceived as a rival is fundamentally immaterial to their measure; the perception could be based on disputed territory, a history of conflict, ideological differences, or a combination of these and other factors.[25] Critically, Thompson and others recognize that the expectation of conflict and the perception of serious levels of threat can exist without states actually engaging in militarized violence against one another. Hence, it overcomes a key disadvantage of the dispute density approach. Additionally, by exploring the actual perceptions of a state's decision makers, it overcomes a key disadvantage of the PRIE approach.

Thompson (2001) and Colaresi, Rasler, and Thompson (2007) identify 173 strategic rivalries between 1816 and 2001, covering a wide range of states. A number of large states perceived one another as rivals (e.g., Austria and Russia starting in 1816), but rivalries also existed between smaller states (e.g., Albania and Greece starting in 1913) and between small states and large states (e.g., Poland and Russia starting in 1918 or Germany and Czechoslovakia in the 1930s). Rivalries can fluctuate in their intensity. Rivals may even cooperate under particular circumstances. For instance, naval and colonial competition led the British and French to perceive one another as rivals throughout the nineteenth century and the Fashoda crisis of 1898 nearly brought them to war.[26] Yet Britain and France also signed the Cobden-Chevalier reciprocal trade treaty in 1860, jointly intervened in the Crimean War (1853–56), and cooperated during the Second Opium War (1857–60).

The major advantage of using strategic rivalry to identify threats is that it corrects for the overstating of threats associated with both the MID density and PRIE approaches. However, there is the possibility that strategic rivalry achieves this objective by overcorrecting. Strategic rivalry only includes states that mutually perceive one another as threats. Dyads are not counted as rivals when state A feels threatened by state B but state B does not perceive state A as a threat. This leads the Thompson data to omit highly asymmetric dyads where the smaller state may view the larger state as a threat but this perception is not reciprocated.[27] For example, while Germany is considered a strategic rival of Czechoslovakia in the 1930s, Russia is not. This is surprising since relations between the two parties were tense throughout the 1920s and early 1930s (Lukes 1996). But the coding might be due to the perception of threat not being shared: after all, Czechoslovakia did not pose a threat to the Soviets. In a sensitivity analysis in chapter 3, I will attempt to partially account for this shortcoming by expanding the Thompson list of strategic rivals.

Variable Construction and Coding Plausibility

Using strategic rivals to identify the threats faced by each negotiation participant, I can now construct my measure of strategic compatibility. Regardless of the data used to define when a country is a threat, strategic compatibility occurs when negotiation participants agree on the states to target with the alliance. It seems obvious that participants will agree to target a common threat, as the existence of a common threat likely drove them to begin negotiating an alliance treaty in the first place. But states rarely share the exact same "portfolio" of threats. There are probably differences in the extent to which the participants perceive other states as threats. As discussed in the previous chapter, determining whether the alliance should be extended to include protection against nonshared threats could be a key point of discussion during the negotiations and might have the ability to undermine the negotiation. Hence, coding strategic compatibility requires capturing the differences in which states the negotiation participants perceive as threats.

To construct such a measure, I use the strategic rivals' data to identify all states that any of the negotiation participants perceive as threats. I then determine the number of these threats that are common among the participants. This allows me to construct a ratio

$$\frac{\text{Threats Perceived in Common}}{\text{All Threats among Negotiation Participants}}$$

This ratio can range from 0 (all perceived threats are different) to 1 (all perceived threats are common threats). For a sense of the range of values taken on by this ratio and how they can fluctuate over time, see figure 2.2. This figure plots the ratio of common threats to total threats for Britain and France from 1815 to 1945 (based on the strategic rivals data). This ratio is shown by the black line in figure 2.2. The ratio varies substantially, ranging from a low of 0.14 to a high of 0.6. The notable nonlinear fluctuation over time suggests that the threat ratio likely contains noise, meaning it is an imprecise year-to-year measure of strategic compatibility. Stated differently, I am reluctant to place immense interpretative weight on a small change in this ratio, say from 0.30 to 0.31. For this reason, I use the threat ratio to create a binary variable, *high strategic compatibility*, coded 1 if the parties to the negotiation have a ratio greater than or equal to the median value for the sample, 0 otherwise.[28] Dichotomizing the ratio in order to place negotiations into two categories (high strategic compatibility negotiations and low strategic compatibility negotiations) minimizes the importance of small changes in the threat ratio's value. Making *high strategic compatibility* a dichotomous variable also makes it easier to combine (and compare) this variable with the *high operational compatibility* variable that I generate below.

Having created this variable, it is useful to check the threat ratio's validity as a basis for creating the variable. The threat ratio is essentially a threat-derived measure of similarity in foreign policy interests, which means it is worth comparing it to a widely used measure of similarity in foreign policy interests: the s-score of Signorino and Ritter (1999). Therefore, figure 2.2 also plots the British-French s-score of foreign policy similarity (the gray dashed line in figure 2.2).[29] The s-score uses the alliance treaty relations between states to construct a measure of common foreign policy interests between two states. The assumption underpinning the s-score, whose value ranges from −1 to 1, is that two states with the exact same alliance partners (a score of 1) likely have highly similar (if not identical) foreign policy interests. In essence, the s-score offers an alliance-derived measure—rather than a threat-derived measure—of strategic compatibility.[30] Unsurprisingly, the s-scores and the threat ratio have some similarities in movement. Both indicators have peak values in the 1830s and the late 1930s, and both have short declines at the end of the time series. But there are also notable differ-

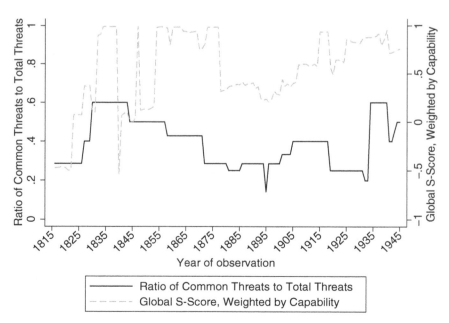

FIGURE 2.2. British-French Common Threat-to-Total-Threat Ratio Compared to Global S-Score, 1815 to 1945

ences between the two graph lines. The s-scores are more volatile, especially in the early years of the time series. The relatively high s-scores starting in the mid-1850s (always above 0.6 on a −1 to 1 scale) suggest relatively common interests between the two states. The lower threat ratio, in contrast, suggests less commonality in interests for much of the mid- to late 1800s. The historical record of the late nineteenth century suggests that the threat ratio offers a more accurate depiction of British-French relations: Britain and France had colonial rivalries and stark differences in perception of the threat posed by Germany and Russia. Moreover, the two states nearly came to war during the Fashoda crisis of 1898. The Fashoda crisis is a particularly useful event for benchmarking the two measures. The 1898 s-score for the two countries was 0.317, well above the standard cut point value for similar foreign policy interests (0). In contrast, the threat ratio value in 1898 was 0.285. This is below the value used as the cut point between high and low strategic compatibility (0.375). Stated differently, the threat ratio, unlike the s-score, suggests that France and Britain had incompatible security interests in 1898, which is consistent with the reality that they nearly went to war that year.

Coding Operational Compatibility

The strategic component is just one of the two components that determine ideal war plan compatibility. The other is the high-level operational component. A war plan's high-level operational component specifies the general guidelines for using military force against a threat. As discussed in chapter 1, this is closely tied to a state's military doctrine. This suggests that I can use the military doctrine of each negotiation participant to determine when participants have operational compatibility in their ideal war plans. However, as I describe below, existing data on the military doctrines of states are not easily applicable to my research design. I will have to manipulate, reformat, and extend the data, as well as address flaws in the data that could render them inappropriate for my study. Only then will I be able to code the operational compatibility between negotiation participants.

Data Source and Limits

In a series of mid-1990s studies, Allan Stam drew on several collections written by military historians to code the wartime military doctrines of all COW interstate war participants (Stam 1996; Bennett and Stam 1996; Reiter and Stam 1998).[31] These data code a state's military doctrine as the general military posture of its armed forces during the war. This posture is either offensive or defensive and is separable from the state's goals during the war.[32] Offensive doctrines call for taking the fight to the threat. The aim is to disarm the enemy by destroying its armed forces with an early and intense attack, typically via a first strike. In contrast, a defensive doctrine aims to deny or impede an attacking enemy's advance. If a state used multiple strategies, the strategy coded is the one that absorbed the majority of the state's military assets (Bennet and Stam 1996, 247).[33] This approach was also applied when a state switched strategies during a war, such as from offensive to defensive strategies shortly after the beginning of World War I.[34]

These data have two problematic features that I must address before they are suitable for coding the operational components of ideal war plans. First, for many European countries between 1816 and 1850, data are missing. For example, I do not have a military doctrine observation for the British until 1854, when Britain participated in the Crimean War. This is because the first observations in the Bennett and Stam data come from the Franco-Spanish War of 1823 (as this is the first COW interstate war), followed by the Russo-Turkish war of 1828. The next European war is not until the Austro-Sardinian War of 1848. The second limit is that these data only pertain to wartime. However, states also have operational plans during peacetime. Moreover, many of the negotiations in my data set take place outside of an active war. Hence, the Stam and Bennett data, as given, do not provide military doctrine information for many of my observations. I must address these two limitations before the data are suitable for my purposes.

Overcoming the first limitation requires data on military doctrines during the later stages of the Napoleonic Wars, specifically the wars of the Sixth Coalition (1812 to 1814) and the Seventh Coalition after Napoleon's return from Elba (1815).[35] To acquire such data, I turn to one of the sources underlying the Stam and Stam and Bennett data on wartime strategies: the Historical Evaluation and Research Organization (HERO) data set.[36] This data set codes a variety of details for 660 battles fought between 1600 and 1982, such as troop strength, weapon counts, casualties, and, most important for my purposes, the primary battlefield scheme deployed by each state's forces during a battle. Scholars have questioned the accuracy of particular battle details found in the HERO data (see Mearsheimer 1989; Desch 2002).[37] Their criticisms are primarily focused on how HERO codes the effectiveness of battlefield strategies, the course of particular battles, or specific intangible aspects of the combatants (such as "quality of leadership" or "troop morale").[38] I am not using the HERO data to code battlefield details of this nature.[39] Instead, I am drawing on these data to identify belligerents' general operational plans, which will allow me to code the doctrines of participants in the Napoleonic Wars.[40]

To code the strategies used during the Napoleonic Wars, I begin with the *primary tactical scheme* variable in HERO.[41] This variable can take on one of twelve different values, but only four were used during the Napoleonic Wars: DO (defensive/offensive plan), DD (defensive plan), EE (single envelopment), and FF (frontal attack).[42] Comparing HERO to Bennett and Stam data, these HERO strategies translate to Bennett and Stam strategies as follows: FF corresponds to an offensive doctrine, DD corresponds to a defensive doctrine, DO corresponds to a defensive doctrine, and EE corresponds to an offensive doctrine.[43] I then code the strategy used most frequently by each state or, if there is a tie in frequency, the one that absorbed the largest number of a country's troops.[44] This allows me to code the doctrines of eighteen countries for the Napoleonic Wars.[45] Of these eighteen countries, eight are coded as using an offensive doctrine and ten as a defensive one.[46]

I can overcome the second limitation—that the data do not code states' peacetime war doctrines—with two assumptions: (1) military planners "fight the last war" and (2) military planners base doctrines on their own state's war experiences. These assumptions are grounded in an extensive literature (see Jervis 1976; Ralston 1990; Khong 1992; Posen 1993; Reiter 1996)[47] and have strong empirical support (Reiter and Meek 1999; Weisiger 2013).[48] These two assumptions imply that victory in war will reinforce the existing doctrine, but defeat leads to a complete reevaluation of that doctrine. For example, in describing the lessons drawn by Israel and Egypt from the 1967 Six-Day War, Newell (1991, 86–87) observes that "Israeli success in 1967 led her to leave her basic doctrine on how to conduct war essentially unchanged, but the Egyptian failure prompted that country to examine her doctrine for the conduct of war rather closely." I assume that only victories reinforce an existing doctrine, consistent with this example. A loss or stalemate will lead policy makers, as part of an effort to determine why victory was not achieved, to change doctrines.

In order to use these two assumptions to code the peacetime war doctrines of states, I must identify the outcome of a war for each participant. I do so using the Stam (1996) coding of war outcomes. In Stam's coding, a war can end in one of three ways: win, lose, or draw. These outcomes are primarily based on the Dupuy and Dupuy (1986) military encyclopedia (Stam 1996, 75). The coding rule is that the state benefiting in the new territorial status quo after the war is the winner, while the state harmed by the new territorial status quo is the loser. An outcome is coded as a draw when there is a cease-fire (with or without an internationally recognized treaty) with no notable changes in the territorial status quo that benefit one party over the other. For example, according to Stam's data, the First Schleswig-Holstein War between Prussia and Denmark was a draw. The Second Schleswig-Holstein War was a win for Prussia and Austria and a loss for Denmark, who ceded territory. For the Napoleonic Wars, I code the forces aligned with Britain at the end of the war as the victors (England,

Austria, Prussia, Russia, Spain, Portugal, Switzerland, Bavaria, the Netherlands, Italy, and Württemburg).[49]

Using these two assumptions, I code a state's military strategy during a given peacetime year in two steps. First, if the state won its most recent war, I code each subsequent peacetime year (until the next war) with the strategy that was used during the war. Second, if a state lost its most recent war, I code each subsequent year (until the next war) with the opposite strategy to the one used during that war. In a sensitivity analysis test described in chapter 3, I allow the doctrine to change during peacetime rather than remain the same for each year after a war.

This procedure enables me to create a country-year data set of the military doctrines for fifty-eight states from 1816 to 1945. To make the coding procedure concrete, consider the codings for France and Prussia/Germany in 1872. The year 1872 was the first full year of peace following the 1870–71 Franco-Prussian War. France used an offensive strategy during the war, but France lost the war. Therefore, I code France's military doctrine in 1872 as defensive. Prussia/Germany is coded as using a defensive strategy during the war. Since it won the war, I coded Prussia/Germany's military doctrine in 1872 as defensive.

Before moving on to evaluate the plausibility of my coding of military doctrines, I should make clear that I do not use Stam's "fine grained" strategy typology of attrition, maneuver, or punishment. These subcategories will be familiar to scholars who have used the Stam and HERO data. Stam explains how these fit within an offensive or defensive doctrine. A maneuver strategy means the state primarily used tactics that entailed encircling and dividing an opponent (Bennett and Stam 1996, 246).[50] An attrition strategy means the state's forces fought engagements aimed at denying an attacking force the ability to cross a border or at destroying a defending state's army and taking prisoners (Bennett and Stam 1996, 246; Stam 1996, 82, 84). A punishment strategy means that either the state adopted guerrilla tactics or civilians were the principal military target (Bennett and Stam 1996, 247). I do not use these categories because they sit between the low-operational and tactical components of war planning. As explained in chapter 1, this level of planning is not central to whether alliance treaty negotiations end in agreement or nonagreement. Moreover, even if the subcategories were conceptually relevant, little is to be gained empirically: for the 1816 to 1945 period, the preponderance of observations in the Bennett and Stam data use an attrition strategy.[51] There were 156 country-war observations where a state used an attrition strategy but just 2 country-war observations where a state used a punishment strategy and 16 where a state used a maneuver strategy. Hence, the true variation in the data comes from differences in doctrines (offensive versus defensive), not in substrategies (maneuver, attrition, and punishment).

Coding Plausibility and Variable Construction

How plausible is my country-year measure of military doctrine? Does it provide a reasonable measure of military plans during peace and war over the period from 1816 to 1945?[52] One way of answering this question is to determine whether my measure adequately captures the known prevalence of offensive and defensive doctrines at a point in history. For instance, scholars widely argue that a "cult of the offensive" existed just prior to the onset of World War I.[53] This means states generally held offensive military doctrines just prior to the war. As described by Van Evera (1984, 58): "During the decades before the First World War a phenomenon which may be called a 'cult of the offensive' swept through Europe. Militaries glorified the offensive and adopted offensive military doctrines, while civilian elites and publics assumed that the offense had the advantage in warfare, and that offensive solutions to security problems were the most effective."

For example, the French army, declared Chief of Staff Joseph Joffre, "no longer knows any other law than the offensive. . . . Any other conception ought to be rejected as contrary to the very nature of war."[54] Similarly, British general W. G. Knox wrote, "The defensive is never an acceptable role to the Briton, and he makes little or no study of it," and General R. C. B. Haking argued that the offensive "will win as sure as there is a sun in the heavens."[55] Critical to the moniker of "cult" is the notion that the focus on offensive plans was misplaced: it was out of alignment with the technology of the day. This point is made forcefully by Jack Snyder (1984, 108): "Military technology should have made the European strategic balance in July 1914 a model of stability, but offensive military strategies defied those technological realities, trapping European statesmen in a war-causing spiral of insecurity and instability. As the Boer and Russo-Japanese Wars had foreshadowed and the Great War itself confirmed, prevailing weaponry and means of transport strongly favored the defender. . . . Even if the outbreak of war is taken as a given, the offensive plans must still be judged disasters."

The cult of the offensive suggests that, looking at the years preceding World War I, offensive doctrines should have been more prevalent than defensive doctrines. If my measure shows this not to be the case, I should question the measure's validity. To conduct this evaluation, for each year from 1816 to 1945 I computed the percentages of states with each doctrine. I then subtracted the number with defensive doctrines from the number with offensive doctrines. The yearly values of this difference are plotted in figure 2.3. When the line in this figure is above zero, more states have offensive doctrines than defensive doctrines. The higher the value, the more dominant are offensive doctrines.

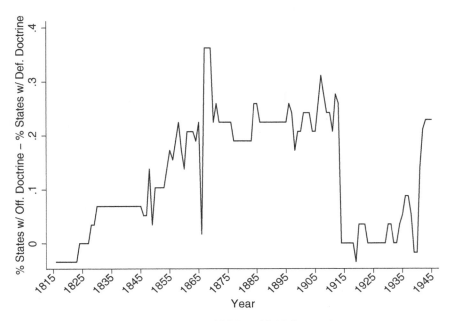

FIGURE 2.3.   Offensive Dominance, 1815 to 1945 (by year)

Figure 2.3 clearly shows the dominance of offensive doctrines preceding World War I. Throughout the second half of the nineteenth century and into the early twentieth century, offensive doctrines were quite prevalent. This prevalence peaks in 1912 and 1913, before plummeting with the outbreak of war in 1914. This plummet occurs because the data sources code states as primarily using defensive doctrines during the war. While states opened the war with offensive doctrines, the fighting soon bogged down into ridged trench warfare, especially on the western front. This led states to shift their strategies from offensive to defensive. Following the war, offensive dominance would not recover until World War II. Overall, figure 2.3 suggests that my coding of military doctrines maps well to the received historical understanding of general military strategies during the early twentieth century. This supports the plausibility of my measure of doctrine.

Having described my yearly measure of a state's military doctrines, I can use it to create a variable capturing the operational compatibility of alliance treaty negotiation participants' ideal war plans. This is captured in the variable *high operational compatibility*. This variable draws on the notion, discussed in chapter 1, that tensions can arise from conflicting doctrines, such as one negotiation participant adhering to an offensive doctrine and another following a defensive doctrine. For each negotiation, this variable is coded with a 1 when at least one

TABLE 2.1.   Summary of key variables

VARIABLE	CODING	DATA SOURCES
Agreement	Binary variable equal to 1 if negotiations end in a signed treaty	ATOP (v. 3.1); author coding from diplomatic histories
Strategic Compatibility	Binary variable equal to 1 when the ratio of common threats to total threats is above the median value of the sample	Thompson Strategic Rivalries
Operational Compatibility	Binary variable equal to 1 when the participants do not have opposing military doctrines	HERO; Bennett and Stam 1998

negotiation participant has an offensive (defensive) doctrine and no participant has a defensive (offensive) doctrine, 0 otherwise. Hence, the Franco-Russian negotiations of 1876 are coded with a 0, since France had a defensive doctrine and Russia had an offensive doctrine. In contrast, the Serbian-Greek negotiations of 1913 are coded with a 1 since both Serbia and Greece had defensive doctrines.[56]

I have described the data used to construct my unit of analysis, outcome variable, and key explanatory variable. Drawing on data from the Alliance Treaty Obligation and Provision data set and on original data based on diplomatic histories, I created a data set of alliance treaty negotiations to serve as my unit of analysis. I used the same data sources to code when negotiations ended in agreement or nonagreement. I then explained how I operationalized the two components of ideal plan compatibility: strategic compatibility and operational compatibility. Strategic compatibility is captured using the proportion of all threats faced by any of the negotiation participants that are shared by all of them. Operational compatibility is captured using the negotiation participants' military doctrines.

The variables I created and the sources of data used in their construction are summarized in table 2.1. The next step is to analyze these data to see if they exhibit patterns supportive of the hypotheses drawn from my theory. This will involve techniques ranging from basic cross tabulations to a variety of sophisticated sensitivity analyses. I do all of this in the next chapter.

ANALYZING ALLIANCE TREATY NEGOTIATION OUTCOMES

Does war planning explain agreement and nonagreement in alliance treaty negotiations? War planning is central to my theoretical claims, and the previous chapter detailed the data I can use to evaluate those claims. This chapter analyzes those data. The goal is to see if patterns in the data support the hypotheses derived from my theory. One hypothesis holds that ideal war plan compatibility is associated with a higher rate of success in alliance negotiations. A second hypothesis holds that ideal war plan compatibility determines when outside options influence the outcome of negotiations: the existence of outside options should influence agreement only when ideal war plan compatibility is low.

It is important to see what the data say willingly through inspection, not just what they confess when squeezed by the machinery of parametric modeling (Achen 2002). Patterns that are clearly observable without leveraging strong modeling assumptions tend to be reliable (Achen 2005, 334–36). To be clear, I will eventually use parametric modeling via multivariate regression, but I begin with basic cross tabulations. These tabulations show that having strategic and operational compatibility is strongly associated with a higher rate of agreement. The rate of agreement is over 30 percentage points higher for negotiations with high ideal plan compatibility than for those without it. This supports the direct effect of ideal war plan compatibility, as expressed in hypothesis 1.1. The cross tabulations also show that agreement can be reached, though less often, even between states that lack ideal war plan compatibility. This suggests that further analysis might support hypothesis 1.2, namely, that another variable—the unattractiveness of outside options—makes agreement more likely when ideal war plan compatibility is low.

The suggestive evidence offered by these cross tabulations is useful, but the cross tabulations also raise questions. The observed direct relationship between agreement and ideal war plan compatibility could be spurious. Accounting for complicated features of the data—namely, omitted variable bias and selection effects—could diminish or even eliminate the observed direct relationship. This necessitates turning to parametric modeling by using multivariate regression analysis. The goal is to see if the positive direct association between agreement and ideal war plan compatibility will hold across a range of models and sensitivity analyses. The positive relationship does hold in most of these tests, though some sensitivity analyses reveal the limits of the data to support hypothesis 1.1 (as sensitivity analyses are intended to do).

With respect to evaluating hypothesis 1.2, I begin by briefly reviewing recent attempts, largely found in studies of international political economy, to empirically capture the effect of outside options on negotiation outcomes. I then describe my measure of when outside options exist among participants in alliance treaty negotiation: whether a state already has an alliance partner when it begins negotiations. After some initial analysis of the data using simple cross tabulations, I turn to matching analysis in order to identify how and under what conditions the existence of an outside option influences the outcome of alliance treaty negotiations. Besides evaluating how ideal war plan compatibility could modify the influence of outside options on negotiation outcomes, these tests set up the subsequent chapters that qualitatively trace the details of key alliance treaty negotiations.

Preliminary Analysis and Data Complications

Having dedicated the previous chapter to measuring negotiation participation and war plan compatibility, I begin empirically investigating the constructed variables by considering some basic patterns in the data. Table 3.1 reports the agreement rate under four conditions: when the negotiation participants have low strategic and operational compatibility, when they have high strategic compatibility but low operational compatibility, when they have high operational compatibility but low strategic compatibility, and when the participants have high strategic and operational compatibility. Recall from chapter 2 that strategic compatibility is high when the common threat–to–total threat ratio is above the median value for the sample, and operational compatibility is high when the participants do not have contradictory military doctrines.

The evidence reported in table 3.1 supports the direct effect of war plan compatibility on alliance negotiation outcomes (hypothesis 1.1). According to

TABLE 3.1.   Agreement rate by strategic compatibility and/or operational compatibility

		Strategic Compatibility	
		High	Low
Operational Compatibility	High	77% [89%, 65%] (37/48)	46% [60%, 31%] (22/48)
	Low	53% [69%, 38%] (24/45)	41% [54%, 28%] (23/56)

Note: 0.95 confidence intervals in brackets. Ratio of negotiations ending in agreement to total negotiations in parentheses.

hypothesis 1.1, plan compatibility should be associated with a higher rate of negotiations ending in agreement. Table 3.1 shows that 77 percent of the negotiations where the participants have both strategic and operational compatibility end in agreement. In contrast, when the participants had neither type of compatibility, the agreement rate was only 41 percent. Notice that this is 36 percentage points lower than the agreement rate for the negotiations with both strategic and operational compatibility. Besides considering the average rates, I should also consider the variation around each agreement rate. Because the agreement rate is based on a sample that likely has measurement errors, is missing observations, or does not account for the future, the actual agreement rate for a given set of conditions (e.g., high strategic and operational compatibility) may not be exactly the same as the rate reported in the observed sample. It could be higher or lower. The variation of the sample data around the agreement rate provides an indication of the likely value of the true (unobservable) agreement rate. The wider the variation in values, the wider the range of possible values for the true agreement rate. I account for the variability by computing confidence intervals around each agreement rate. The 0.95 confidence intervals are reported in table 3.1. The confidence interval for when the negotiation participants have both strategic and operational compatibility (89 percent to 65 percent) does not overlap with the confidence interval for when the participants have neither strategic nor operational compatibility (54 percent to 28 percent). This offers further evidence that war plan compatibility makes agreement more likely.

A few more observations should be gleaned from table 3.1. First, when negotiation participants had just one form of compatibility, the rate of agreement was either slightly better than a coin flip (53 percent when the participants had only strategic compatibility) or slightly worse than a coin flip (46 percent when the participants had only operational compatibility).[1] Second, notice that agreement is not completely absent when states lack plan compatibility. While the agreement rate is below 50 percent when the participants had neither strategic or operational compatibility, 41 percent of these negotiations still end in agreement. This is still consistent with my theory. The theory does not predict a complete absence of agreement when the participants' ideal war plans are incompatible. Instead, it predicts that agreement will be less likely but still possible. The possibility of agreement when ideal war plans are incompatible depends on the absence, for at least one of the participants, of attractive outside options. However, such an expectation must be subjected to further empirical investigation.

Overall, the results in table 3.1 support the claim that ideal war plan compatibility plays an important role in determining the probability that negotiations will end in agreement. However, there are potential complications and features of the data that could limit the inferences one can draw from table 3.1. Indeed, the patterns revealed in table 3.1 could deceive: they may suggest a relationship where one does not actually exist. The empirical patterns revealed in table 3.1 could be deceptive for two reasons: selection bias and omitted variable bias.[2]

Selection Bias?

The first possible complication is selection bias. All studies using observational data suffer from selection bias.[3] The key for researchers is to theorize about the nature of the selection and then determine whether the bias induced by the selection is, in the words of Berk (1983, 392), "small enough to be safely ignored." There are three sources of selection bias that could create complications for my inferences: (1) missing data, (2) selection into the treatment, and (3) selection into the sample.

The first source of selection bias is missing data. Using diplomatic histories is not unproblematic for identifying alliance treaty negotiations that end in nonagreement. More precisely, one could reasonably suspect that historians systematically overlook failed negotiations, especially compared to how often they overlook negotiations that end with a signed treaty. Overlooking negotiations that end in nonagreement could be due to the absence of a treaty signing event or because some failed negotiations leave little or no documentary evidence. Particularly susceptible to omission are failed negotiations exclusively involving minor powers, either due to the historian's bias (if he or she is primarily interested in the foreign policy activities of major powers) or a lack of suitable archives in minor powers. In short, a fair number of negotiation failures may have gone unreported in the histories, so my sample likely undercounts the negotiations ending in nonagreement.[4]

Overlooking a sufficient number of failed alliance treaty negotiations will create problems for my analysis if the missing failed negotiations are systematically more likely to have participants with highly compatible war plans. Stated differently, it is possible that my sample of alliance treaty negotiations overstates the rate at which high war plan compatibility is associated with agreement. Of course, checking this requires knowing whether the missing failed negotiations are systematically more likely to have participants with highly compatible war plans. One could tell a plausible story supporting this claim—one could claim that minor powers, due to their strategic vulnerability, are all likely to have defensive doctrines and view all major powers as threats. But one could also tell a plausible story countering this claim—another could claim that since minor powers are more varied in their capabilities and regional/geostrategic situations than major powers, they are likely to have differing military doctrines and perceptions of threats. The reality is that we simply do not know the full distribution of failed alliance treaty negotiations.

While we are uncertain of the full distribution of alliance treaty negotiations that ended in nonagreement, the data collected from the diplomatic histories give us a sense of the likely distribution. This is because those data could be viewed as representing the minimum number of negotiations that ended in nonagreement. Therefore, a sensitivity analysis below will use the data on failed negotiations collected from the diplomatic histories as a basis for creating an alternative (and larger) set of nonagreement negotiations. This set of "synthetic" nonagreements can then be used to gauge the extent to which the potential for missing failed negotiations is problematic for my inferences.

The second source of possible selection bias is selection into the treatment.[5] Within the context of my study, it is possible that states know the plans of other states before entering negotiations and, therefore, choose whether to enter negotiations with compatible or noncompatible plans. This would mean my data on plan compatibility is not "as if" randomly assigned: states are selecting into the "treatment" of having a compatible plan. This is similar to the selection bias that concerns scholars studying the effects of treaties on state behavior: treaty effects could merely be reflections of underlying state preferences rather than evidence of the treaty having an independent influence on behavior (Mearsheimer 1994/95; Downs, Rocke, and Barsoom 1996; Von Stein 2005; Simmons and Hopkins 2005; Lupu 2013). Of course, if the determinants of state preferences are observable, they can be accounted for by including control variables. But what if the determinants of state preferences are unobservable? On the one hand, I could rely on an "ignorability" assumption (Rubin 1978). This means assuming that unobservable confounders can be safely ignored. On the other hand, this is a rather strong assumption: Is it ever the case that one can observe all relevant influences on an outcome? Imbens (2003, 126) states bluntly that "often this assumption [selection on observables] is not realistic, and researchers are concerned about the robustness of their results to departures from it." Hence, I should gauge the sensitivity of my findings to the presence of an unobservable variable. I attempt to do so below using generalized sensitivity analysis.

The third source of selection bias is selection into the sample, which is closely related to selection into the treatment. States do not randomly walk into a negotiation and take a seat at the table.[6] They choose to enter alliance treaty negotiations. Consequently, data on negotiations will be inherently biased, as there is something about the states that enter negotiations that distinguishes them from states that do not enter negotiations.[7] If this something is correlated with my key explanatory variable (or *is* my key explanatory variable), this could undermine the inference I draw from that variable's parameter estimates.[8] In other words, similar to selection into the treatment, my inferences will be threatened if states enter negotiations because they have compatible ideal war plans.

However, there are four reasons that I am not concerned about this source of selection bias undermining my findings. First, my theory offers reasons why a state's ideal war plan is not perfectly known to outsiders prior to negotiations: threats are a matter of perception, and military doctrine is a product of internal planning sessions. Second, it appears that high war plan compatibility could not in any feasible way be viewed as a necessary condition for entering alliance treaty negotiations. Turning again to table 3.1, the largest of the four groups is negotiations with low compatibility, not high. Table 3.1 clearly shows that ideal war plan compatibility is not necessary for a group of states to be in the sample of alliance treaty negotiations. Negotiations where both the strategic and operational components have low compatibility comprise the plurality of the cases: fifty-six negotiations. Indeed, in only 24 percent (48/197) of negotiations do the participants have high operational and high strategic compatibility.

Third, consider how the groups of states that entered alliance treaty negotiations compare to groups of states that entered ad hoc military coalitions. Like groups of states that entered alliance treaty negotiations, groups of states in ad hoc coalitions saw a need to cooperate on defense. But unlike groups of states that entered alliance treaty negotiations, groups of states that entered military coalitions did not seek to sign a treaty to underpin their cooperation. This suggests that a variable that might explain why groups of states enter treaty negotiations is one that is systematically different between those groups and the groups of states in ad hoc military coalitions.[9] If that variable is war plan compatibility, then one could plausibly claim that war plan compatibility likely leads states to enter alliance treaty negotiations (and, hence, leads groups of states to select into alliance treaty negotiations). To test this, I first find all ad hoc military coalitions involving a European state prior to 1945 (so that the ad hoc coalition groups are comparable to the groups in alliance treaty negotiations). I focused only on coalition members that fought from the beginning of a conflict, meaning late joiners to a coalition, such as the United States in World War I, were not included.[10] I then identified which of these military coalitions were truly ad hoc, meaning they did not have a formal alliance underpinning their cooperation as a group.[11] Using the COW interstate war data set to identify conflicts, I find eleven ad hoc military coalitions. Within this set of coalitions, 27 percent had highly compatible ideal war plans. This is close to the 24 percent among the groups of states that entered alliance treaty negotiations. If I instead use the MID data set to identify conflicts, I find ninety-five ad hoc military coalitions. The larger number of coalitions is due to MIDs representing a lower intensity of conflict than interstate wars (and, hence, a lower threshold for identifying when a group of states are involved in a conflict).[12] The percent of these ad hoc coalitions with highly compatible ideal war plans is 25 percent, which is again very close to the 24 percent among the groups of states that entered alliance treaty negotiations.[13] Overall, this evidence suggests that war plan compatibility is not a plausible reason why states enter alliance treaty negotiations rather than form ad hoc military coalitions.

Fourth, I acknowledge that the scope of my analysis applies only to the variables associated with agreement for those groups of states that are actually negotiating an alliance treaty. This is important because it is unlikely that I could directly model the sample selection process in a satisfactory manner. A standard approach to "correct" for selecting into a sample is to use a two-equation model, such as that introduced by Heckman (1979).[14] The first equation captures the determinants of selection (the selection equation), and the second equation captures the determinants of the main outcome of interest (the outcome equation). However, the selection equation must contain at least one variable that influences selection but not the outcome. This is known as an exclusion restriction (Achen 1986, 38).[15] It is unlikely that I can satisfy the exclusion restriction in this study. The variables that factor into the decision of a state (or group of states) to enter negotiations are likely to play some role (though perhaps an attenuated one) in the negotiations themselves. Indeed, this is explicitly part of my theory. The theoretical discussion implied that having a common threat or perceiving the need to protect a single region are reasons why two states will consider each other as potential alliance partners. But since shared threats are a component in my calculation of strategic compatibility, they play a role in both the selection stage and the outcome stage.[16] While some scholars offer selection models that do not require valid exclusion restrictions (e.g., Sartori 2003), identification in these models is achieved solely through a distributional assumption.[17]

Omitted Variable Bias?

The second complication is omitted variable bias.[18] Omitted variable bias can manifest itself in two ways.[19] First, an omitted variable might be confounding. The patterns revealed in table 3.1 could be driven by some unaccounted-for factor that leads negotiation participants to have compatible plans and reach agreement.[20] Accounting for the influence of this confounding factor could eliminate the observed relationship between plan compatibility and negotiation outcomes. Second, an omitted variable might be complementary, meaning it is included because it accounts for an alternative explanation for the outcome of interest (Kadera and Mitchell 2005, 319). On the one hand, this second reason for including control variables could actually harm my ability to make proper inferences. Including a large number of control variables can lead to multicollinearity and high-dimensional interdependencies, which can enlarge the bias in the variable of inference.[21] On the other hand, controlling for complementary variables can, in the words of Ray (2003, 10), "relieve Variable A [the explanatory variable of interest], so to speak, of the necessity to account for variation in Variable B [the outcome variable] with which it has no causal connection. . . . Thus unburdened, as it were, Variable A can be shown in fact to correlate quite strongly with Variable B." However, when including controls for this reason, they should not be conflated with controls for the purpose of accounting for confounding: control for a complementary cause "should be clearly distinguished theoretically, and in discussions or explanations of research findings from the process in which control variables are intended to expose the relationship of key interest as spurious" (Ray 2003, 10). As suggested in the introductory chapter, the competing explanations that most concern me are reliability concerns and uncertainty over the capabilities of the negotiation participants. Hence, I must include control variables that account for these two competing explanations.

I include control variables by using maximum likelihood multivariate analysis. This entails estimating the relationship between a variable and the probability of observing an outcome while simultaneously accounting for how other variables (i.e., the control variables) also influence the probability of that outcome. In this approach, the analyst is asking, "For a given set of variables (and assumptions about how to model those variables), how likely are the data I observe?" Of particular interest are the parameters reported for each of the variables. One of these parameters is the coefficient, which indicates the relationship between a particular variable and the outcome (while accounting for how the other variables relate to the outcome).[22] Stated differently, a coefficient's value indicates whether that variable is associated with an increase (or decrease) in the probability of an event and, once the coefficient is properly transformed, the estimated magnitude of that increase (or decrease). Additionally, maximum likelihood allows one to compute standard errors and confidence intervals around this coefficient, which can be used to gain confidence (though not confirm) that the estimated relationship is distinguishable from random chance.[23]

Using regression techniques to account for the influence of control variables requires being mindful of the abovementioned complications that can arise from the inclusion of control variables (e.g., multicollinearity and complex interdependencies between the variables). For this reason, a prudent approach is to begin with the simplest regression model and then progressively include controls.[24] If the inference on the main explanatory variable is consistent across specifications, this increases the researcher's confidence in the empirical relationship identified for that variable.

While I will not immediately turn to a model with control variables, I must eventually include them. In particular, I am interested in controlling for the competing explanations of reliability concerns and capability concerns. (I will be better able to address the disagreements over a treaty's language induced by entrapment concerns in my qualitative analysis.) Therefore, I will now describe the three variables used to capture reliability concerns—*power asymmetry*, *reputation*, and *regime type*—and then describe how I capture capability concerns using uncertainty over the participants' capabilities. I will then briefly describe additional control variables.

ACCOUNTING FOR RELIABILITY CONCERNS

The alliance literature suggests that reliability considerations play a key role in alliance formation. This extensive literature identifies several variables that appear to capture considerations of reliability in alliance treaties, with three of the most important being *power asymmetry*, *past behavior*, and *regime type*. In this section, I will explain how I operationalized all three concepts.

Before describing these variables, I recall a point raised in the introduction: even if I show that reliability considerations did not play a critical role in alliance negotiations, this will not refute reliability's overall role in the formation of alliances. As Fearon (1998) argued, because negotiation participants probably accounted for reliability concerns before entering negotiations, one will not see reliability concerns playing a role in the negotiations themselves. The possibility still exists, however, that reliability concerns have a residual influence that overshadows efforts to craft an agreement.

The first determinant of reliability is the power asymmetry among the negotiation participants when the negotiations are between a single major power and one or more minor powers (Morrow 1991; Palmer and Morgan 2006; Mattes 2012b).

To understand this, consider a simple bilateral negotiation between a major power and a minor power.

Since minor powers have few capabilities and major powers have many, minor powers can expect an obvious benefit from an alliance with a major power: additional capabilities that the major power can project against a threat. Given the benefit of a major power projecting power on its behalf, a minor power should be willing to do what it takes to form an alliance with a major power. This is likely to include incurring the cost of allowing a major power to base troops on its territory in order to enhance the major power's capacity to project power. This action is indeed costly to the minor power: the minor power is compromising its sovereignty by allowing foreign troops on its territory. However, the expected net benefit of the alliance is large enough that the minor power can incur these costs and still gain a net benefit from the alliance. The minor power has reasons to be reliable due to its dependence on the security provided by the major power.

For its part, the major power is gaining an obvious benefit from the alliance: enhanced power projection. Given this benefit, major powers should be willing to do what it takes to form alliances with minor powers. This is likely to include incurring the costs of stationing troops on the territory of the minor power. This action is costly to the major power; it incurs both the financial costs of supplying the troops and the opportunity costs of committing troops to one location, thereby preventing it from quickly mobilizing them to another location. But, as with the minor power, the expected net benefit of the alliance is large enough that the major power can incur these costs and still benefit from the alliance.

Because major powers can provide security and minor powers can offer power projection enhancements, Morrow (1991, 914–15) writes that "deals between major and minor powers are natural in this situation. . . . Asymmetric alliances should be easier to form because each side receives different benefits, and both sides can deliver their end of the bargain."[25] Morrow (1991, 918) argues that such deals will be easier to form because there is an expectation that the parties will uphold the agreement:

> Asymmetric alliances are less likely to break in a given period than symmetric alliances and so tend to last longer. . . . [C]hanges in the weaker power's capabilities will not greatly alter the nature of the trade. Because it provides autonomy to the major power, its contribution to the alliance is unaffected by changes in its capabilities. Its security is primarily provided by its major power ally, so its benefits from the alliance will not change greatly with changes in its capabilities. Consequently, these shifts in capabilities are unlikely to break the alliance.[26]

I follow Morrow (1991) and Mattes (2012b) by coding the variable *asymmetric negotiation* as equaling 1 if a negotiation contains a single major power, 0 otherwise. To identify major powers, I use the widely applied COW classification of major powers as described in chapter 2 (Small and Singer 1982). This variable equals 1 for approximately 35 percent of the negotiations, indicating that a little over a third of the negotiations are between a single major power and one or more minor powers.

A second determinant of reliability draws on a notable body of scholarship emphasizing the relationship between past behavior and alliance formation (Reiter 1996; Miller 2003; Leeds and Savun 2007; Gibler 2008; Leeds, Mattes, and Vogel 2009; Crescenzi et al. 2012; Mattes 2012b).[27] For instance, Crescenzi et al. (2012, 262–63) write, "States seeking alliance partners must, by some mechanism, assess the likely reliability of potential partners beyond simple assurances, given that such assurances may evaporate in a crisis. One way states achieve this objective is by observing one another's compliance with past obligations." Similarly, Mattes (2012b, 684) writes, "One important source of information on a potential ally's reliability is its past behavior. Past behavior informs a country's reputation that is then used by others as the basis for predictions about the country's future actions." In other words, one state can rely on another's history of alliance commitments and abrogation as a useful indicator of its underlying, inherent preference for alliance commitments. This argument would hold that states are most likely to sign agreements with states that have a history of reliably following agreements.

Crescenzi et al. (2012) recently developed a useful measure of a state's alliance reliability reputation. This measure uses the *termmode* variable found in the ATOP data set described in the previous chapter. Specifically, a *termmode* value of 3 indicates that an alliance was broken before the scheduled termination date.[28] Equipped with this variable, Crescenzi et al. create their measure using a two-step process. First, for country I in year T, Crescenzi et al. compute I's *alliance history* with each state in the system. *Alliance history* ranges from −1 (indicating that country J perfectly fails to uphold is obligation to I) to 1 (indicating that country J perfectly upholds its obligation to I). *Alliance history* equals 1 if, in year T, country J had an opportunity to uphold the alliance (perhaps during a crisis or war) and fulfilled that obligation. *Alliance history* equals −1 if, in year T, country J had an opportunity to uphold the alliance and failed to do so. For each year in which no event takes place, the score begins to decay toward 0 (a score of 0 indicates no information).[29] Second, Crescenzi et al. then compute an *alliance reputation* score between countries I and J. The *alliance reputation* between I and J is determined by the average *alliance history* score of state J relative to all other states K in the system.[30] It is important to note that Crescenzi et al. assume reputation is a state characteristic rather than a characteristic of particular leaders. While foreign policies may be influenced by the opinions of individuals, the realm of possibilities is constrained by state-related factors, including the nation's capability, geopolitical stature, existing relationships with other states, and the similarity of its national interests to those of others in the system. Moreover, attributing reputation to leaders requires assuming that reputations need to be reset with each new administration, thereby providing little information about the state's historical behavior. This necessitates the odd assumption that other states and leaders lose all knowledge of their historical relationships as soon as leadership changes occur. Even if country I violated its alliance treaty obligation in year $T - 10$ due to a decision by previous leader H, other states in year T will consider the fact that country I was able to have a leader like H in the past (i.e., country I could again have a leader who is able, within the institutions of that country I, to violate the agreement).

Having obtained the *alliance reputation* measure for each pair of negotiation participants, I then create a dichotomous variable, *highly reliable past behavior*, which is set to 1 if the minimum alliance reputation score for all of the participant pairs in the negotiation is above the median value for the whole sample, and to 0 otherwise.[31] This is in line with recent work arguing that state behavior must be viewed in the context of all states, not given an absolute value (LeVek and Narang 2017).

A third determinant of reliability acknowledges the role of regime type. The empirical alliance literature consistently finds that alliances between democratic states last longer, that democracies are less likely to violate the terms of their alliance agreements, and that democracies are less susceptible to the termination of alliances due to swings in the societal support for the leader (Gaubatz 1996; Leeds and Savun 2007; Leeds et al. 2009). The literature has put forward a host of theoretical reasons for this finding, ranging from domestic political constraints to democratic polities intrinsically valuing law (Gaubatz 2006). Of these varied explanations, those based on domestic political constraints have received the most attention (Leeds 1999; Lai and Reiter 2000; Mattes 2012a). According to the domestic political constraint explanation, democratic political institutions necessitate that democratic leaders answer to public opinion. From the public's perspective, international agreements are a commitment and the public wants the country to be perceived as honoring its commitments. A leader who reneges on an agreement can look untrustworthy or even incompetent (Guzman 2009; Smith 1998). Both factors can compromise the leader's, and perhaps even the country's, ability to conclude future agreements. Hence, the leader will suffer heavy domestic political costs by being voted out of office. Fearing punishment by voters, democratic political leaders are especially likely to stand by their commitments. The end result is that states recognize democracies as attractive alliance partners.

This suggests that if country *I* has a democratic regime, other negotiation participants may expect it to be more likely to uphold an agreement. Hence, a negotiation among democracies should have fewer reliability concerns and, consequently, be more likely to end in agreement. To capture this claim empirically, I turn to the Polity IV data set used in many of the above-cited studies on the relationship between regime type and alliance commitment (Marshall and Jaggers 2002). The Polity IV data set captures the political system of a country using the *polity* variable. This variable is on a 21-point scale, ranging from −10 to 10. A score of −10 indicates that the country is the most restrictive and least politically competitive sort of autocratic regime (such as Saudi Arabia in the year 2000). A score of 10 indicates that a country is a liberal democracy (such as Sweden in the year 2000). More precisely, a country's *polity* score is determined by combining its scores on six key indicators: (1) regulation of chief executive recruitment (the extent to which a polity has institutionalized procedures for transferring executive power); (2) competitiveness of executive recruitment (the extent to which prevailing modes of advancement give subordinates equal opportunities to move upward); (3) openness of executive recruitment (the extent to which all members of the politically active population have an opportunity, in principle, to attain the position); (4) constraints on the chief executive (the extent to which there are institutionalized constraints on the power of the chief executive, such as legislatures in democracies or councils of nobles in monarchies); (5) regulation on participation (the extent to which there are binding rules on when, whether, and how political preferences are expressed); and (6) competitiveness of political participation (the extent to which alternative preferences for policy and leadership can be pursued in the political arena).[32]

To capture when states are democracies, applied work commonly dichotomizes the *polity* variable rather than using the 21-point scale. This is because the 21-point scale is not a continuous measure of regime type. Gleditsch and Ward (1997) described how the *polity* data are rather coarse, with countries clumping together at the ends and in the middle of the scale. More importantly, scholars commonly want to make statements about "democracy" itself rather than about incremental changes in a scale (Wiens, Poast, and Clark 2014). There is no standard in international relations for when a state should be considered a democracy on the *polity* scale. Some studies use a rather conservative measure of *polity* ≥ 7 (e.g., Mansfield and Pevehouse 2008), while others adopt a more generous coding of *polity* ≥ 5 (e.g., Lai and Reiter 2000; Gibler 2008). I follow Jaggers and Gurr (1995) and Jaggers and Gurr (2010) by using the middle of these two options (*polity* ≥ 6).

Having used the *polity* variable to identify which members of a negotiation are democracies, I then create the variable *all participants are democracies*. This is a dichotomous variable equal to 1 if all participants in the negotiation are democracies, 0 otherwise. Using a dichotomous measure is reasonable since, given the above claims in the existing literature, participants in negotiations composed solely of democracies, such as the 1941 Anglo-American negotiations, should have fewer reliability concerns than participants in negotiations composed entirely of autocratic regimes, such as the 1882 negotiations to form the Triple Alliance, or negotiations with a mixture of regimes, such as the 1939 Triple Alliance negotiations.

I should add that there are notable criticisms of the view that democracies are more reliable. First, the need to answer to a domestic audience is not unique to democracies. Some autocratic leaders, such as those in single-party dictatorships, rule only with the support of a particular audience (Weeks 2008). Second, this explanation presumes blanket public support of adherence to all alliance commitments. Joe Clare (2013) maintains that the domestic public will only punish a failure to uphold an alliance commitment if the public deems the ally to be of great strategic importance.[33] Moreover, Matthew S. Levendusky and Michael C. Horowitz (2012) find that leaders are commonly able to avoid the domestic punishment associated with defection by claiming that "new information" led to the decision to defect.[34]

Given these weaknesses, Michaela Mattes (2012a) clarifies the mechanism underpinning the finding of democratic reliability by emphasizing the role played by domestic institutions. Mattes considers two types of security cooperation agreements: defense pacts and consultation pacts. Defense pacts—in contrast to consultative pacts—commit future leaders to close military cooperation with an ally. Such precommitment is critical in a democracy, where the threat of leadership turnover, particularly in a state marked by highly fractious partisan politics, means there is no guarantee of ally credibility (Gartzke and Gleditsch 2004). Precommitment devices raise the cost to the opposition party of overturning the leader's policies in the interregnum. The opposition could still overturn the treaty, but this is exceedingly difficult if the defense pact was ratified through a legislative process (and, hence, became part of the country's laws) (Kydd 2009, 298; Martin 2000; Dai 2005). As Leeds et al. (2009, 462) note, "once a treaty becomes law, there are specific institutional procedures required for changing that law, and perhaps, negative repercussions for executives who do not adhere to established law." For this reason, Mattes argues that the link between democracy and alliance reliability should only apply to defense pacts. Since my analysis focuses on the formation of defensive and offensive pacts, then, given Mattes's argument, I should account for the potential reliability enhancements brought about by democracy.

ACCOUNTING FOR CAPABILITY UNCERTAINTY

The second competing argument put forward in the introductory chapter was that of pure capability aggregation. This argument holds that negotiations do not fail over either disagreements about how capabilities should be used in war or uncertainty about the alternatives to a joint war plan. Instead, this argument holds that some negotiations ultimately fail because the parties to the negotiation were uncertain about each other's capabilities and that the greater this ex ante uncertainty, the more difficult it is for the parties to reach agreement. Stated differently, nonagreement is due to uncertainty about the aggregation that will be created by the treaty, which is caused not by ineffective plans but by uncertainty about the participants' capabilities.

To empirically capture uncertainty around a participant's capability, I begin by coding, for each negotiation participant I in negotiation N in year T, its military capability for the preceding five years. Data on military capabilities over the time frame of my analysis (1816 to 1945) are readily available via the COW project. COW offers two measures of military capabilities: personnel and expenditure. Military personnel data are a more useful measure of capability than military expenditure data because they are more widely and accurately available for the nineteenth century (Bean 1973, 209). Measurement error for military expenditure—defined by COW as a state's total military budget for a given year (with the exclusion of civil ministries, such as a national police force, under military control)—is largely due to inaccurate national-level data, problems with conflicting sources, and concerns about currency conversions.[35] These problems were especially pronounced in the earlier years of my sample.[36]

Having obtained the military personnel data for country I for the five years preceding negotiation N, I then compute the variance over that five-year period. This gives me a measure of volatility in country I's military personnel heading into negotiation N. I then use these values for each participant in negotiation N to compute *capability uncertainty* for negotiation N. More precisely, I apply a "weakest link" assumption (Poast 2010). For each negotiation, I determine which participant had the highest variance in military personnel levels over that time period. That value becomes the *capability uncertainty* for the group of participants. This variable has a large range, with a minimum value of 0 and a maximum value of 2.24×10^7. Finally, I use *capability uncertainty* to create the variable *high capability uncertainty*. This is a dichotomous variable, coded 1 when *capability uncertainty* is above the median for the sample, 0 otherwise. To evaluate the plausibility of this variable, I conducted a simple t-test, comparing the agreement rate for the negotiations where *high capability uncertainty* = 0 (0.61) to the agreement rate for negotiations where *high capability uncertainty* = 1 (0.46). That *high capability uncertainty* is associated with a lower agreement rate is consistent with the claim that uncertainty about the participants' capabilities leads to non-agreement.[37]

An important limit of this measure of capability uncertainty is that it does not account for one negotiation participant believing that another is trying to hide or obscure its capabilities. This factor could be difficult to measure directly across a large number of negotiations.[38] However, in the robustness check section, I will describe an alternative model-based measure that attempts to capture when the observed level of military personnel deviates from the expected level.

ACCOUNTING FOR OTHER CONSIDERATIONS

When analyzing negotiations, I should account for their structure, meaning the set of issues and the payoffs associated with agreement (McKibben 2013). Fortunately, by focusing only on alliance negotiations, I am, in essence, keeping much of the bargaining structure constant. Nevertheless, there are a few remaining observable characteristics of negotiations for which I must control explicitly using control variables. Many of these variables were identified by and used in my study on the effect of offers of issue linkage in alliance treaty negotiations (Poast 2012). Therefore, I follow that work by including these variables.

First, since the number of states involved in a negotiation can influence its dynamics, I control for the number of participants in the negotiation, with a value of 2 (the minimum number of states involved in a negotiation), 3, 4, or 5 (the maximum number of states involved in any negotiation in my data set). Second, I control for whether the specific group of states appears in my data set as having been involved in a prior alliance negotiation that either ended in agreement or nonagreement. The first alliance negotiation involving a particular group of states should have very different dynamics than if this group of states was involved in past alliance negotiations. For instance, there will be more uncertainty about the intentions and motivations of states that are involved in their first-ever alliance negotiation as a group. Additionally, if a group of states tried to form an alliance in the past but failed, one could reasonably suspect that the group will have different incentives for reaching an agreement than a group of states with no previous attempt to form an alliance. Third, and related to the second variable, I use the ATOP data to code whether this exact group of negotiation participants had a previous alliance agreement.

Fourth, I code when the negotiation participants are contiguous states. It is widely recognized in the theoretical and empirical alliance literature that distance plays a key role in determining alliance partners (Walt 1987). The variable capturing contiguity equals 1 if all states in the negotiation are geographically proximate, 0 otherwise. Contiguity is determined using the geographic distance data computed by the EUGene software of Bennett and Stam (2007). Fifth, since expanding alliance negotiations along an economic dimension may increase the likelihood of agreement (Davis 2009; Poast 2012), I include a variable equal to 1 if there is an offer to expand the negotiation along an economic dimension (such as a trade or aid offer), 0 if not. Sixth, I use my measure of threat to create an indicator variable coded 1 if any of the negotiation participants are rivals, 0 otherwise.

Finally, recall from chapter 2 (table 2.2) that five countries participated in far more negotiations than any others: Russia, Prussia/Germany, Britain, France, and Austria. Given the sheer volume of negotiations involving these states, it is reasonable to expect that a negotiation involving one of these states is systematically different from negotiations not involving these states. Moreover, their frequent participation opens a potential source of nonindependence between cases (e.g., the negotiations involving Russia are likely not independent of one another). Therefore, I include a dummy variable, *high participation*, which is coded 1 if one of these five countries is a negotiation participant, 0 otherwise. Since these five countries were also five of the most important European powers during this period (Italy being another major power), this variable could also be considered simply a "major power" indicator.

All the control variables are listed in table 3.2. Table 3.2 also provides a brief description of the variables and basic summary statistics. Having created these variables, I am now ready to conduct multivariate analysis.

Direct Influence of War Plan Compatibility

Hypothesis 1.1 expresses the expected direct influence of ideal war plan compatibility on negotiation outcomes: negotiations whose participants have high compatibility in their ideal war plans are more likely to end in agreement than negotiations whose participants have low compatibility in their ideal war plans. The previous section described the features of my data that could complicate evaluating this hypothesis. Having described these issues and my procedures for addressing them, I am now ready to conduct multivariate analysis.

My goal is to know whether the pattern identified in table 3.1 holds once I account for the influence of confounding variables. To conduct multivariate analysis, I presume that the outcome of negotiations, agreement or nonagreement, is explained by a set of observable factors, call these **X**, and some nonobservable random element.[39] When these observable factors and nonobservable element are placed in the appropriate functional form equation, I can obtain an estimate of the probability that a negotiation will end in agreement.[40] I presume that this

TABLE 3.2. Summary of control variables

VARIABLE	CODING	MEAN	MIN	MAX	N
Highly Reliable Past Behavior	= 1 if lowest Crescenzi et al. reputation score of pairs in negotiation is above sample median	0.09	0	1	197
Asymmetric Negotiation	= 1 if only one major power participant	0.35	0	1	197
All Participants are Democracies	= 1 if all participants have Polity IV score ≥6	0.10	0	1	197
High Capability Uncertainty	= 1 if lowest 5-year variance of participants' COW military personnel data is above sample median value	0.50	0	1	197
Previous Negotiations among Participants	= 1 if same group of participants in an earlier alliance treaty	0.51	0	1	197
Previous Alliance among Participants	= 1 if same group of participants were in an earlier alliance treaty	0.39	0	1	197
Economic Linkage Offer	= 1 if negotiation witnessed offer to include economic cooperation according to Poast (2012)	0.08	0	1	197
Number of Participants in the Negotiation	Count of number of states in the negotiation	2.37	2	5	197
Negotiation Participants are Contiguous	= 1 if participants are geographically contiguous according to COW contiguity data	0.41	0	1	197
Any of the Participants are Rivals	= 1 if any two participants are rivals according to Thompson coding	0.36	0	1	197
"High Participation" Country	= 1 if a participant involved in 50+ negotiations	0.91	0	1	197

functional form is a linear model containing each observable factor (along with a coefficient expressing the extent to which it contributes to the outcome) and a logistically distributed error.[41] Given that I am assuming a logistic distribution, I will use a logit estimator whose parameter values are determined via maximum likelihood estimation.[42]

I begin by creating three binary variables that account for plan compatibility. The first variable is *operational only*, coded 1 for negotiations where *high operational compatibility* = 1 and *high strategic compatibility* = 0, and 0 otherwise. The second variable is *strategic only*, coded 1 for negotiations where *high operational*

TABLE 3.3. Main regression results (DV = Negotiation Ends in Signed Treaty)

	MODEL 1 BASE	MODEL 2 + RELIABILITY VARIABLES	MODEL 3 + CAPABILITY UNCERTAINTY	MODEL 4 + OTHER CONTROLS	MODEL 5 + "HIGH PARTICIPATION" DUMMY
Planning Variables					
Strategic Compatibility Only	0.49 (0.40)	0.49 (0.42)	0.38 (0.43)	0.81 (0.50)	0.76 (0.51)
Operational Compatibility Only	0.19 (0.40)	0.03 (0.42)	0.04 (0.43)	0.11 (0.46)	0.13 (0.46)
Both Strategic and Operational Compatibility	1.57*** (0.44)	1.26*** (0.47)	1.17** (0.47)	1.50*** (0.53)	1.44*** (0.53)
Alternative Explanation Variables					
Highly Reliable Past Behavior		1.20 (0.82)	1.00 (0.83)	0.76 (0.88)	0.59 (0.89)
Asymmetric Negotiation		1.04*** (0.34)	1.15*** (0.35)	1.14*** (0.43)	1.28*** (0.44)
All Participants Are Democracies		1.03* (0.57)	1.11* (0.58)	1.14* (0.64)	0.94 (0.66)
High Capability Uncertainty			−0.57* (0.33)	−0.52 (0.36)	−0.54 (0.37)
Constant	−0.36 (0.27)	−0.76*** (0.31)	−0.45 (0.35)	−1.20 (1.03)	−0.11 (1.23)
Number of observations	197	197	197	197	197

* $p < 0.10$; ** $p < 0.05$; *** $p < 0.01$ (two-tailed). Coefficients and standard errors on other control variables and "High Participation" dummy variable available in replication files.

compatibility = 0 and *high strategic compatibility* = 1, and 0 otherwise. The third variable is *both strategic and operational compatibility*, coded 1 for negotiations where *high operational compatibility* = 1 and *high strategic compatibility* = 1, and 0 otherwise. The coefficients on the variables should be interpreted relative to a base category. In this case, the base category is "no plan compatibility." Hence, a positive coefficient on *both strategic and operational compatibility* indicates the extent to which having both strategic and operational plan compatibility raises the probability of agreement relative to having neither.

Having created these three variables, I am now ready to conduct multivariate analysis. Table 3.3 reports the results from this analysis. Each column of table 3.3 reports, for each variable, a coefficient and a standard error around that coefficient. The coefficient can be used to compute the substantive effect of the corresponding variable on the outcome. The standard errors can then be used to compute a confidence interval around that effect. For economy of presentation, the substantive effect and confidence intervals are not reported in table 3.3. Instead, I use stars (*, **, or ***) to indicate statistical significance, meaning a conventional confidence interval (at the 0.90, 0.95, or 0.99 level, respectively) around the estimate does not include 0.[43] Model 1 is a baseline model containing only the key explanatory variables, in particular *both strategic and operational compatibility*. Model 2 adds the control variables accounting for reliability concerns. Model 3 adds the capability uncertainty variable, and model 4 includes the additional negotiation variables from Poast (2012). Finally, model 5 is the full model with all controls and the dummy variable indicating if a negotiation involved one of the five "high-participation" countries. Progressively adding variables in this manner helps to address concerns that my key finding is being driven by inclusion or exclusion of a particular set of control variables.[44]

Across all five models the coefficient on the key variable, *both strategic and operational compatibility*, is positive. Also, this coefficient remains statistically significant regardless of the control variables included in the model. But perhaps the two most important pieces of information that can be taken from multivariate results are the substantive effect associated with a coefficient's value and the confidence interval around that substantive effect. In particular, I should compute the substantive effect and confidence interval of the key variable, *both strategic and operational compatibility*. This means using the coefficients in the model to determine the change in the predicted probability of a negotiation ending in agreement when *both strategic and operational compatibility* changes from a value of 0 to a value of 1. To do this, I first set both *strategic compatibility only* and *operational compatibility only* to 0. If I also set *both strategic and operational compatibility* to 0, I can use a logit link function to compute the probability of agreement when *both strategic and operational compatibility* = 0. Next, keeping all other variables unchanged, I set *both strategic and operational compatibility* to 1 to compute the probability of agreement when *both strategic and operational compatibility* = 1. The confidence intervals around both of these substantive effects are obtained using standard errors computed via the delta method.[45]

Using model 1 in table 3.3, figure 3.1 shows the predicted probabilities of agreement (with 0.95 confidence intervals) when *both strategic and operational compatibility* = 0 and when *both strategic and operational compatibility* = 1. A couple of observations should be drawn from this figure. First, notice that the change in the predicted probability of agreement is 36 percentage points. Specifically, the probability increases from 41 percent (with confidence intervals between 29 percent and 54 percent) to 77 percent (with confidence intervals between 63 percent and 87 percent). This is exactly the same as the change in the agreement rates reported using simple cross tabulations in table 3.1. This is unsurprising, since I have not yet included the control variables. However, it serves as a useful sanity check to ensure that the assumptions required for regression analysis, especially applying maximum likelihood to a logit estimator, are not by themselves

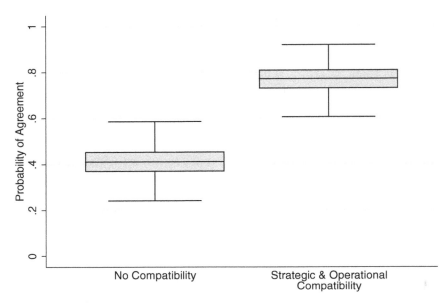

FIGURE 3.1. Predicted Probability of Agreement

Note: Computed by using coefficients from model 1 of table 3.3 to compute predicted probability of agreement when both strategic and operational compatibility set to 0 and predicted probability of agreement when both strategic and operational compatibility set to 1. The 0.95 confidence intervals acquired using ten thousand simulated values of each computed predicted probability.

generating strange inferences. Second, notice that there is no overlap in the confidence intervals around the two probabilities. This shows that the difference in the predicted probabilities is statistically distinguishable from 0; the difference is likely not due to random chance.

Of course, the purpose of multivariate analysis is to see if the change in the predicted probability of agreement associated with strategic and operational compatibility can be eliminated by the addition of control variables. To this end, for models 2 through 5 in table 3.3, figure 3.2 reports the substantive change in the predicted probability of agreement associated with the coefficient on *both strategic and operational compatibility*.[46] It shows quite clearly that the change in the probability of agreement associated with having strategic and operational compatibility is fairly steady across the models. The estimated substantive effects, and the confidence intervals around that effect, are similar across the models. Overall, this is useful support for hypothesis 1.1.

Before moving on to additional tests, it is useful to pause to consider the substantive effects for the key control variables. In model 5 of table 3.3, the model containing all of the control variables, all three reliability variables have positive coefficients. A positive coefficient is consistent with the idea that expecting an ally

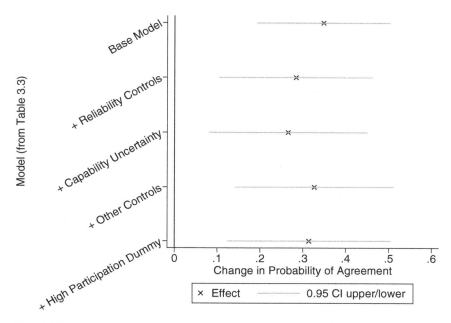

FIGURE 3.2. Substantive Effect of Both Strategic and Operational Compatibility on Probability of Agreement

Note: Computed using the coefficients from the models in table 3.3. To compute each effect, the both strategic and operational compatibility variable is changed from 0 to 1 with the remaining continuous variables set at their means and the dichotomous variables set to their proportions. Procedure performed using Stata command mfx.

to be more reliable is associated with an increase in the probability of the negotiations ending in agreement. The positive sign on *highly reliable past behavior* means that if the negotiation participants have been reliable in the past, the negotiation is more likely to end in agreement. The positive sign on *asymmetric negotiation* means that a negotiation with a single major power is more likely to end in agreement. The positive sign on *all participants are democracies* means that if all the negotiation participants are democracies, the negotiation is more likely to end in agreement. Only the latter two variables, *asymmetric negotiation* and *all participants are democracies*, are statistically distinguishable from 0. But only *asymmetric negotiation* is statistically significant at the highest confidence level (the 0.99 confidence level). Substantively, I find that, holding all other variables at their means (if continuous) or at their proportions (if dichotomous), going from being a symmetric negotiation (*asymmetric negotiation* = 0) to an asymmetric negotiation (*asymmetric negotiation* = 1) raises the probability of agreement by approximately 29 percentage points.[47] This is notable, since it suggests that the effect of asymmetry is less than the effect of the participants having plans that are both strategically and operationally compatible. With respect to the *high capability uncertainty* variable, the negative coefficient suggests that increasing the uncertainty about the military capabilities of the participants is associated with a decrease in the likelihood of the negotiation ending in agreement. While this is consistent with my expectations for this variable, the effect is not statistically significant at conventional confidence levels.

Analysis Using Other and Alternative Control Variables

As mentioned above, my selection of control variables was based on the need to account for two main alternative explanations for agreement or nonagreement in alliance treaty negotiations—reliability concerns and capability uncertainty—and to include the set of control variables used in my previous study of alliance treaty negotiations (Poast 2012). However, these were not the only control variables that I could have included in the model. Moreover, there are other ways I could have operationalized some of the control variables used in the above models. This section presents results that include additional control variables or use alternative means of operationalizing the concepts.

To conduct each additional test, I begin with model 5 of table 3.3. I then either add the additional control variable or replace the relevant existing control variable. These tests were not reported above either because the control variable did not have an obvious connection to a single category of control variables already in the model (reliability controls, capability uncertainty controls, or negotiation feature controls) or because it is an alternative coding of a variable already in the model. Since I am primarily interested in how the inclusion of these variables or use of an alternative measure could influence the estimated relationship between the negotiation participants having strategic and operational compatibility and the likelihood of negotiation agreement, I do not report the full regression results here. Instead, I summarize the results in figure 3.3. Figure 3.3 is similar to figure 3.2, except that it reports the substantive effect of *both strategic and operational compatibility* computed from ten different models.

Before describing the new variable used in each of these ten models, one important observation should be drawn from figure 3.3: the substantive effect of *both strategic and operational compatibility* is highly consistent from model to model. More precisely, each model estimates that changing *both strategic and operational compatibility* from 0 to 1 will raise the probability of agreement by approximately 31 percentage points. In other words, the use of the other variables does not result in an inference that deviates from figure 3.1 (or table 3.1, for that matter).

In the first model of figure 3.3, I replace the single *high participation* dummy variable with five dummy variables, one for each of the individual

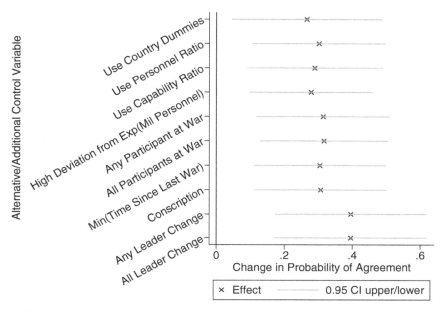

FIGURE 3.3. Substantive Effect of Both Strategic and Operational Compatibility, Models with Alternative or Additional Controls

Note: To compute each effect, the both strategic and operational compatibility *variable is changed from 0 to 1 with the remaining continuous variables set at their means and the dichotomous variables set to their proportions. Procedure performed using Stata command mfx.*

high-participation major powers: Russia, Prussia/Germany, Britain, France, and Austria. While I do not report the regression table from this model, it is useful to note that the coefficients on each of the five dummy variables were negative, indicating that the presence of each country is indeed associated with a lower probability of agreement. However, only the dummy variables for Prussia/Germany and France were statistically significant at or above the 0.95 confidence level. In the sensitivity analysis tests described below, I will return to these countries in order to determine how each or any could drive the results in my analysis.

In the second and third models in figure 3.3, I use alternative measures of *asymmetric negotiation.* In the main analysis, I used an asymmetry measure based on the COW identification of major powers. A negotiation was considered asymmetric when it had only one major power. However, given that this variable was consistently found to be statistically significant, one may wonder if a finer-grained measure of power asymmetry would produce different results. Therefore, the second model in figure 3.3 uses the military personnel data described above (for coding *high capability uncertainty*) to compute the following ratio:

$$\text{Power Asymmetry} = \frac{\max\left(M_1, \ldots, M_k\right)}{\sum_{i=1}^{k} M_i}$$

where M_i is the level of military personnel for country I in negotiation N. This measure ranges from 0.3 (highly symmetric) to 1 (highly asymmetric). As another alternative, the third model in figure 3.3 includes a variable computed using equation 1 but with a measure of capabilities used across a host of studies: the Composite Index of National Capabilities (CINC) score (Singer and Small 1966).[48] As the name suggests, CINC is measured by combining a variety of indicators of a country's active and latent military strength: iron and steel production, energy consumption, total population, urban population, military expenditure, and military personnel. To obtain a country's CINC score for a given year, start with the global totals of iron and steel production, energy consumption, population, urban population, military expenditure, and military personnel. Next, for each of these six components, divide the state's value by the global total. This gives the proportion of each of these indicators held by the state in that year. Finally, the CINC score is the average of these six proportions. This variable ranges from 0.33 (highly symmetric) to 1 (highly asymmetric). Not only does using either alternative measure of asymmetry not alter the estimated substantive effect of *both strategic and operational compatibility*, but I continue to find that the value of *asymmetric negotiation* is positive and statistically significant at the 0.95 confidence level.[49]

In the fourth model in figure 3.3, the measure of capability uncertainty attempts to account for one participant believing that another is trying to hide or obscure its capabilities. As I mentioned above, this could be quite difficult to measure directly across a large number of negotiations. However, one way to capture this notion of capability uncertainty is to assess whether a participant's actual observable level of military personnel deviates greatly from the level that one should reasonably expect. For each negotiation participant in negotiation N in year T, I generate an estimated level of military personnel. This estimate is obtained by using the coefficients from a statistical model that, using data from 1816 to 1945, regresses, via an ordinary least squares estimator, the military personnel of country I in year T on country I's total population in year $T-1$, urban population in year $T-1$, military personnel in year $T-1$, and whether country I was in a war in year $T-1$. I then take this estimated level of military personnel, subtract from it the actual number of military personnel in year T, and take the absolute value of the difference. This provides the deviation in country I's expected military personnel. Next, I find the maximum deviation from expected military personnel for all the participants in negotiation N. These values range from 0 to

6,293. Finally, I create a binary dependent variable equal to 1 for negotiation N if its maximum deviation from the expected number of military personnel is above the median, 0 otherwise. Figure 3.3 shows that using this alternative measure of capability uncertainty induces no notable change in the estimated relationship between *both strategic and operational compatibility* and the negotiation ending in agreement.

In the fifth, sixth, and seventh models in figure 3.3, I include variables that account for the participants being involved in war. War participation is not an alternative argument to my overall theory per se, but it is a mechanism that could induce compatibility of war plans. Stated differently, war participation is an alternative source of a plan: plan compatibility may not emanate from doctrines but from the immediacy of war. To this end, I create three variables using the COW data on interstate wars (described in chapter 2). The fifth model controls for whether any participant is at war in the year of the negotiation. The sixth model controls for whether all of the participants are at war in that year. For the seventh model, I begin by computing the amount of time since the most recent war for each participant. I then find the shortest time since a war among the negotiation participants and use this to create an indicator variable, coded 1 if the shortest time is below the median duration for the sample, 0 otherwise.[50] As shown in figure 3.3, including these controls does not notably alter the estimated relationship between *both strategic and operational compatibility* and the negotiation ending in agreement.

In the eighth model in figure 3.3, I include a variable that was not included in the main analysis since it was unclear whether it was an indicator of reliability or if it helped to reduce uncertainty over capabilities. Specifically, Horowitz, Poast, and Stam (2017) argue that a particularly important means of signaling military strength is a state's military recruitment policy. States have two main ways to recruit for their armed forces: (1) recruit volunteers by offering sufficient inducements to join the military instead of entering the private labor force, or (2) use conscription. This decision has important implications for national defense, including military effectiveness (Horowitz, Simpson, and Stam 2011), doctrine (Kier 1997), and even such domestic policy choices as tax rates (Scheve and Stasavage 2010) and political rights (Alesina and Angeletos 2005). From the Napoleonic era until very recently, the decision to utilize conscription signaled a commitment to a strong national defense posture.[51] Conscription was something that powerful countries did when necessary; for example, all of the major combatants in World War II used conscription. Therefore, I used the Horowitz, Poast, and Stam (2017) data on the recruitment systems of states for all years from 1816 to 2005. I then used these data to code whether all of the states in the negotiation have conscription, indicating that they are committing to bringing military power to bear. As can be seen in figure 3.3, the inclusion of this variable again leaves the estimated substantive effect of *both strategic and operational compatibility* virtually unchanged.

In the ninth and tenth models in figure 3.3, I include control variables that indicate if one participant or all of the participants experienced a change in leadership in the previous year. A new leader might have different policy preferences than the previous leader. In turn, this may be a source of policy uncertainty that ultimately leads to nonagreement. Hence, these leadership change variables are an alternative means of capturing whether uncertainty in a negotiation participant's domestic politics can undermine efforts to reach agreement. To capture leadership change, I draw on the Archigos data set of political leaders from Goemans, Gleditsch, and Chiozza (2009). This data set records information on leaders in 188 countries from 1875 to 2004. In particular, I draw on these data to identify when a country experienced a change in leadership. A limitation of these data is that they only begin in 1875. Hence, the ninth and tenth models in my analysis can only include negotiations between 1876 and 1945. Despite the smaller sample, figure 3.3 shows that the estimated effect of *both strategic and operational compatibility* is consistent with the other eight models. However, it is worth noting that the effect is slightly larger (approximately 40 percent rather than approximately 30 percent).

Sensitivity Analyses

The above results show, across a host of model specifications, that strategic and operational compatibility lead to a notable and statistically significant increase in the probability of agreement. But all of the above results pertain to potential confounders or alternative explanations. They did not probe the assumptions used to create the underlying failed negotiation data, the coding of the key explanatory variables, or possible selection bias. Therefore, this section presents results from tests that evaluate the robustness of the core findings to deviations from these assumptions. The tests can be grouped into four categories: tests that drop observations, tests that recode the planning variables, tests that use an alternative set of nonagreement negotiations (using a synthetic set of nonagreements), and generalized sensitivity analysis. Before going into detail, figure 3.4 summarizes the results from the first three categories of tests. (The fourth category, generalized sensitivity analysis, does not produce a single coefficient estimate that can be used to compute substantive effects.) Each estimated effect is produced using model 1 in table 3.3. Notice that while each set of sensitivity analyses continues to find that the variable *both strategic and operational compatibility* has a positive association with the probability of agreement; the magnitude of this as-

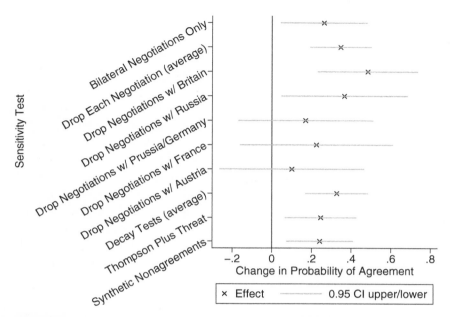

FIGURE 3.4. Substantive effect of Both Strategic and Operational Compatibility, Sensitivity Analyses Results

Note: Computed using the coefficients from model 1 in table 3.3, but with specified sensitivity adjustment. To compute each effect, the both strategic and operational compatibility variable is changed from 0 to 1 with the remaining continuous variables set at their means and the dichotomous variables set to their proportions. Procedure performed using Stata command mfx. For the results where one observation is dropped and the model is estimated with that one observation removed, the figure reports the average effect, average 0.95 confidence interval upper bound, and 0.95 confidence interval lower bound. For the decay results, the figure reports the average effect, average 0.95 confidence interval upper bound, and 0.95 confidence interval lower bound.

sociation varies greatly from test to test. Moreover, the estimated effect is no longer statistically different from zero in some of the tests. I will now describe exactly how I conducted each test.

TESTS THAT DROP CASES

The first several models listed in figure 3.4 drop observations from my sample. These tests drop the multilateral negotiations, drop each negotiation, or drop each negotiation involving a particular high-participation state (e.g., all the negotiations involving Russia).

For the first test that drops observations, I drop all the multilateral negotiations. Given that the theoretical discussion in chapter 1 focused on bilateral negotiations, one might contend that I should only test my theory using such negotiations. To this end, I drop the multilateral negotiations from the sample and test the model using this smaller sample (145 negotiations). This reduces the estimated effect to approximately a 20-percentage-point increase in the probability of agreement. While the substantive effect is smaller, the confidence intervals still do not include 0. This suggests that the inclusion of multilateral negotiations, particularly trilateral negotiations (which make up 38 of the 52 multilateral negotiations), does have an important influence on the above-estimated effects. They are not the sole driver of my finding (as the effect without them is still statistically different from 0 at the 0.95 confidence interval), but they should not be ignored.

For the second test that drops observations, I consider the sensitivity of the results to removing a single negotiation. To do this, I drop one observation from my sample, reestimate the model, and then compute the substantive effect of *both strategic and operational compatibility*. This produces 197 estimates of the substantive effect of having war plans that are strategically and operationally compatible, each obtained from a sample that only contains 196 observations (since one observation has been removed). Rather than report all of these estimated coefficients (and the corresponding confidence intervals) on *both strategic and operational compatibility*, figure 3.4 reports the average estimated effect, as well as the average 0.95 confidence interval upper and lower bounds. It is important to report that the maximum effect identified by this procedure is 0.315, and the minimum effect is 0.294. The maximum 0.95 upper bound is 0.476, and the minimum 0.95 upper bound is 0.459. The maximum 0.95 lower bound is 0.154, and the minimum 0.95 lower bound is 0.129. In sum, this suggests that removing any one negotiation from the sample does little to alter the estimated relationship identified by the model.

For the final test that drops observations, I remove observations associated with one of the high-participation countries (Russia, Prussia/Germany, France, Britain, or Austria) rather than running the model with a control variable indicating when a negotiation has a high-participation country (or, as in one of the robustness checks, a separate variable for each high-participation country). This test usefully illustrates the limits of my analysis. Dropping negotiations with Russia, Prussia/Germany, France, or Austria nullifies the identified relationship between plan compatibility and negotiations ending in agreement. Dropping the negotiations involving Britain, however, does not nullify the effect. In fact, dropping the British negotiations raises the identified substantive effect to 0.366 (with 0.95 confidence intervals of [0.656, 0.076]). The null effect from negotiations without Russia, Prussia/Germany, France, or Austria can only be partially explained by the reduction in sample size. It is true that dropping Russia, Prussia/Germany, France, or Austria substantially reduces the sample size. Dropping Russia reduces the sample from 197 observations by 67 observations. Dropping Germany/Prussia reduces the sample by 71 observations. Dropping France reduces the sample by 60 observations. Dropping Austria reduces the sample by 46 observations. However, dropping Britain also substantially reduces the sample by 66 observations. Instead, the null effect resulting from the removal of Russia, Prussia/Germany, France, or Austria suggests that the negotiations involving these countries are critical to my study.[52] On the one hand, this suggests that Britain may be the major power that most poorly fits my theory. On the other hand, I populated chapter 1 almost exclusively with examples drawn from British negotiations to illustrate my theory. Hence, there are instances in British history that fit my theory well. Nevertheless, this points to the need to further interrogate a negotiation involving the British. I will take up this challenge in the qualitative chapters (chapters 4 and 5).

TESTS THAT RECODE COMPATIBILITY VARIABLES

The next two models in figure 3.4 evaluate the sensitivity of key assumptions used to code the operational or strategic compatibility of the negotiation participants. For strategic compatibility, I assumed that a state's identification of threats was based on strategic rivals (based on data from Thompson [2001] and Colaresi, Rasler, and Thompson [2007]). But it is possible that strategic rivals data understate the threats perceived by a given state. This is because strategic rivalry does not capture situations where threats are not shared. For this reason, I recode strategic compatibility to account for situations where threat perceptions are not shared, such as a small state perceiving a large state as a threat, but the large state not deeming the small state a threat. Based on the discussion of PRIE in chapter 2, I add to each state's threats any contiguous major power state that was not originally listed as a strategic rival. For example, Romania's strategic rivals in 1935 were Bulgaria and Hungary (Thompson 2001, 570–72). To this list, I add Russia, a contiguous major power. This modification to the identification of threats has little influence on my results. The estimated substantive effect is 0.25 and remains statistically significant.

For operational compatibility, I assumed that a state's choice of doctrine is based solely on its experience in the most recent war. While I gave reasons for considering this to be a reasonable assumption in chapter 1, one might consider it inappropriately strong. In particular, the lessons from the previous war might "decay" with time: as time passes without a war, a state becomes more likely to discount the lessons from the most recent war. Therefore, I recode states' doctrines in a way that allows for a doctrine to change during peacetime. To begin, I generate a count of years since war. Next, for each year T and country I, I compute the probability of no doctrine change, which is $100 - W$, where W is the number of years since the most recent war.[53] After computing the probability of no doctrine change for country I in year T, I generate a random number between 0 and 100. If the random number is greater than the probability of no doctrine change, the doctrine is switched. More concretely, suppose country I had an offensive doctrine in year $T-1$. Suppose that the probability of no doctrine change in year T is 25 and that the random number is 27.8. In this case, country I's doctrine in year T will be changed to defensive, the probability of no doctrine change will be reset to 100, and the doctrine will remain defensive for all subsequent years until the random number is again larger than the probability of no doctrine change. After using this procedure to recode the doctrine of each country for all years, I recode the planning compatibility variables for all of the negotiations. I then reestimate the statistical model and store the estimated substantive effect (and 0.95 confidence interval) associated with *both strategic and operational compatibility*.

Since this procedure uses a random number, I repeat it one thousand times. This generates one thousand estimated substantive effects associated with *both strategic and operational compatibility*. Figure 3.4 reports the average effect, average 0.95 confidence interval upper bound, and average 0.95 confidence interval lower bound.[54] The average estimated effect was again approximately 31 percent, with average confidence intervals indicating that the effect is statistically distinguishable from 0.

SYNTHETIC NONAGREEMENTS

The next model in figure 3.4 evaluates the sensitivity of the procedures used to create my set of failed alliance treaty negotiations. Recall that my coding of failed negotiations entailed qualitatively coding events reported in diplomatic histories. One might be concerned about the subjectivity inherent in this coding, or that diplomatic histories are biased toward not identifying cases of failed alliance treaty negotiations. Therefore, I consider an alternative approach for creating observations of alliance negotiations that ended in nonagreement. Specifically, I create a synthetic set of failed alliance treaty negotiations.

I do so using the procedures introduced by Alberto Abadie and Javier Gardeazabal (2003). Abadie and Gardeazabal want to identify the economic effect of terrorism in the Basque region of Spain.[55] Unfortunately, the economic characteristics and performance of the Basque region are unique among Spain's regions. This means Abadie and Gardeazabal lack a control region. Therefore, they create a synthetic control region by taking a weighted average of the economic characteristics of other regions in Spain and using them to create a fictional region that is similar economically to the Basque region but without terrorist attacks. This allows them to gauge the economic impact of terrorist attacks.

I follow a similar logic. Using the procedures described by Poast (2010), I begin by creating a data set of all k-ads of European states from 1816 to 1945, where $2 \leq k \leq 5$. For instance, this data set will include all dyads that include France from 1816 to 1945 (e.g., France-Britain 1857, France-Britain 1858, etc.), all triads that include France from 1816 to 1945 (e.g., France-Britain-Russia 1857, France-Britain-Russia 1858, etc.), all tetrads that include France from 1816 to 1945 (e.g., France-Britain-Russia-Turkey 1857, France-Britain-Russia-Turkey 1858, etc.), and all pentads that include France from 1816 to 1945 (e.g., France-Britain-Russia-Turkey-Austria 1857; France-Britain-Russia-Turkey-Austria 1858; etc.). This generates a total of 7,486,776 k-ad-year observations.

Next, for each of these observations, I code a variety of variables that will be used to create a model that predicts alliance formation. These variables are drawn from Fordham and Poast (2016), who use a k-adic data set to study alliance formation.[56] First, the model includes the total COW CINC score of the k-ad and the square of this score, as well as the number of states in the k-ad and the square of this number. Second, the model includes the foreign policy similarity within the k-ad, using the average s-score of all the dyads within the k-ad (Signorino and Ritter 1999). Third, the model includes two measures of the presence of democratic regimes in the k-ad. One measure applies to the "weakest link" principle of Oneal and Russett (1997) by using the lowest of the 21-point Polity scores of states in the k-ad (ranging from -10, complete autocracy, to 10, complete liberal democracy) (Marshall, Jaggers, and Gurr 2013). The other measure uses the largest difference in Polity scores between members of a k-ad. Fourth, the model includes two measures of the geographic distance between the states in the k-ad.[57] One measure captures the maximum distance between any two states in the k-ad, while the other captures "compactness," the proportion of states in the k-ad that are contiguous to one another. Finally, I capture the magnitude of possible threats facing members of the k-ad using the measure of international threats proposed by Leeds and Savun (2007).[58]

Having coded these variables for all 7,486,776 k-ad-year observations, I then use the ATOP data set to identify which k-ads formed an alliance in year T. This is used to create a dependent variable, *alliance formation*, equal to 1 if k-ad I formed an alliance in year T, 0 otherwise. Using a logit model, I can regress alliance formation on the above-described variables. Having run this regression, I compute each k-ad-year's probability of alliance formation. After removing the k-ads that actually formed an alliance in year T, I keep the 200 remaining k-ad-years with the highest predicted probabilities of alliance formation. These are my synthetic failures. Given that my original data set had ninety-one failed negotiations, this means that I am now using more than twice as many failures as were identified in the diplomatic record.

Having identified my synthetic failures, I now code, for each synthetic failure, whether the participants had compatibility in their strategic plans only, in their operational plans only, or in both. I code these using the procedures described above. Combining these failures with the true successful negotiations, I then re-estimate the basic planning model. As figure 3.4 shows, this results in an attenuated estimated effect of approximately a 24-percentage-point increase in the probability of alliance treaty negotiation agreement. While the estimated effect is smaller, it is still substantial, and the 0.95 confidence intervals do not include zero.[59] Hence, allowing the set of failed negotiations to be more than twice as large did not dramatically alter my findings. Overall, while these results should be viewed with a degree of caution (as the nonagreements are, after all, synthetic), they give me confidence in the findings I identified with my own data set of failed alliance treaty negotiations.

EFFECT OF UNOBSERVABLES?

A final test evaluates the extent to which my core finding is driven by an unobserved confounder. An unobserved variable might determine when negotiation participants enter a negotiation with compatible ideal war plans. If I can somehow account for this unobservable, it could nullify my core finding. The procedure below essentially determines how much hidden bias can be present before a key finding is nullified (Rosenbaum 2005). I must emphasize that the following procedure does not correct for selection on unobservables. Instead, it provides guidance for deciding whether the possibility of hidden bias should lead a researcher to lose confidence in his or her findings.

To evaluate the sensitivity of my key finding to hidden bias, I use the generalized sensitivity analysis (GSA) procedure developed by Harada (2013).[60] GSA is conducted in four steps. The first step is to define the target value. In my case, I wish to know when the positive coefficient on the *both strategic and operational compatibility* variable is no longer statistically significant at the 0.95 confidence level. Hence, my target is the t-statistic value of 1.96 for this variable. In the second step, a "pseudo-unobservable" variable is created using the residuals from an outcome model (i.e., the main model of interest), the residuals from a treatment model (one in which the main explanatory variable of interest, *both strategic and operational compatibility*, is regressed on the other observable control variables), and a random element. Third, the pseudo-unobservable variable is then placed in both the outcome model and the treatment model as an additional variable. The two models are regressed and the t-statistic corresponding to the coefficient on the *both strategic and operational compatibility* variable in the outcome model is stored. Steps two and three are repeated until a pseudo-observable variable is found in which the outcome model produces the target value (i.e., the t-statistic corresponding to the coefficient on the *both strategic and operational compatibility* variable falls to exactly 1.96). Fourth, once the third step is complete, the partial effects of the pseudo-unobservable variable in the outcome and in the treatment model are calculated and recorded. The second, third, and fourth steps are repeated (usually more than one hundred times). Iterating these three steps enables the researcher to plot the range of effect magnitudes associated with an unobservable variable that induces the desired target value.

For my analysis, I use a model in which *agreement* is regressed on *both strategic and operational compatibility*, on the control variables used in model 5 of table 3.3, and on the *all participants at war* variable.[61] The analysis reveals that the statistical significance of *both strategic and operational compatibility* will be nullified if an unobserved variable explains 12 percent of the variation in the outcome that is not explained by the observed covariates, and explains 10 percent of the variation in the treatment assignment. To understand this result, consider how it compares to the *asymmetric negotiation* variable. Recall from above that this is one of the most robust control variables, with the largest substantive effect. This variable explains approximately 6 percent of the variation in the outcome (which is the most of any of the control variables) and 1 percent of the variation in the treatment (which is approximately the same as all of the other covariates). Hence, an unobserved variable would have to be twice as important to negotiation outcomes as *asymmetric negotiations* in order to undermine my key finding. Given the notable literature suggesting that *asymmetric negotiations* (as well as the other control variables) should be accounted for in a study of alliance formation, it is unlikely that I am leaving out a variable that is substantially more influential than asymmetry (or the other variables already included in the analysis). In other words, the results suggest that my key finding is quite insensitive to hidden bias.

Indirect Influence of Ideal War Plan Compatibility

To this point, the empirical analysis has focused on testing the direct effect of war plan compatibility on negotiation outcomes. This was captured in hypothesis 1.1: negotiations where the participants have high compatibility in their ideal war plans are more likely to end in agreement than negotiations where the participants have low compatibility in their ideal war plans. But the direct effect of war plan compatibility is only one way that my theory predicts war planning will influence the outcomes of alliance treaty negotiations. A second hypothesis considers how ideal war plan compatibility modifies the influence of outside options on negotiation outcomes. Hypothesis 1.2 holds that attractive outside options will influence reaching agreement in a negotiation only when the participants have low ideal war plan compatibility.

I now evaluate this indirect influence of ideal war plan compatibility. Measuring outside options has proven challenging to previous scholars. After discussing how previous scholars, mostly studying international political economy, attempted to empirically capture the effect of outside options, I describe my approach to measuring outside options. After some initial analysis using simple cross tabulations, I turn to matching analysis in order to identify how and under what conditions the existence of an outside option influences the outcome of alliance treaty negotiations. This provides a natural transition to the subsequent chapters that qualitatively trace the details of key alliance treaty negotiations.

Measuring Outside Options

Testing this implication requires empirically capturing when the negotiation participants have attractive outside options. This is not a trivial task. McKibben (2013, 420), in seeking to empirically analyze the bargaining strategies adopted by states within European Union (EU) institutions, laments that "states' outside options are another factor for which a consistent and systematic empirical measure does not currently exist."

In the face of this challenge, scholars have adopted a variety of approaches to measuring outside options. McKibben (2013) uses interviews of EU negotiators to code the extent to which they placed importance on "reaching an agreement, in and of itself." McKibben's approach is based on the assumption that states with more attractive outside options will have less need to reach an agreement. This is a useful approach, but it does not offer a direct measure of the outside option that led the negotiator to view reaching agreement as important "in and of itself." Another approach was adopted by Phillip Lipscy (2015).[62] Focusing on the International Monetary Fund and the World Bank, Lipscy argues that the outside options available to states will vary between the two institutions. Regional development banks and bilateral country-to-country development aid are both viable outside options to working with the World Bank. In contrast, there is no large pool of alternative funds for addressing balance of payment and financial crises outside of the International Monetary Fund. This leads Lipscy to expect and find that states will have more bargaining leverage to alter the rules and procedures of the World Bank than of the International Monetary Fund. However, this approach means that rather than measuring the effect of outside options directly, Lipscy infers it indirectly.[63]

Given the challenges faced in previous studies that attempted to quantitatively evaluate the effect of outside options, what is an appropriate approach for the current study? An extreme approach would be to claim that because the period under study, pre-1945, is one of multipolarity, all states always had available outside options: there was always another major power to which a state could turn. But this is unsatisfying given that it would suggest that the available data cannot be used to study the effect of outside options. Moreover, the examples given in the theory chapter showed that states during the pre-1945 period did vary in their perceptions of having an outside option available or, if outside options were available, of their attractiveness.

A slightly less extreme approach would be to claim that major powers always have attractive outside options. The options available to major powers are not limitless, but relative to minor powers, major powers should always have attractive outside options. However, this approach again runs up against the examples given in the theory chapter. The British, clearly a major power during this period, were a participant in each of the minicases. But they did not perceive themselves as having an attractive outside option in all cases. For instance, there was variation in when the British viewed "splendid isolation" as an attractive outside option.

Indeed, the theory chapter showed that the type of outside options and the attractiveness of a given outside option could vary from negotiation to negotiation. Given the context specificity of outside option attractiveness, one could investigate each case to code the existence of an attractive outside option for each participant. But it can be difficult to know when a particular policy option is viewed by a participant as attractive. Indeed, even for a well-known and extensively studied negotiation, such as the 1939 Triple Alliance negotiations or the 1901 Anglo-German negotiations (see the next chapter), whether the participants had attractive outside options (and when) is still a matter of debate. Adcock and Collier (2001, 535) stress that the coding of context-sensitive indicator variables, while potentially useful, "must be carefully justified." In the present study, a case-by-case specific coding of an *attractiveness of outside options* variable requires judgment calls that are sufficiently subjective that I do not think the variable's creation can be adequately justified.

Fortunately, there is one approach to measurement that offers a relatively straightforward and justifiable indicator of whether a state in an alliance treaty negotiation has an outside option: whether that state already has an ally. This was discussed in the theory chapter as one of the three categories of outside options available to states in alliance treaty negotiations (along with unilateral action and buck-passing). This approach has the advantages of being more nuanced than the extreme approaches of using system polarity or being a major power to code outside options, while also minimizing the inherent subjectivity of coding outside option attractiveness. The drawback is that this approach will overcount attractive outside options in some cases (as a participant may not actually perceive its existing allies to be attractive outside options) and undercount attractive outside options in others (as a participant may view another policy, such as buck-passing, as an attractive outside option). Hence, this approach provides a reasonable, if imperfect, means of capturing the existence of outside options.

Given this approach, I use the ATOP data to identify when a negotiation participant had existing alliances with any other state (whether or not those other states are parties to negotiations). I create the variable *outside option exists*, which is coded 1 if any of the negotiation participants enters the negotiation already having an alliance partner, 0 otherwise. Why do I use the existence of an outside option for any negotiation participant? After all, figure 1.1 in chapter 1 emphasized whether "all" or "not all" participants had an outside option. I use the existence of an outside option for any one participant because the discussion in chapter 1 made clear that when ideal war plan compatibility is low, any one of the participants having an attractive outside option can lower the probability of agreement. This was particularly evident when I unpacked the Standard Bargaining negotiations. In those negotiations, a participant with an attractive outside option could hold firmly to its ideal plan. Even if the other participants lacked attractive outside options, negotiations could collapse due to these participants believing that the recalcitrant participant was misrepresenting the attractiveness of its outside option.

To illustrate how this variable is coded, consider four pre–World War I negotiations involving Serbia: the 1904 negotiation between Serbia and Bulgaria, the 1912 negotiation between Serbia and Bulgaria, the 1913 negotiation between Serbia and Greece, and the 1914 negotiation between Serbia, Austria-Hungary, and Romania. The *outside option exists* variable is coded 0 in the first two negotiations, as neither Serbia nor Bulgaria had alliance pacts when they entered the negotiations.[64] The variable is coded 1 in the latter two negotiations: the 1913 negotiation between Serbia and Greece and the 1914 negotiation between Serbia, Austria-Hungary, and Romania. The variable is coded 1 in the 1914 negotiation because Serbia had an existing alliance with Greece and Montenegro, Austria-Hungary had the Triple Alliance with Germany and Italy, and Romania was also in an alliance with Austria-Hungary, Germany, and Italy.[65] The variable is coded with a 1 in the 1913 negotiation because Serbia had an existing alliance with Bulgaria, and Greece also had an existing alliance with Bulgaria.[66]

I should emphasize that my *outside option exists* variable is by no means a perfect measure of an alliance treaty negotiation participant having an attractive outside option. Given the wide range of outside options and how states could perceive nearly any alternative policy as an attractive outside option (or, conversely, not actually view an existing alliance as attractive), there probably is no perfect measure of outside option attractiveness that will be applicable to a large number of alliance treaty negotiations. But given difficulties in empirically measuring outside option attractiveness in general, as well as the specifics of measuring this concept in alliance treaty negotiations, my measure is reasonable.

Initial Analysis

My analysis of war planning's indirect effect on alliance treaty negotiation outcomes begins with table 3.4. This table uses the *outside option exists* variable and the *both strategic and operational compatibility* variable to sort all 197 negotiations into four cells: negotiations with high ideal war plan compatibility and no participants having outside options (i.e., *both strategic and operational compatibility* = 1 and *outside option exists* = 0), negotiations with low ideal war plan compatibility and no participants having outside options (i.e., *both strategic and operational compatibility* = 0 and *outside option exists* = 0), negotiations with high ideal war plan compatibility and at least one participant having an outside option (i.e., *both strategic and operational compatibility* = 1 and *outside option exists* = 1), and negotiations with low ideal war plan compatibility and at least one participant having an outside option (i.e., *both strategic and operational compatibility* = 0 and *outside option exists* = 1).

To place table 3.4 in context, consider how each of Serbia's four negotiations described above fits into one of the cells in the table. In the 1904 negotiation between Serbia and Bulgaria, the parties had low war plan compatibility (Serbia had an offensive doctrine, and Bulgaria had a defensive doctrine), but neither had an attractive outside option. This negotiation ended in agreement. In the 1912 negotiation between Serbia and Bulgaria, the parties had high plan compatibility and continued not to have attractive outside options. Unsurprisingly, this negotiation also ended in agreement. In the 1914 negotiation between Serbia, Romania, and Austria-Hungary, the parties had both low war plan compatibility (Serbia and Romania had defensive doctrines, and Austria-Hungary had an offensive doctrine) and outside options (indeed, all three parties had existing alliance pacts). This negotiation ended in nonagreement. Finally, in the 1913 negotiation between Serbia and Greece, the parties had high war plan compatibility, and, according to how I code the variable *outside option exists*, both parties had an attractive outside option. However, this negotiation highlights how it can be difficult to identify if a party truly finds an outside option attractive. In this case, the outside options for both parties were their respective bilateral alliances with Bulgaria. But Serbia and Greece had begun negotiating an alliance treaty with one another in January 1913 in anticipation of entering war against Bulgaria. Hence, their existing alliances were not truly an outside option for this particular negotiation. This negotiation ended in agreement.

Seeing how each of these Serbian negotiations fits in table 3.4 helps make the evidence and data concrete, but my main interest is in seeing how the evidence in table 3.4 maps onto my theoretical expectations. This can be done by recognizing that each of the four cells in table 3.4 essentially represents one of the four ideal negotiation types introduced in chapter 1. Same Page negotiations are represented by the cell where the negotiation participants have high ideal war plan compatibility and none of them have outside options. My theory expects this combination to be highly conducive to agreement, and, indeed, these negotiations have a 100 percent agreement rate. At the other extreme are the Revealed Deadlock negotiations, which are found in the cell where the negotiation participants have low ideal war plan compatibility and outside options do exist.[67] The negotiations in this cell had the lowest agreement rate among the four cells (42 percent). This is consistent with my theory's expectation that negotiations are most likely to fail in the case of both low ideal war plan compatibility and the existence of outside options. The agreement rates of the remaining two negotiation types, Pleasant Surprise and Standard Bargaining negotiations, should lie between the extremes of Same Page and Revealed Deadlock negotiations. The Pleasant Surprise negotiations are found in the cell where the negotiation participants have high ideal war plan compatibility and outside options do exist.[68] Standard Bargaining negotiations are represented by the cell where the participants have low ideal war plan compatibility and none of them have outside options. The reported agreement rates of these two negotiation types, at 73 percent and 86 percent respectively, do indeed lie between the agreement rates of the extreme negotiation types.

I now turn to evaluating how war plan compatibility modifies the effect of outside options on the probability of agreement. When war plan compatibility is high, table 3.4 shows that the existence of outside options appears to reduce the probability of agreement. The apparent decrease in the probability of agreement is 27 percentage points (from 100 percent to 73 percent). However, the

TABLE 3.4. Agreement rate by war plan compatibility and existence of outside option

		Outside Option Exists?	
		No	Yes
Both Operational and Strategic Compatibility	High	100% [100%, 100%] (7/7)	73% [87%, 59%] (30/41)
	Low	86% [100%, 65%] (12/14)	42% [51%, 34%] (57/135)

Note: 0.95 confidence intervals in brackets. Ratio of negotiations ending in agreement to total negotiations in parentheses.

0.95 confidence interval around this difference of 27 percentage points (0.27) is [0.61, −0.07].[69] This means the difference is not statistically distinguishable from 0. This is consistent with my theoretical expectation that the existence of outside options should have no effect when ideal war plan compatibility is high. When war plan compatibility is low, the existence of outside options reduces the probability of agreement by 44 percentage points (from 86 percent to 42 percent). Not only is this a sizable difference in the probabilities, but the 0.95 confidence interval around this difference is [0.70, 0.17]. This means the difference is statistically distinguishable from 0.[70] This is consistent with my theoretical expectation that the existence of outside options should influence the probability of agreement when ideal war plan compatibility is low.

Overall, table 3.4 suggests that the data support hypothesis 1.2. The table shows that attractive outside options have a large and statistically significant influence on the probability of agreement only when ideal plan compatibility is low. It also shows that moving from my theory's ideal conditions for agreement (no outside options and high ideal war plan compatibility) to my theory's least favorable conditions for agreement (the existence of outside options and low war plan compatibility) is associated with a substantial 58-percentage-point reduction in the probability of agreement (from 100 percent to 42 percent). However, as when I evaluated the direct effect of ideal war plan compatibility on negotiation outcomes, it is possible that the associations found in table 3.4 are the result of omitted variable bias. After all, this table focuses only on the core variables of my theory; it does not attempt to contextualize the negotiations. Therefore, I now turn to multivariate analysis.

Matching Analysis

Evaluating hypothesis 1.2 within a multivariate framework is more challenging than evaluating hypothesis 1.1. I must evaluate two subsets of data: when ideal war plan compatibility is high and when it is low. The need to split my sample raises three concerns about the appropriateness of using a logit, the type of estimator I used to evaluate hypothesis 1.1.[71] First, for small samples, identification in a logit model is driven primarily by the parametric structure imposed on the data by the model, not the data itself. Second, the statistical power of my tests will be questionable given the inclusion of numerous control variables in a parametric model with few observations. Third, table 3.4 shows perfect separation in the data when ideal war plan compatibility is high and no outside options exist (and near-perfect separation when ideal war plan compatibility is low and no outside options exist). Under conditions of perfect or near-perfect separation, we cannot estimate a multivariate model.[72]

Given these concerns about using a fully parametric approach, I turn to the semiparametric approach of propensity-score matching.[73] I have a binary key independent variable (*both strategic and operational compatibility*), a binary outcome variable (whether alliance treaty agreement is reached), and a variety of covariates that account for contextual factors. Therefore, propensity-score matching is a sensible approach.[74] Matching, as developed and described by Cochran (1953) and Rubin (2006), is a preanalysis procedure that uses minimal structural or parametric assumptions to separate treatment effects from shared background characteristics.[75] It consists of pairing each subject in a treatment group with a subject in a control group that has similar though perhaps not identical values for a series of covariates. For example, suppose the covariates are gender and age. Then a perfect match for a thirty-seven-year-old male in the treatment group would be a thirty-seven-year-old male in the control group.[76] The goal of this process is to minimize (if not eliminate) systematic differences between the treated and control groups other than exposure to the treatment. In the context of my study, matching ensures that I am comparing relatively similar negotiations. This, in turn, should eliminate the bias caused by selection on observable characteristics.[77]

The key for matching is that two groups of states are similar on a variety of characteristics, with the only observable difference being the presence (or absence) of an outside option. With respect to the observable covariates, I use all the controls from my main analysis (as reported in model 5 in table 3.3), along with the variable from the additional control tests capturing war participation by all participants in the year of the negotiation (since this variable was found to have a substantively large, positive, and statistically significant relationship with negotiations ending in agreement). To make the two groups—negotiations with outside options and negotiations without outside options—similar on the observable covariates, I use the nearest-neighbor matching algorithm developed by Abadie and Imbens (2002 and 2006), which matches the treated subjects and control subjects that are the closest match (rather than requiring an exact match). The determination of a match is made in three steps. First, I identify the variables on which matches should be based. I call these variables **X**. Second, I determine the probability of each observation receiving the treatment (in this case, an outside option) by regressing the treatment on **X**. This probability is called the propensity score. Third, I use the propensity score to match observations to one another. The Abadie and Imbens (2002 and 2006) procedure also allows cases to be used as a match more than once.[78] Once matches are made, one can estimate the average effect of the treatment, or average treatment effect (ATE). This is computed by a simple difference-of-means t-test between the treated observations and control observations.[79]

Table 3.5 reports the results from matching treated negotiations (i.e., negotiations with an outside option) to control negotiations (i.e., negotiations with no outside option) and then computing the difference of means. The results in table 3.5 are consistent with those found in table 3.4. First, table 3.5 shows that, regardless of whether the negotiation participants have high or low war plan compatibility, the existence of an outside option is associated with a reduction in the probability of the negotiation ending in agreement. Second, table 3.5 shows that the reduction in the probability of a negotiation ending in agreement is larger when the participants have ideal war plans with low compatibility than when their ideal war plans are highly compatible. Third, when the participants have highly compatible ideal war plans, the confidence interval around the effect of the existence of outside options includes zero (and a fair number of positive values). This suggests that while the estimated effect of an outside option existing is negative, one cannot rule out the possibility that the effect is zero or positive. Fourth, when the participants have low ideal war plan compatibility, the confidence intervals around the effect of outside options do not include zero, suggesting that the effect of an outside option under this condition is truly negative.

All of these results continue to support hypothesis 1.2. But table 3.5 also lays bare an important caveat to my findings. The confidence intervals around the effect of the existence of outside options are quite wide. When the negotiation participants have low war plan compatibility, the confidence interval is 60 percentage points (−0.65 to −0.05). When participants have high war plan compatibility, the confidence interval is 70 percentage points (−0.59 to 0.11). The large confidence intervals mean one cannot rule out that the effects are the same for both groups. More precisely, the intervals around the effect of outside option existence when the participants have high (low) ideal war plan compatibility include the estimated effect of outside option existence when the participants have low (high) ideal war plan compatibility. The larger width of the confidence intervals is likely due to the smaller sample sizes used in these tests (149 observations and 48 observations, compared to 197 observations in the analysis reported in table 3.3). This suggests that I have reached the limit of the inferences I can draw from my data on alliance treaty negotiations.

In summary, the tests in this section lend support to hypothesis 1.2. But these tests capture only one kind of outside option: being a member of an existing alliance. I described other outside options in chapter 1. These include unilateral action, buck-passing, or even simultaneously negotiating a different alliance treaty. Moreover, this test does not account for the attractiveness of the existing alliance: a state might have an alliance partner but be unsatisfied with that partner. Indeed, that may have been the case during the 1913 negotiations between Serbia and Greece, as Serbia was seeking to form an alliance to guard against the state

TABLE 3.5. Effect of outside option existence on alliance formation: matching analysis

SAMPLE	ESTIMATED EFFECT	0.95 CONFIDENCE INTERVALS	NUMBER OF OBSERVATIONS
Negotiations with High War Plan Compatibility	−0.24	[0.11, −0.59]	48
Negotiations with Low War Plan Compatibility	−0.35	[−0.05, −0.65]	149

with which it already had an alliance: Bulgaria. However, capturing whether or how a nuanced concept like attractiveness drove the outcome of a negotiation is likely ill-suited for large-n analysis. It is instead likely to be highly case and context specific. This suggests that empirically evaluating the influence of outside options on alliance treaty negotiations requires that the highly suggestive large-n results offered in this section be complemented by careful qualitative analysis. I turn to such analysis in the next two chapters.

This chapter used data introduced in chapter 2 to evaluate my theory empirically. The goal was to take a large number of alliance treaty negotiations and look for patterns consistent with my theoretical explanation for why negotiations end in agreement. Using a variety of analysis methods, robustness checks, and sensitivity analyses, I consistently found that when the ideal war plans of negotiation participants are strategically and operationally compatible, the negotiation is substantially more likely to end in agreement. I then offered evidence supportive of my theory's claim that war plan compatibility has an additional, indirect effect on negotiation outcomes: it modifies when the existence of outside options will influence the probability of agreement.

It is important to recognize the limits of these large-n results. The consistency between the empirical hypotheses offered at the end of chapter 1 and the patterns in the data observed in chapter 3 is suggestive of a causal relationship, but doubts about the chain of events and decisions influencing the outcomes of alliance treaty negotiation remain. The large-n results do not shed light on the chain of events and decisions that link war plan compatibility and negotiation agreements. They also have difficulty capturing the variety of nuanced ways in which outside option attractiveness can be found in a negotiation. For these reasons, I turn to qualitative analysis.

A KEY NONAGREEMENT

The 1901 Anglo-German Negotiations

Incompatible war plans appear to undermine alliance treaty negotiations. When their ideal war plans are incompatible, states are more likely to walk away without a signed treaty. How is that decision made? Was it because a participant with a highly attractive outside option decided not to sign the treaty? If so, did the other participants have different ideal war plans? Did the state with the attractive outside option attempt to convince the others to adopt its ideal war plan? Was war plan compatibility even discussed during the negotiations?

These questions pertain to process: the chain of decisions or events that leads to an outcome. While the previous two chapters presented data and analysis suggestive of an overall pattern linking ideal war plan compatibility to alliance treaty negotiations ending in agreement, the results are largely silent about process. This chapter and the next turn to case study analysis. A case study allows me to look closely at the links between background variables (i.e., the characteristics of the negotiation participants) and the outcome variable (i.e., whether the negotiation ends in agreement or nonagreement) (Collier 1999; Levy 2008). It allows me to detail the sequence of events between decision making and outcomes (George 1979; King, Keohane, and Verba 1994; Brady, Collier, and Seawright 2004; Bennett and Elman 2006; Levy 2008).

This chapter explores an important example of an alliance treaty negotiation that ended in nonagreement: the 1901 Anglo-German negotiations. I explore this case chronologically, starting with the initiation of the negotiations in January 1901 and ending with their effective collapse in late May 1901. In exploring the Anglo-German negotiations, I draw from a host of sources, notably several official document collections. These include volume 17 of the German-language *Die Grosse Politik der Europäischen Kabinette* (*Grosse Politik*), volume 3 of the English-language *German Diplomatic Documents, 1871–1914* (*German Documents*), volume 2 of the *British Documents on the Origins of the War* (*British Documents*), volume 4 of *The Holstein Papers*, and the English translation of the diary of Friedrich von Eckardstein.

The next section describes my case selection criteria: why is the 1901 Anglo-German negotiation appropriate for exploring the mechanisms of alliance treaty negotiations? I then begin the actual case study by describing Britain's outside options on entering the negotiation and explaining why the British considered their outside options to be attractive. Focusing on the British outside options is important, because the British were the party that walked away from the negotiation. (The Germans were still hoping to reach an agreement when the British called off the negotiations.) It is critical that I evaluate why Britain considered an alliance treaty with Germany less attractive than its outside options. Was it for the reason put forward by my theory—ideal war plan incompatibility—or is one of the alternative explanations correct? To this end, I preview the possible sources of incompatibility in the two countries' ideal war plans (my explanation) and the possible sources of reliability concerns, a key alternative explanation highlighted by other studies of this negotiation. I then explore the negotiations themselves. I consider evidence that supports both explanations for the British choosing

TABLE 4.1. Key participants

NAME	OFFICE HELD DURING THE NEGOTIATION
Bernhard von Bülow	German Chancellor
Francis Bertie	British Assistant Undersecretary of State
Baron Hermann von Eckarstein	First Secretary in the German London Embassy
Paul von Hatzfeldt	German Ambassador to London
Count Tadasu Hayashi	Japanese Foreign Minister
Friedrich von Holstein	German Undersecretary of Foreign Affairs
Lord Lansdowne	British Foreign Minister
Sir Frank Lascelles	British Ambassador to Berlin
Oswald von Richthofen	German State Secretary of Foreign Affairs
Lord Salisbury	British Prime Minister
T. H. Sanderson	Permanent Undersecretary of State for Foreign Affairs
Kaiser Wilhelm II	German Emperor

their outside options. I conclude the chapter by summarizing my findings and pointing to the case explored in chapter 5: the 1948–49 negotiations of the North Atlantic Treaty.

Before beginning the case, turn to table 4.1. This table lists the key participants in the negotiations. A number of individuals were involved in these negotiations, which can make it difficult for the reader to follow the narrative. While I mention each participant's official position at first instance, this table should help the reader to keep track of who is speaking to whom.

Case Selection

My analysis will focus on the 1901 Anglo-German negotiations, which ended in nonagreement. There are three reasons this case is useful for evaluating my theoretical claims: it is predicted well by the main statistical model in chapter 3; it is historically important; and it is commonly viewed as supporting a competing explanation.

First and foremost, this case "lies directly on the regression line," meaning it is well predicted by the statistical model from chapter 3 (Seawright and Gerring 2008, 300). Levy (2008) and Dafoe and Kelsey (2014) encourage using statistical models to identify cases for qualitative analysis.[1] This is done in two steps. The first step is to use the statistical model to identify a case that is predicted well by the model. The second step is to explore the case to see if it fits the model due to the mechanisms identified by the theory. Carrying out this technique necessarily requires selecting on the dependent variable, as the objective is to identify cases with a particular outcome that the statistical model predicts accurately. Selecting on the dependent variable can be problematic because it attenuates estimates of causal effects (King, Keohane, and Verba 1994, 130).[2] However, my objective here is not to establish that the presence or absence of a particular variable raises the likelihood of agreement. That was the objective of the large-n analysis. Instead, my objective is to trace the mechanism by which variable X is associated with a particular outcome (Levy 2008, 8). More precisely, I want to know the role of ideal war plan incompatibility in nonagreement and how—in this case—its role compared to that of competing explanations.

When using this selection method, it is useful to have a model that fits the overall data well. The full statistical model from chapter 3 (model 5 in table 3.3) fits the data quite well, as it correctly predicts the outcome (agreement or nonagreement) in 74 percent of the negotiations.[3] Of 91 actual nonagreements, the model predicts that 67 will end in nonagreement. Of 106 actual agreements, the model predicts that 79 will end in agreement.[4] The 1901 Anglo-German alliance nego-tiation is one of the negotiations predicted especially well by the model. This ne-gotiation ended in nonagreement, and, consistent with this outcome, the model assigns it only a 17 percent probability of ending in agreement.[5]

One reason the model from chapter 3 predicts this particular case well is that the case was coded as 0 on the *both strategic and operational compatibility* vari-able.[6] This score means that Germany and Britain had incompatible ideal war plans. Strictly following the coding rules laid out in chapter 2 (i.e., using the most recent war to code a state's military doctrine), Britain had an offensive doctrine.[7] In contrast, Germany had a defensive doctrine.[8] There were also important dif-ferences in the parties' conceptions of the strategic environment. But the differ-ences did not lie in the identity of the exact threats (a key part of the coding rules described in chapter 2). Both Germany and Britain perceived France and, most importantly, Russia as key strategic rivals.[9] But while both Germany and Britain perceived Russia as a threat, they disagreed on where Russia posed the greatest threat. This will be a key component of my case study narrative and highlights the nuances one uncovers by carefully exploring a particular case.

Second, the 1901 Anglo-German negotiations are historically important. In-deed, a number of observers following World War I viewed these negotiations as the great "missed opportunity" to set Anglo-German relations on a path that might have avoided the war.[10] The contention that this was a missed opportunity is predicated on the idea that Britain and Germany would have been allies going into the July crisis of 1914 (not unreasonable, given the duration of the French-Russian alliance formed in 1892 and the British-Japanese alliance formed in 1902). The British and Germans being allies during the July crisis would have altered the dynamics of the crisis. On the one hand, an alliance with Britain might have em-boldened Germany in its crisis bargaining with Russia. On the other hand, an alliance pact could have better positioned Britain to manage its ally, by convinc-ing Germany not to enter Belgium. This latter point is important, as Levy (2003) claims that Britain's inability to convince Germany not to send forces through Belgium (for the purpose of attacking France) is perhaps the main reason that World War I became a general war, not just a local Balkan war.

Due to their historic importance, these negotiations have been the subject of much study by diplomatic historians. Indeed, by 1929 Lord Newton (1929, 207) wrote that "much has been written concerning the breakdown of the proposed Anglo-German alliance," and this was even more so when historian Paul Ken-nedy noted in 1980 that the negotiations had been "recounted and scrutinised in innumerable studies" (244). Two of the most prominent early studies were George Monger's book *End of Isolation* (1963) and H. W. Koch's 1969 article in the jour-nal *History*. For Monger (1963, 37), the negotiations ultimately failed due to Prime

Minister Salisbury's desire to maintain the flexibility accorded by British non-alignment: "[Salisbury] had a deep-rooted aversion to any form of commitment in advance and remained attached to the ease of manoeuvre and empiricism of policy which formed the virtues of Splendid Isolation." Monger adds, "Salisbury's attitude was probably decisive." Of course, Britain would align, signing the Anglo-Japanese pact in January 1902. This is why Koch (1969, 392) emphasizes the divergent geographic priorities of the two parties: "From Germany's point of view, her interests in the Far East were too small to risk the security of her frontiers in Europe. . . . If Britain had to give up her traditional policy of a free hand, it was, for the time being, only in the Far East."[11] But the historians' emphasis on a lack of common interests between the two parties is not fully consistent with the claims made more recently by international relations scholars. Building on the work of Miller (2003; 2012), Crescenzi et al. (2012, 260) write that the failure was not due to Britain being uninterested in assisting Germany in Europe but to British fear that Germany would not reliably fulfill its obligations: "Despite the perceived value of an Anglo-German military alliance, negotiations between the two ultimately broke down in 1901 in large part due to British skepticism of Germany's likelihood of upholding its alliance commitments. . . . British policymakers feared that despite the obvious military advantage of a formal alliance with Germany, an alliance could become a strategic vulnerability if Germany were to shirk on its responsibilities to the UK in any subsequent crisis with Russia."

This leads to the third reason for evaluating this case: it is useful for contrasting my war-planning explanation with the competing explanation of reliability concerns. International relations scholars have used this negotiation as an example of reliability concerns undermining the possibility of alliance formation (Miller 2012; Crescenzi et al. 2012).[12] For example, Miller (2003, 71) quotes a November 9, 1901, memorandum by Francis Bertie (the British assistant undersecretary of state in charge of the African and Asiatic Departments). The memorandum does raise the issue of reliability concerns, as Bertie writes of a tendency for Germany to renege on its past commitments: "in considering offers of alliance from Germany it is necessary to remember the history of Prussia as regards alliances and the conduct of the Bismarck Government in making a treaty with Russia concerning and behind the back of Austria the ally of Germany."[13] But the majority of Bertie's memorandum focuses on Germany's precarious strategic position and the benefits to Britain of remaining isolated from commitments on the European continent: "The German government lay stress on the danger to England of isolation. . . . There may be some danger but there are also advantages to us in isolation." Miller himself acknowledges that the letter may simply convey Bertie's preference for an alternative ally rather than serving as a definitive piece of evidence that reliability concerns led to the negotiation's failure (Miller

2012, 73). Moreover, this memorandum comes later in 1901, when the British had already abandoned negotiations with Germany and were deep in negotiations with Japan.

My goal is to determine whether the British pursued outside options due to a lack of ideal war plan compatibility (my explanation) or reliability concerns (the alternative explanation). Did reliability concerns undermine agreement? Or was the ultimate cause the incompatibilities between the powers' policies for countering Russia? Was it both? Neither? I will use my theory to reevaluate the evidence and offer insights into these remaining questions regarding this important case.

The British Outside Options

It is well known that the negotiation ended in nonagreement because the British had two outside options that they ultimately perceived as more attractive than an alliance with Germany. The first was nonalignment with any major power in Europe. The second was an alternative ally in East Asia. What is under debate is why the British found those options more attractive than an alliance with Germany. Before I can explore British decision making, it is useful to describe the two outside options available to the British.

Regarding the first outside option, the British found the policy of nonalignment in Europe—"splendid isolation"—to be attractive. By "nonalignment," I am referring to not having an alliance with a major power.[14] When Prime Minister Lord Salisbury effectively ended the negotiations on May 29, he referred to the advantages historically offered by the English Channel:

> [German ambassador] Count Hatzfeldt speaks of our "isolation" as constituting a serious danger for us. *Have we ever felt that danger practically?* If we had succumbed in the revolutionary war, our fall would not have been due to our isolation. We had many allies, but they would not have saved us if the French Emperor had been able to command the Channel. Except during his reign we have never even been in danger; and, therefore, it is impossible for us to judge whether the "isolation" under which we are supposed to suffer, does or does not contain in it any elements of peril. It would hardly be wise to incur novel and most onerous obligations, in order to guard against *a danger in whose existence we have no historical reason for believing.*[15]

Salisbury's point is made clear with a map of Europe in 1901 (figure 4.1). The map shows, with respect to Russia (in black), the geographically precarious posi-

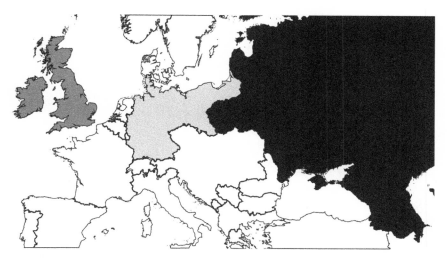

FIGURE 4.1. Europe in 1901

Note: Britain (in dark gray), German Empire (in light gray), Russian Empire (in black). Map created using shapefile from Euratlas Historical Atlas of Europe (http://www.euratlas.com/) and the spmap and shp2dta commands in Stata version 14.0. See the replication materials for more details.

tion of Germany (in light gray) compared to the secure position of the British mainland (in dark gray). But it is important to emphasize that splendid isolation pertained to Britain in Europe. Nonalignment was less feasible in other regions.[16]

This leads to the second outside option: an alternative alliance partner in East Asia. The port of Weihaiwei was the only British foothold in northern China and the Yellow Sea region (see figure 4.2). Acquired by the British in 1898, the Weihaiwei naval station was more important symbolically than functionally, as the harbor was too shallow, exposed to northerly winds, and had limited capacity.[17] Geographically, Weihaiwei was in a less-than-ideal location. The German naval base at Kiaochow was to the south, and Port Arthur, then under Russian control, was ninety miles to the north.[18] Hong Kong, the nearest British naval station, was almost one thousand miles away to the south (Otte 1995, 1166).

An arrangement with Germany was one option for Britain to improve its influence in the region, but Japan also offered to fulfill this need. The British and Japanese had cooperated previously, though on a limited scale. For instance, after Japan's victory over China in the 1894–95 Sino-Japanese War, Britain had refused to join France, Germany, and Russia in pressuring Japan to evacuate Port Arthur and abate other demands on China.[19] The prospect of a formal alliance with Japan opened in April 1901 when the Japanese foreign minister Count Tadasu Hayashi broached the idea to the British foreign minister Lord Lansdowne. Interestingly, it was a March 1901 German inquiry into the possibility of Japan

Port Arthur

Weihaiwei

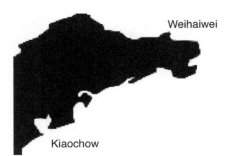

Kiaochow

FIGURE 4.2. Yellow Sea Region, 1901

Note: China (in black), Korea (in gray). Map created using Cshapes shapefile (Weidmann, Kuse, and Gleditsch 2010) and the spmap and shp2dta commands in Stata version 14.0. Map based on map in Davis and Gowen (2000, 89).

joining Germany and Britain that induced Hayashi to begin talks with just Britain.[20] Of the meeting between Hayashi and Lansdowne, Lansdowne writes: "The Japanese Minister spoke to me today with some anxiety about the position of his country in respect to Chinese affairs. He told me that, in his opinion, Japanese interests were seriously threatened by the policy of Russia, and he added that it seemed to him highly necessary that the Japanese Government and that of His Majesty should endeavour to arrive at some permanent understanding for the protection of their interests in that part of the world."[21]

In his "Secret Memoirs" published in 1915, Hayashi describes a subsequent meeting between himself and Lansdowne on May 15.[22] Hayashi again raised the idea of an Anglo-Japanese agreement, in reply to which Lansdowne asked him to outline the general parameters of such an agreement.[23] Hayashi stressed that Japanese interests were "the maintenance of the open door and the territorial integrity of China," which Hayashi felt were identical to Britain's interests in the region. Hayashi writes that Lansdowne thought the "main lines" of an agreement would be easy to reach and that he would refer the matter to Salisbury.[24] This shows that by mid- to late May 1901, Salisbury was aware that a bilateral alliance treaty with Japan could serve as an alternative to an alliance with Germany. This alternative was eventually pursued, with the negotiations beginning in full during the autumn of 1901. An alliance treaty between Japan and Britain was signed on January 30, 1902.

Why did Britain choose its outside options? Was it because the British and Germans had incompatible joint war plans? Alternatively, did British concerns about German reliability drive them to accept "splendid isolation" in Europe and an alliance with Japan in East Asia? Answering this question is the goal of the remainder of the chapter, where I explore the negotiations to determine which factor played the primary role in the British decision.

Why Britain Chose Its Outside Options

To establish why Britain pursued its outside options, it is useful to review the course of the negotiations. I will first consider the state of Anglo-German relations just prior to the negotiations. This sets the stage by providing the diplomatic context in which the negotiations took place. I then explore the negotiations themselves, starting with the offering of initial proposals in January 1901 and ending with their collapse in May 1901.

Before Negotiations

Operationally, the turn of the twentieth century was a time of doctrinal adjustment for both Germany and Britain. Immersed in the Boer War in South Africa, British military planners were in the midst of rethinking the use of defensive firepower, instead beginning to stress the "necessity for developing a resolutely offensive spirit" (Travers 1978, 537).[25] Jones (2012, 66) writes of how "attitudes toward the offensive were malleable throughout the time period." As for Germany, Alfred von Schlieffen, the chief of the Imperial General Staff from 1891 to 1906, was still developing his war plans in 1900 and 1901. His primary plan called for taking the initiative and launching an offensive against France. However, even as late as 1904 German military planners recognized that personnel levels were still inadequate for executing such a plan (Gross 2014, 106). In this case, the secondary option was a counteroffensive (Gross 2014, 100). As the historian Annika Mombauer (2014, 43) writes, "We simply do not know what [Schlieffen] would have done [i.e., if Germany would have entered Belgian and French territory first or would have instead prepared for a counterattack on German soil] if his demands for preemptive war, for example in 1905, had led to a European war."

Strategically, Germany and Britain both perceived Russia as a threat, but they differed widely in why. For Britain, Russia was primarily a threat to its colonial interests in central and East Asia. With respect to central Asia, the historian Michael Hughes (2000, 2) writes, "As Russia moved its frontiers ever southward, while the British continued to strengthen their rule in India, the whole of central Asia became a critical flashpoint between the two countries." With respect to East Asia, the British wished to check Russian incursions into China. So concerned was Britain about Russian influence in China that in August 1898, responding to Russian attempts to block the construction of British rail lines in northern China, acting foreign secretary Alfred Balfour proposed that the cabinet consider cutting off diplomatic relations with Russia and declaring war (Otte 2007, 165). While the dispute between Russia and Britain was temporarily settled, the historian T. G. Otte (2007) rightfully observes, "The fact that a military conflict with Russia was actively considered was indicative not only of the strains in Anglo-Russian relations; it also highlighted the explosive potential of the China Question" (165).

Make no mistake; British concerns about Russia were not limited to Asia. For decades the British had sought to check Russian incursions into Ottoman territory and the threat of Russia closing off the Bosporus Straits. This concern became acute with the signing of the Franco-Russian alliance treaty in the early 1890s. As the historian George Kennan (1984) writes, "The British were haunted, particularly in the years of the 1890s, by the fear that the Russians might either force the Straits with these vessels or dragoon the Sultan into acquiescing in their passage; after which the Russian ships would emerge into the Mediterranean and associate themselves with the French navy, thereby overshadowing the British Mediterranean force and establishing a Franco-Russian naval supremacy in that sea" (127).

For Germany, Russia was a direct threat to its territorial integrity in Europe. Again, this should be evident by consideration of figure 4.1. But Germany did have growing interests in Asia.[26] Sir Frank Lascelles, the British ambassador to Berlin, informed Salisbury in August 1900 of Germany's acute commercial interests in the Yangtze region: "now German commercial interests were second and not far inferior to those of England in the valley of the Yang-tsze, and if Her Majesty's Government could see their way to give assurances that they would maintain the policy of the open door, they would find the German Government on their side."[27] This led Germany to sign the "Yangtze agreement" with Britain in October 1900.[28] The agreement's core provision was clause 3, which read: "In case of another Power making use of the complications in China in order to obtain under any form whatever such territorial advantages, the two Contracting Parties reserve to themselves to come to a preliminary understanding as to the eventual steps to be taken for the protection of their own interests in China."[29] This provision did not obligate the two countries to defend China from incursions by a third party,[30] but scholars recognize that the intent of the agreement, which will be referenced again below, was to prevent Russian expansion into China (Miller 2012, 67–74).[31] Hence, it would be incorrect to say that Germany had no interests in Asia. But Germany's core concern with respect to Russia lay in Europe, not Asia.

In short, the parties agreed on Russia as a threat but had different views about the region to emphasize. Reaching agreement on an alliance treaty would require settling that difference, either by agreeing to focus on one region or by creating a comprehensive alliance that covered Europe and Asia. The former seemed unlikely given that it would require one party to sacrifice a key element of its core security interests. The latter seemed unlikely given the sheer scope and scale of such an agreement.

Before entering the negotiations, the British had concerns about German reliability. Consider a letter by Salisbury to Lord George Curzon from October 17, 1900. In the letter, Salisbury writes: "As to Germany I have less confidence in her than you. She is in mortal terror on account of that long undefended frontier of hers on the Russian side. She will therefore never stand by us against Russia; but is always rather inclined to curry favour with Russia by throwing us over. I have no wish to quarrel with her; but my faith in her is infinitesimal."[32] This statement clearly conveys reliability concerns. Interestingly, it came one day after England and Germany signed the abovementioned "Yangtze agreement." Salisbury's views appeared justified, as by January 1901 Britain perceived Germany as having broken the agreement.[33] The precipitating event was Russia obtaining a concession from China at Tientsin in Manchuria. From the British viewpoint, this appeared to be a direct case of a "Power making use of the complications in China in order to obtain under any form whatever such territorial advantages" which, according to clause 3, called for a response (Monger 1963, 23). But Germany responded that Russia's actions did not directly involve German interests (Kennedy 1980, 244). As the German chancellor Bernhard von Bülow remarked to the Reichstag in reference to the Anglo-German agreement, "that agreement was in no sense concerned with Manchuria."[34] This was not an unreasonable interpretation of the treaty, as the German government had negotiated it with the understanding that their obligations applied only to the Yangtze River basin region, not to Manchuria (Kawai 1939, 424). Friedrich von Holstein, the German undersecretary of foreign affairs and a highly influential senior official in the German State Department,[35] remarked in an October 31, 1901 memorandum to Bülow that the records of the treaty negotiations "showed that from the very start Lord Salisbury agreed that Manchuria was not to come within the scope of the arrangement."[36] To this comment, Bülow remarked, "we disappointed Lord Salisbury, since he imagined that we meant the agreement to include Manchuria." In addition to the limits of their treaty obligations, Kaiser Wilhelm conveyed to Francis Bertie, the assistant undersecretary of state in charge of the African and Asiatic Departments, that "the length of the Russo-German frontier . . . forces Germany to walk warily."[37] Given that these events happened just prior to the alliance treaty negotiations, it is reasonable to suppose that they shadowed British ideas about the prospects for agreement.

Initial Proposals: January through Early March

It is unclear from the historical record exactly who initiated the idea of an Anglo-German alliance in 1901. The initial proposal might have come from Germany. Kaiser Wilhelm visited England in January 1901. The main purpose of the visit was for Wilhelm to see his grandmother Queen Victoria before her death. Following the funeral—Victoria died on January 22—a farewell dinner was held for the kaiser. During the dinner, Wilhelm stood and remarked to those in attendance, "We ought to form an Anglo-German alliance, you to keep the seas while we would be responsible for the land."[38] Of course, this comment could be dismissed as simply a sentiment voiced in light of the occasion. In his assessment of the event, Koch (1969, 389) writes, "The Kaiser's visit for the funeral of Queen Victoria may have softened public feelings towards Germany, but it was quite another matter for the public to be asked to fight over Alsace or the Balkans."

The kaiser's remarks aside, Paul Von Hatzfeldt, the German ambassador to London, in a memo to the German Foreign Ministry dated January 18, 1901, identified the British as making the initial proposal: "Recently, Baron Eckardstein was with Mr. Chamberlain in the country with the Duke of Devonshire, when Chamberlain remarked that he and his friends in the cabinet now recognized that the time for 'splendid isolation' was over. . . . [Chamberlain] was convinced that joining forces with Germany and connection to the Triple Alliance was preferable. He personally will do everything possible to bring about a gradual initiation in this direction."[39] Paul von Metternich, a member of the German embassy in London who would be appointed German ambassador to England in November of 1901, also viewed the British as making the initial proposal. Metternich wrote to Bülow on January 22 that "the English were in a mess and therefore felt the desire for a rapprochement."[40] The "mess" was both Russian incursions in China and the ongoing Boer War. In a marginal note, Bülow declared Metternich's observation "correct!"[41] Metternich's view was that Germany "should neither lend the Russians our money nor the English our soldiers."[42] Holstein was also skeptical of the proposal. In a memo to the first secretary in the London embassy, Baron Eckardstein, Holstein conveyed his fear that an alliance with Britain would, given British rivalry with Russia and France, place Germany at risk of war. Accepting such a risk required compensation. This was a problem, because Holstein felt that Salisbury would rebuke any compensation request with a flippant "You ask too much for your friendship."[43] In a telegram dated February 14, Holstein advised Ambassador Hatzfeldt that "we should not run after the English with proposals for a rapprochement" but instead leave it to the British to bring forward a proposal to cooperate against Russia.[44] He then cautioned Eckardstein to be wary of

Salisbury's "policy of a confidence trickster," which Holstein pointed to as the cause of "England's present isolation."[45]

Regardless of who initiated the proposal, more substantial negotiations over the matter began in March 1901.[46] On March 8, 1901, the British foreign secretary Lord Lansdowne asked Hatzfeldt about the possibility of Germany keeping France at bay in case of a war in the Far East between Russia and Japan. In other words, England wanted Germany to help "localize" the war. Landsdowne proposed that Germany "make a statement in Paris with England that, in the event of a Russo-Japanese conflict, both powers, in the interest of peace in Europe, desired localizing the conflict in Europe and maintain strict neutrality."[47] The reason for making the statement in Paris was to make clear to the French that "should any European power meddle in a Russo-Japanese War, Germany and England would 'reconsider their neutrality.'"[48] Hatzfeldt, in a memo to the foreign office (not shared with Landsdowne), felt that a statement in Paris was likely "superfluous" because France was unlikely to meddle in a "Japan-Russia or Japanese-English-Russian conflict in China."[49]

On March 9, 1901, Holstein wrote to Eckardstein (because Holstein suspected that Hatzfeldt was ill) that Germany "can't go beyond benevolent neutrality" because the Yangtze agreement "provides no Anglo-German solidarity in case the Russians and French both attack us in Europe on account of our proceedings in Eastern Asia."[50] However, Holstein then proceeded to lay out the provisions of an agreement that could induce Germany to go beyond neutrality:

> I may observe for your personal information that the position would be very different if there were a defensive alliance between Great Britain and Germany. This might be to the effect that each contracting party should fight one adversary on its own account, the treaty to come into force as soon as there were two or more adversaries. If in that case, England, probably with Japan, fought Russia alone, we should be neutral unless and until France joined in, which in that case it would certainly not do. Indeed, England and Japan would be so superior to Russia that the latter would give way without fighting when it came to the point.[51]

Holstein concluded the letter by lamenting how the existing agreements with England—namely, the Zanzibar and Portuguese agreements—did not produce more "real material advantage" for Germany.[52] In the first of the agreements, signed in 1890, Germany gained access to the island of Heligoland but lost the Zanzibar region in Africa, while in the second, signed in 1898, the two parties agreed on their right to preemptively divide Portugal's African colonies. Here, Holstein said that, "the Zanzibar agreement, where England got the lion's share, has left a bad impression, so has the Portuguese agreement which is still unrealised."[53] Hence, he apparently shared the view that a primary benefit to Germany of an agreement with England was the acquisition of colonies. But Holstein made clear to Eckardstein that "you must on no account raise this idea. It must come from them."[54] Holstein felt that such a proposal from England was unlikely with Salisbury in office. On March 17, 1901, Holstein reiterated to Eckardstein the need for holding back the proposal of an alliance, "I forbid you EXPRESSLY, my dear friend, even to breathe a word about alliance. The proper moment, if it ever comes, is certainly not now."[55]

Further Proposals: Mid-March

Events started moving quickly in mid-March. In his memoir, Eckardstein writes that before he received the abovementioned March 17 note from Holstein, he had a conversation with Landsdowne about the possibility of an alliance agreement. The conversation took place on March 18, 1901. Both Eckardstein and Landsdowne wrote about the conversation. It can prove insightful to compare their accounts.

ECKARDSTEIN'S ACCOUNT

Eckardstein wrote to Holstein of how the conversation began two days before, with Lansdowne again raising the question of Germany joining with England to ensure that a Russo-Japanese conflict remained "localized" in East Asia: "Lord Lansdowne, with whom I dined the day before yesterday, asked me in the strictest confidence whether I thought there was any hope of a joint Anglo-German action for localising a possible Russo-Japanese war by influencing France."[56] Eckardstein reports that he replied that such an arrangement was unlikely because it would not oblige England to provide for any of Germany's needs: "I replied, that I did not think there was the least prospect of such a proposal being accepted by the Imperial Government, as Germany would thereby commit itself without getting any assurance of backing from England."[57]

The very next day, according to Eckardstein, Lansdowne again broached the subject, this time with an offer—a more complete defensive alliance—that might be more appealing to Germany: "Yesterday afternoon Lord Lansdowne again raised this question, and said that he had been contemplating the possibility of bringing about a defensive arrangement between Great Britain and Germany which should be concluded for a considerable period. He believed that several of his most influential colleagues would favour the idea. England was now at a turning point and must make up its mind as to what line it would take in future." However, Lansdowne added that the cabinet would first need to know if the German government would be inclined to accept the offer: "But, should such an idea be put into concrete form by the Cabinet, no official proposal would be made to Germany until there was some certainty that Germany would be disposed in principle to accept it."[58] Eckardstein responded that he would first need to know the nature of the proposal before he could say if the German government would be inclined to sign a treaty: "I replied that I was not in a position to tell him whether and to what extent the Imperial Government would favour such a proposal when made. If he would put forward a definite idea I would not fail to report it to Berlin."[59]

Eckardstein concluded his note to Holstein by saying that he would wait to hear more from Lansdowne in the next few days but would also appreciate guidance from the German foreign office.[60] He also added his personal impression, which was "that the Cabinet here, including Salisbury, are really now at a parting of the ways as to their future policy in general and as to China in particular, and that in the course of the next few days we shall know definitely."[61] Of particular interest is what Eckardstein did not say in his memo to Holstein. Eckardstein writes in his memoir that he withheld a key piece of information from Holstein: "The fact was that, when dining with Lord Lansdowne on March 16th, I had given him a strong hint to approach us with an offer of alliance, for I had said to him: 'If there were a defensive alliance between Great Britain and Germany, covering all possibilities, it would be obvious that Germany could at once agree to localise a war between Russia and Japan by influencing France.'"[62] His reason for not offering this detail is that Holstein would have criticized him for "going too far" because "Holstein's motto always was: 'Make me an omelette but break me no eggs.'"[63]

In response to Eckardstein's note, Holstein wrote that now was an important opportunity, but it would be difficult to seal the deal:

> Anyone can see that the present moment is decisive. Both Great Britain and Germany are at a parting of the ways. . . . Such an understanding between Great Britain and Germany as I desire is made difficult by mutual distrust. The English have of late become distrustful, but Germany has for long had occasion to be so . . . Germany's good will has been shown in its attitude over the Tientsin question, which has pleasantly surprised a follower of Salisbury like Frank Lascelles. As for English mistrust, it cannot be anything like as great as that which we are entitled to entertain against Salisbury. Nevertheless, we won't give up hope of a satisfactory result in the end. I believe the right way is via Vienna.[64]

The final sentence is in reference to the idea, also expressed in the letter, that connecting England with the Triple Alliance would be the most practical approach: "In order to facilitate an exchange of views and to conciliate public opinion, it would be more practical to give the rapprochement the character of an accession by England to the Triple Alliance rather than of an Anglo-German Alliance."[65] Holstein also viewed Japan as a potential negotiation participant: "I see moreover no reason why Japan should not also be brought into such a defensive alliance. This would make such a combination in some ways easier, for Japan is popular in Germany. Japan, being only out for what it can get, would probably attach no great value to a mere insurance treaty. But all the same its general position would be improved by a treaty which would bring it into good company."[66]

Holstein's response is important, as it shows that he initiated the idea of Britain joining the Triple Alliance, not just forming a bilateral agreement with Germany. This view was shared by other German officials. For instance, in response to the question of the conditions under which Germany would accept an alliance with Britain, Bülow informed Hatzfeldt, "best of all in the form of an arrangement between the Triple Alliance and England."[67] The reality is that German officials had reliability concerns about their Triple Alliance partners, Italy and Austria-Hungary. Holstein believed the Triple Alliance allies were "shaky," and Britain was a means of strengthening the alliance.[68] He wrote in a March 27, 1901, memorandum: "For obvious reasons it would not benefit us, with no other support than that of the shaky Triple Alliance, to incur the kind of suspicion which would bring into the foreground the chauvinistic elements and tendencies of the Dual Alliance. All would be quite different if England would make up her mind to link herself at some time with the Triple Alliance."[69] Holstein's rationale was that Britain "in Asia and Europe is genuinely for a defensive policy," which would help strengthen the Triple Alliance in Europe and restrain Japanese efforts to enter Korea or push Russia out of Manchuria.[70] In an April 14, 1901, letter to Hatzfeldt, Foreign Secretary Baron Oswald von Richthofen wrote that "enemies of the Triple Alliance" were spreading reports that Germany intended the partition of Austria-Hungary following the death of Emperor Franz Joseph.[71] Richthofen thought that the best way of dispelling such rumors was to make Austria-Hungary a central figure in the negotiations: "there can be no more practical way of disarming this suspicion than by the realisation that the Austro-Hungarian Monarchy is being allotted a leading part by Germany in the formation of the projected new alliance [with England]."[72] To drive home the point, Richthofen ends the note by writing, "This is why we set so much store on making Vienna to some extent the centre for the alliance negotiations."[73]

LANSDOWNE'S ACCOUNT

Lansdowne shared his view of the conversation in a letter to Ambassador Lascelles dated March 18, 1901. His account is largely consistent with Eckardstein's: Germany did not favor an arrangement solely focused on Germany and England "keeping a ring" around a third party (read: France) entering a Russo-Japanese war.[74] The type of agreement favored by Germany, Lansdowne writes, is oriented toward security on the continent of Europe itself: "The kind of arrangement which he contemplated might be described as a purely defensive alliance between the two Powers, directed solely against France and Russia. So long as Germany or England were attacked by one only of the other two Powers the Alliance would not operate, but if either Germany or England had to defend itself against both France and Russia, Germany would have to help England, or England Germany, as the case might be."[75] This account by Lansdowne is consistent with the information that Eckardstein chose not to share with Holstein. Hence, one can conclude that, regardless of the origins of the idea for an Anglo-German alliance, the general structure of the treaty was first offered by Eckardstein.

Lansdowne then shared Eckardstein's reasoning for why such an arrangement would be in England's favor: "[Eckardstein] thought England, which had scattered and vulnerable possessions all over the world, was more likely to require help than Germany."[76] Lansdowne did not rebut this claim, but he proceeded to highlight his thoughts as to why such an agreement would benefit Germany: "I told Baron Eckardstein that the proximity of Russia to Germany along so extensive a frontier made the situation of Germany quite as vulnerable as ours."[77] In short, Germany viewed Britain as overextended, and Britain viewed Germany as highly vulnerable to a direct Russian invasion.[78]

Lansdowne's letter suggests a British openness to a comprehensive alliance treaty, but he would have to share the idea with the British cabinet: "[Eckardstein's] project was a novel and very far-reaching one, which would require careful examination, and which obviously I could not encourage without reference to my colleagues."[79] However, even if such an agreement was reached, Lansdowne was highly concerned about the reliability of the parties and how they would interpret particular events that could trigger mutual assistance: "It occurred to me, moreover, that it was far from easy to distinguish between the case in which a country was acting on the defensive and the case in which it was not. The first blow might be ideally struck in self-defence; or, conversely, an attack might be brought on by political action of a deliberately provocative character. How were our mutual obligations to be defined so as to meet all such cases fairly?"[80]

In response to Lansdowne's note, Lascelles said Eckardstein's proposal harkened back to a conversation he had with Kaiser Wilhelm in August 1898 where the emperor "alluded to an 'arrangement.'"[81] Interestingly, from the standpoint of diplomats viewing alliance treaties as plans, Lascelles adds the following: "I will make enquiries and in the meantime I would suggest that Eckardstein should be reminded of a conversation I had with the Emperor in December 1898 in the course of which His Majesty endorsed Count Hatzfeldt's opinion that no formal alliance between England and Germany was necessary because if it became advisable for them to take common action the necessary arrangements could be made in a very short time. See my despatch No. 338 of 21st December, 1898."[82]

This 1898 conversation was recorded by Lascelles in a December 21, 1898, memorandum to then foreign minister Salisbury. In the memorandum, Lascelles recounts a dinner conversation with Kaiser Wilhelm on December 19. When the conversation turned to the possibility of an alliance treaty, Lascelles shared with Wilhelm "an observation, made to me by Count Hatzfeldt, that no formal alliance was necessary between England and Germany, as, if it became advisable for them to take common action, the arrangements could be made in twenty-four hours."[83] Wilhelm concurred, but "with the alteration of half-an-hour instead of twenty-four hours, and said there was certainly no necessity for a formal alliance."[84]

Questions and Details: Late March through April

With the idea proposed and with Eckardstein offering the general outline of an agreement, the parties dove into the details. A telegram from Hatzfeldt to the German foreign office dated March 23, 1901, provides an informative starting point for considering the details of an eventual treaty. As recorded in the *German Diplomatic Documents* collection, the telegram contains marginal notes by German chancellor Bülow that capture his response to Hatzfeldt's comments. Hatzfeldt begins by stating Lansdowne's eagerness to "bring declarations on the subject as fully as possible into agreement."[85] Bülow's response is "Good." Hatzfeldt then states that Lansdowne agreed that Manchuria "had been expressly omitted from the negotiations" and that the agreement did not oblige "a third [party] to observe its principles."[86] To this, Bülow noted, "Correct." Hatzfeldt then shared how Lansdowne had composed a memorandum that was shared with the British foreign minister Arthur Balfour and Prime Minister Salisbury.[87] According to Hatzfeldt, Lansdowne said that Salisbury, after studying the memorandum, was in principle "for a strictly defined defensive alliance," but it depended on the details of the agreement and the meaning of "all means found."[88] Otherwise, it would be difficult to ensure that the agreement was accepted by Parliament, which was commonly opposed to long-term agreements.

This point about gaining parliamentary approval deserves a bit more discussion. In his memoir, Eckardstein recalls a conversation with Lansdowne (around the same date in March) where a scheme was described by which treaties "were to be kept strictly secret, but it was contemplated that after a sufficient education of public opinion in both countries the Parliaments concerned could be consulted."[89] Hence, while public opinion and the need for parliamentary ratification surely constrained the actions of the diplomats, these would not prohibit treaties if the leadership of the countries valued the treaties enough to incur the effort of "educating" the public.

Returning to Hatzfeldt's memorandum, he next describes how Lansdowne then asked a series of questions. This led Hatzfeldt to suspect that Lansdowne—or, more precisely, Balfour and Salisbury—was considering the details of an agreement.[90] The questions were as follows:

1. Do you think personally that the Imperial Government will eventually consent to a binding defensive agreement with England? And will this be possible in the face of the acutely anti-British feeling in Germany?
2. Assuming that the Imperial Government favours such an idea, how, in your opinion, would such an alliance be conceived? Would an absolutely defensive alliance be preferred or one in which the *casus foederis* would only arise when one of the parties was attacked on two or more sides?
3. Would a secret agreement or one to be accepted by Parliament be included?
4. Would Japan, in connection with the Far East, eventually be included?[91]

Though Hatzfeldt offered opinions on each question, the most relevant responses are found in Bülow's marginal notes. With respect to the first question, Bülow wrote, "Best of all in the form of an agreement between the Triple Alliance and England."[92] This does not suggest that a linkage between the Triple Alliance and England was the only means of reaching agreement, only that it was the preferred means. With respect to the second question, Bülow wrote, "The second."[93] With respect to the third question, he wrote, "Only the second." Whether this meant the agreement must be made immediately public or whether it could be subjected to the above scheme described by Eckardstein is unclear.[94] With respect to the fourth question, Bülow wrote, in French, "It depends." Bülow elaborated on this comment in his March 24, 1901, formal response to Hatzfeldt: "Japan is inclined for acquisition and may not therefore see any particular advantage to herself in a purely defensive alliance. But it would do her good insofar as it would introduce her into good political society."[95]

Lansdowne appears to confirm Hatzfeldt's description of events. However, rather than referring to the March 23 exchange (likely because he could have oral discussions with the members of the British cabinet), Lansdowne, in a March 29 dispatch to Lascelles, discusses a conversation that day with Eckardstein. Lansdowne wrote that now was the time to add precision to the proposal: "If the matter was to be advanced we ought to endeavour to form a more precise conception of the contingencies for which we desired to provide. There was one which he and I had already discussed, that of Japan going to war with Russia and being threatened by a combination of that Power with France. [Eckardstein's] proposal, as I had understood it, would not have provided for such a contingency, but only for cases in which either we or Germany were attacked by both Powers."[96]

In mid-April, following the Easter holiday, Eckardstein sought to continue the alliance discussions with Lansdowne.[97] In a memo to Lascelles dated April 13, 1901, Lansdowne writes about his uncertainties regarding the project. He is unsure of whether Eckardstein, when discussing the alliance proposal, is speaking for himself or directly for the German government: "It is not always easy to determine how much of Eckardstein's communications are *de son propre cru.*"[98] Lansdowne then told Eckardstein "that I was perfectly aware that this conversation, like those which had preceded it, was unofficial, but that I was not sure whether I was to infer that his advances were made without any encouragement on the part of the Emperor. I had on the contrary formed an impression that H. M. Government had been sounded upon the subject of the proposed alliance with the unofficial concurrence of the Emperor."[99] After some "humming and ha'ing," Eckardstein replied that his proposals had been made "with the knowledge of persons very near the Emperor, and who had means of judging H. M.'s ideas. He mentioned Holstein (have I spelt it right?) as one of these persons. This is perhaps worth passing on to you."[100]

Perhaps a reason for Eckardstein's "humming and ha'ing" was his superior, Hatzfeldt. Hatzfeldt believed that the best approach was for Germany to "hold firmly to the rule of letting the English come to us regarding their political decisions for the future, without showing any anxiety, impatience, or annoyance."[101] He viewed this as the prudent approach, because he saw an agreement with Germany as the only viable option for England. He knew that Salisbury remained reluctant, "but would the other Ministers, such as Lansdowne and his friends, follow him without question along this path to-day?"[102] To Hatzfeldt, that seemed unlikely "provided that for the time being we keep quite still and do not give our political opponents here any pretext to arouse ill-feeling and distrust against us, whether within or outside the [British] Cabinet."[103] Until then, Hatzfeldt saw no need to "make any extra concessions in any one question" nor to seek to "hide or water down" incompatibilities between how the two parties viewed the role of an alliance.[104]

Indeed, Hatzfeldt saw a way to make the British come over to the German ideal plan: make them think the Germans had an attractive outside option, namely, with Russia. The Germans were in the midst of negotiations to provide Russia, along with France, with a £17 million loan. This had the possibility of reconstituting the cooperation France, Russia, and Germany showed in 1895 when the three powers exerted diplomatic pressure on Japan to relinquish some of the territory it acquired at the end of the First Sino-Japanese War. For Hatzfeldt, Germany "should not break the thread which Russia is now spinning" because "this is the best and most effective means of pressure on the political decisions of the English Government at our disposal."[105] It is not clear if Hatzfeldt truly viewed the Russian proposal as an attractive outside option, but this mattered little for the purpose of negotiating with the British. As Hatzfeldt added, "I can see no disadvantage if the English were to believe for the time being that we were considering whether the Russian proposal might not have advantages" for Germany.[106]

Drafts: Early May

This set the stage for May 1901, the negotiation's peak. At the beginning of May, Hatzfeldt wrote to Holstein to give the foreign minister a sense of where the negotiations stood at that moment. (Holstein, in turn, shared the memo with Chancellor Bülow.) At that time, Hatzfeldt felt that Germany's best approach was to continue to wait for Britain to come forward with a formal proposal. He thought the British "cannot make up their minds here yet on what path to follow in world policy."[107] It appeared to Hatzfeldt that the British, "with their well-known indolence," were waiting for some unspecified exogenous change in the geopolitical environment in the hope that it "will save the English Government from the effort of reaching a decision."[108] Still, Hatzfeldt was hopeful, as there were members of the British cabinet—who he referred to as Germany's "friends in the Cabinet"—who "still want to reach an understanding with the Triple Alliance."[109]

Contributing to Hatzfeldt's sense that patience was the best approach was a minor diplomatic mishap that occurred when the German director of the Colonial Division, Oskar Wilhelm Stübel, came to London to discuss compensation to Germans expelled from their homes in South Africa as a consequence of the Boer War.[110] It appears that Stübel arrived unannounced, which the English government saw as "a lack of consideration."[111] Hatzfeldt thought the ill feeling would soon be forgotten, "but as far as possible care should be taken that no new friction and misunderstandings occur."[112] Next to this last comment, Chancellor Bülow inserted a hand-written comment stating, "As if [preventing new frictions] depended only on us and not also England."[113] Still, perhaps concerned about the lack of movement in this effort, Bülow wrote directly to Holstein with the directive of "not letting the possibility of an alliance with England founder."[114]

On May 16, 1901, Hatzfeldt wrote to Lord Lansdowne to again raise the topic of an Anglo-German pact. Lansdowne informed Hatzfeldt that "he and some of his colleagues would much desire a defensive alliance with Germany."[115] He said that Prime Minister Salisbury was "in principle" inclined to consider the treaty but that Austria and Italy should not be included.[116] Lansdowne then posed several questions to Hatzfeldt, two of which Hatzfeldt felt needed to be highlighted in the memo: (1) What did Germany view as England's required attitude if

Austria-Hungary broke up and, as a consequence, Russia encouraged Turkey to reclaim lost territories? (2) What did Germany view as England's required attitude if Italy entered a war with France or Spain?[117] These questions were intended not only to highlight the vulnerability of Italy and Austria-Hungary but to emphasize the potential complications if a treaty specified that the triggering event was an attack by "two or more great powers."[118]

On May 17, 1901, Hatzfeldt wrote a short note adding that Lansdowne, at the end of the above-described conversation, had said that while neither he nor Hatzfeldt was empowered to make proposals, "the time had come to put a draft of a treaty in writing and then discuss the wording of the various points. . . . There was no other way of advancing further than for both of us to set to work and to decide to set down our academic ideas and discuss point by point."[119] At the end of this round of conversations, Lansdowne said he would be away for several days, during which time he expected more insights from his colleagues.[120]

In the spirit of setting down the ideas, Lansdowne instructed the permanent undersecretary of state for foreign affairs, T. H. Sanderson, to draft a treaty. Sanderson presented it to Lansdowne on May 27.[121] He acknowledged that it was only a draft, "but it may be useful for you to have something tangible to look at and to cut about."[122] Table 4.2 compares two drafts of the treaty created by Sanderson, an original version and an amended version. It is unclear from the record who suggested the amendments and revisions, but it can prove instructive to compare the two drafts. The preamble is the same in both drafts and is a fairly standard defensive alliance preamble, along with a nonaggression clause: "disclaiming all aggressive intentions." Article 1 in both drafts calls on the parties to, at minimum, remain neutral if either party becomes involved in a war with just one other power. Article 1 in both drafts also calls on the neutral party to take measures to prevent other countries from intervening in the war. It is worth noting that between Article 1 and the preamble, it is ambiguous whether "maintaining the general peace of Europe" would also apply to any conflicts involving Russia, Germany, and/or Britain in East Asia. In other words, could Article 1 be read as calling on Germany to keep France out of a conflict in East Asia between Britain and Russia?

In both drafts, Article 2 deals with a second power entering the fight against a signatory. Both drafts call on the parties to offer assistance and not to conclude a separate peace. But then the drafts diverge. Article 2 in the first draft includes the phrase "to support it so far as necessary and practicable with all its forces," while the second draft changes the language to "conduct war in common." Though neither is precise, "conduct[ing] war in common" could be interpreted as suggesting the creation of a joint command, while the former phrasing suggests that one side will be the primary belligerent.

The two drafts switch Articles 3 and 4. Article 4 in the first draft and Article 3 in the second draft make clear that the treaty does not apply to the Western Hemisphere. This is useful, because by explicitly excluding the American sphere of influence, it suggests that Articles 1 and 2 do apply to East Asia as well as Europe.

Equipped with these drafts, Lansdowne then met with Hatzfeldt (upon Hatzfeldt's request) to further discuss the details of an Anglo-German alliance.[123] They met on May 23, 1901.[124] Following this conversation, both men sent summary memorandums to their respective governments. It is useful to compare the two descriptions of the conversation.

Hatzfeldt says he began the conversation by laying before Lansdowne the German interests in the treaty and conditions for an alliance.[125] In particular, an alliance treaty would need to "leave no doubt" that Britain would protect Austria and actively assist Germany if Germany were attacked "due to offering to assist Austria."[126] Hatzfeldt reported that Lansdowne, who "listened with the utmost attention and took studious notes," expressed that knowing the German view was "invaluable." Hatzfeldt said he "could not suppress a certain doubt" that Lansdowne would be able to convince the British cabinet, particularly Salisbury. Lansdowne did not deny such difficulties, and Hatzfeldt remarked that he had no intention of telling the British cabinet what was in British interest, be it "an alliance with the Triple Alliance or the continuation of the policy of isolation or even an understanding with Russia and France."[127] But Hatzfeldt added that, having stayed in England for such a long time and thereby gained an impression of the views in Parliament, he felt "all the intelligent men in the powerful government majority" would recognize the "tremendous benefits" that could be obtained by joining the Triple Alliance. These benefits included "mighty help against combined attacks on any part of English territory," a "securing of European peace for another ten or fifteen years," and "a corresponding undisturbed development of English commerce throughout the world."[128] Hatzfeldt then asserted to Lansdowne that Britain could not expect to receive such benefits without costs: "A treaty of alliance, through which one party can secure only benefits without taking the slightest risk in favor of the other party, had not yet been invented." Lansdowne, according to Hatzfeldt, "did not object to this view."[129]

As Hatzfeldt had observed, Lansdowne wrote extensive notes of the conversation. Lansdowne then summarized the notes in a memorandum, which he shared directly with Salisbury.[130] Lansdowne requested that this summary of the conversation be shared with other key members of the cabinet, including Balfour, Beach, Chamberlain, and Devonshire, so that they, Salisbury, and himself could convene and discuss it.[131] Lansdowne begins the memo by briefly reviewing the pre-May conversations with Eckardstein, including that, "on the occasion of one of these interviews, Baron Eckardstein mentioned incidentally that Austria and

TABLE 4.2. Draft Anglo-German treaties

DRAFT TREATY TEXT	AMENDED DRAFT TREATY TEXT
Preamble	
H. M. the King of the United Kingdom of Great Britain, Ireland, Emperor of India, and H. M. the German Emperor, disclaiming all aggressive intentions, and with object of ensuring as far as possible the maintenance of the status quo, and of the general peace of Europe resolved to conclude a defensive Alliance and have for that purpose appointed as their Plenipotentiaries:	H. M. the King of the United Kingdom of Great Britain and Ireland, Emperor of India, and H. M. the German Emperor, disclaiming all aggressive intentions, and with the object of ensuring as far as possible the maintenance of the status quo, and of the general peace of Europe have resolved to conclude a defensive Alliance and have for that purpose appointed as their Plenipotentiaries:
Who, &c., have agreed upon the following Articles:	Who, &c., have agreed upon the following Articles:
Article 1	
If, while pursuing the policy described in the Preamble of the present Convention, one of the High Contracting Parties should be involved in war with another Power for the defence of its legitimate interests, or in consequence of a defensive alliance contracted by it and made known to the other High Contracting Party, the said other High Contracting Party engages to maintain an attitude not less favourable than that of strict neutrality, and to take such pacific measures as may appear to it to be practicable for the purpose of preventing other Powers from attacking its Ally.	If one of the High Contracting Parties, in the defence of its legitimate interests, or in consequence of a defense alliance contracted by it and previously communicated to the other High Contracting Party engages to maintain an attitude not less favourable than that of strict neutrality, and to take such pacific measures as may be in its power to prevent other Powers from joining in hostilities against its Ally.
Article 2	
Should, however, any other Power join unprovoked in hostile measures against the High Contracting Party so involved in war, the other High Contracting Party engages to come to assistance of its Ally thus attacked, to support it so far as necessary and practicable with all its forces and to make peace except with the concurrence of its Ally.	Should any other Power join without provocation in hostilities against the High Contracting Party so involved in war, the other High Contracting Party engages to come to the assistance of its Ally, to conduct the war in common, and only to make not peace in mutual agreement with it.
Article 3	
This Convention shall remain in force for five years from the date of its signature at the expiration of which period it shall be open to renewal for a similar period. Notice of revision or a desire to terminate the Agreement shall be given by either party a year before the expiration of this period.	It is agreed that this Convention shall not apply to questions on the American Continent, nor bind either High Contracting Party to join in hostilities against the United States of America.
Article 4	
It is agreed that this Convention shall not apply to any questions arising in the American Continent or involving war with the United States.	This Convention shall remain in force for five years from the date of its signature, at the expiration of which period it may be renewed for a similar term. Notice of a desire for its termination or revision shall be given by either Party a year before its expiration.
Article 5	
Ratification clause	Ratification clause

Source: Enclosures 1 and 2 of May 27, 1901, Memorandum by Sir T. H. Sanderson, in *British Documents* 2, no. 85.

Italy would have to be included in such an arrangement as he had proposed."[132] Lansdowne writes that Eckardstein's remark immediately raised concerns: "I said that this seemed to me a most important point."[133] Lansdowne told Eckardstein that reaching a formula suitable to both parties in a purely bilateral alliance would be difficult enough, but the problems (and possible objections to the treaty) would "be urged with infinitely greater force if we were asked to enter into similar obligations to Austria and Italy as well as to Germany."[134]

Lansdowne then describes his meeting with Hatzfeldt. According to Lansdowne, Hatzfeldt told him that "the foreign policy of Germany must always be based upon the closest intimacy with Austria."[135] This led Lansdowne to ask Hatzfeldt pointedly, "Was I then . . . to understand that the proposal was simply that we should join the Triple Alliance?" According to Lansdowne, "Count Hatzfeldt answered in the affirmative."[136] The conversation then focused on what Lansdowne considered to be "a most important point": the possible inclusion of Austria-Hungary and Italy in the treaty.[137] Lansdowne expressed concern over British interests being compromised by reckless behavior on the part of the two weaker states: "I had said to him that in my view the objection to such an arrangement was that this country might find itself dragged into a quarrel in which we had no concern, and which might have been in fact provoked by our ally, whose external policy might be quite beyond our control. . . . These objections could, I thought, be urged with infinitely greater force if we were asked to enter into similar obligations to Austria and Italy as well as to Germany."[138] Hatzfeldt told Lansdowne that "the foreign policy of Germany must always be based upon the closest intimacy with Austria."[139] Hatzfeldt felt that there must be "two 'unities'— one consisting of Great Britain and her numerous Colonies—the other of the members of the Triple Alliance, and the Agreement, if it was to be made at all, must be between the two groups."[140] Hatzfeldt continued by posing the question of whether Britain was prepared to continue in "*isolement*" and saying that Britain "must be alive to the dangers which it invoked."[141] He argued that it was in British interests "to join one of the two great groups into which the European Powers were divided." Britain could "try Russia," but "mais cela vous coûtera cher."[142] Upon hearing this, Lansdowne told Hatzfeldt that he would now "lay the matter" before Salisbury.[143]

Collapse: Late May

This takes us directly to the May 29 Salisbury memorandum that opened this case. Salisbury begins by writing, "This is a proposal for including England within the bounds of the Triple Alliance."[144] The strategic clauses, in Salisbury's understanding, amounted to two key points:

1. If England were attacked by two Powers—say France and Russia—Germany, Austria, and Italy would come to her assistance.
2. Conversely, if either Austria, Germany, or Italy were attacked by France and Russia, or if Italy were attacked by France and Spain, England must come to the rescue.

Salisbury then writes: "Even assuming that the Powers concerned were all despotic, and could promise anything they pleased, with a full confidence that they would be able to perform the promise, I think it is open to much question whether the bargain would be for our advantage. The liability of having to defend the German and Austrian Frontiers against Russia is heavier than that of *having to defend the British Isles against France*."[145] This statement is especially useful for untangling reliability concerns from plan incompatibilities. Salisbury says that even if Britain could be assured that the other parties could reliably follow the plan, it does not work for Britain. This is what prompted Salisbury to enter into his discourse provided above regarding the benefits of splendid isolation in Europe. Stated simply, if the strategic element of war planning is "making war on a map," the map proposed by Germany did not work for Britain.

These points are emphasized in a November 11, 1901, memorandum by Lansdowne. The memorandum was essentially Lansdowne's postmortem on the failed negotiations. He acknowledges that Salisbury's May 29 memorandum, coupled with the replacement of Hatzfeldt by Eckardstein, had effectively ended the negotiations (though Lansdowne also mentions that there is some hope among German officials that the negotiations could restart).[146] As Hatzfeldt observed to Holstein in a June 8, 1901, memorandum, following these events, Lansdowne "avoided any mention of the alliance question to me."[147]

In some respects, Lansdowne's memorandum is strange. On the one hand, Lansdowne writes that Salisbury's interpretation of the German proposal did "not, I think, quite correctly represent the proposal."[148] According to Lansdowne, Salisbury understood the German proposal as suggesting "that the only liability which the German Government would assume under the proposed agreement would be that of having to defend the British islands against France, whereas [Britain] should be bound to defend the German and Austrian frontiers against Russia, a much heavier obligation."[149] This is not precisely how Lansdowne understood Hatzfeldt's proposal. Instead, "Hatzfeldt's idea evidently was that the liability of our allies would oblige them to range themselves on our side in any quarrel in which the British Empire might become involved, and we should not be more bound to defend the German and Austrian frontiers than they would be bound to defend Australasia and our African and American colonies."[150]

On the other hand, Lansdowne then proceeds to write that he is "bound to admit, and I did not conceal this from Count Hatzfeldt or Baron Eckardstein, that I see great difficulties in the way of a full-blown defensive alliance with Germany such as that suggested by Count Hatzfeldt, difficulties which are, I should say at the present moment, virtually insuperable."[151] Lansdowne then proceeds to list these difficulties, the first of which was specifying the strategic element of the treaty: "The impossibility of arriving at a definition of the *casus foederis* which would not be either so rigid as to greatly hamper our freedom of action or so vague as to deprive the alliance of all practical value."[152] This is in addition to "complications with the Colonies, which might not at all approve of the idea of hanging on to the skirts of the Triple Alliance."[153] He also mentions concerns about the treaty worsening relations with France, Russia, and the United States and, lastly, that Parliament, at the present moment, might not ratify such a treaty. This seems to echo Salisbury's views.

In the end, Lansdowne's summary point makes clear that specifying the proper strategic formula was the key to any possible future agreement with Germany: "In these circumstances, and in the face of the decided views which the Prime Minister has expressed, I regard it as out of the question that we should entertain the German overture in the form in which it was presented by Count Hatzfeldt. I would not, however, for these reasons refuse all further discussion of the question. The objections to joining the Triple Alliance do not seem to me to apply to a much more limited understanding with Germany as to our policy in regard to certain matters of interest to both Powers."[154]

I have said little about why Germany did not moderate its plans. Even Miller (2012, 74), an advocate for reliability concerns, acknowledges that "the Germans were unwavering in their demands for a 'Quadruple Alliance.'" Why? Miller (2012, 74) states that it was related to Germany incorrectly perceiving Britain as lacking an attractive outside option: "Germany's intransigence seems to have been based largely on its belief that the British had no other possible allies and would eventually realize they needed Germany, at which point the Germans could dictate the terms of the alliance." This fits well with a core tenet of my theory, or any theory of bargaining, about the importance of beliefs about a counterpart's outside options. Such an explanation appears to be confirmed by an August 25, 1901, dispatch from Lascelles to Lansdowne.[155] After a meeting with Kaiser Wilhelm, Lascelles writes that Wilhelm "quite understood that we could not conclude a Treaty of Alliance without giving up our policy of isolation."[156] But Wilhelm viewed continued isolation as unattractive to Britain because Britain "ran the risk of finding a coalition of Powers against us" and that they should not expect the United States to ever help Britain because, as Britain's "most formidable commercial rival," the

United States would "certainly throw us over as soon as it suited her interest to do so."[157] This was confirmed by Wilhelm.[158] The meeting included not only Lascelles and Wilhelm but also King Edward. Wilhelm said to both, "I cannot judge whether it is possible and useful for England to maintain its splendid isolation, or whether it is in its interests to step on the side of the continent or of America. But I would like to consider that perhaps America and Russia are more intimate with one another than one dreams in London. . . . If [England] believes that it is placing its interests alongside the European Central Powers, I will gladly welcome that; it would mean a connection with the Triple Alliance."[159]

The 1901 Anglo-German negotiation collapsed due to the British pursuing their outside options of nonalignment in Europe and an alternative alliance treaty (with Japan) in Asia. This is well established in both the existing historical and international relations literature. What is less clear is why Britain found these options more attractive than an alliance with Germany. Was it primarily due to concerns over Germany's reliability, or was it primarily due to the parties having incompatible visions for the operation of the alliance (i.e., incompatible ideal war plans)? I provide evidence that strategic incompatibilities played the critical role in Britain's pursuit of its outside options: Germany was primarily concerned with protection from Russia in Europe for itself and its Triple Alliance partners; Britain was concerned about assistance in case of Russian incursions in East Asia. Coupled with the British perception of having attractive outside options and the German belief that Britain's outside option was not highly attractive, this incompatibility meant the two parties failed to make the concessions necessary to reach agreement. Hence, returning to the language introduced in chapter 1, it seems that these negotiations can be classified as a Standard Bargaining negotiation that ended in collapse.

A useful next step is to consider the portability of my theoretical claims. While I have had methodological reasons for limiting my exploration to pre-1945 alliance negotiations, the value of my study could be enhanced by applying my theory to an important post-1945 treaty negotiation. To this end, the next chapter demonstrates how my theory offers insights into the negotiations to create the most important post-1945 alliance treaty, if not the most important alliance treaty in history: the North Atlantic Treaty.

AN IMPORTANT AGREEMENT

The 1948–49 North Atlantic Treaty Negotiations

No study of alliances should fail to address what is perhaps the most important military alliance ever formed: the 1949 North Atlantic Treaty. While today pundits, policy makers, and scholars speak of NATO as underpinning an "Atlantic community" or as the American-European core of a "liberal international order," this chapter will show how the negotiations leading to its creation were far from being a classic Same Page negotiation. Instead, the North Atlantic Treaty negotiations epitomize a Standard Bargaining negotiation in which the final product was created through compromise, concessions, and some capitulation.

Ideal war plan incompatibilities led some participants, notably France, to explicitly threaten to leave the negotiations without an agreement. The negotiations revealed nontrivial incompatibilities in the strategic aspects of the participants' plans. The parties agreed that the Soviet Union constituted a threat, but they disagreed on the geographic reach of that threat. The French were gravely concerned about Soviet influence in southern Europe, especially the possibility that Italy could enter the communist bloc. For the British and Americans, the primary concern was coercive Soviet threats toward states in northern Europe, especially Norway. The United States had a viable outside option of unilateral action and, therefore, could afford to walk away. Whether France or any other participant perceived itself as also having an attractive outside option is less clear. What is clear is that the participants were unwilling to test this possibility: France's threats to walk away induced its negotiation partners, believing that France had an attractive outside option, to concede to its demands.

The parties had both entrapment concerns and reliability concerns and faced real incompatibilities in their ideal war plans. Though reliability concerns were largely addressed early in the negotiations, entrapment concerns induced debate over the wording of key treaty provisions, and such debates consumed a fair portion of the time spent negotiating. The parties needed to find language that assuaged U.S. concerns over entrapment while also fulfilling European desires for a strong treaty that could deter Soviet aggression. I conclude, however, that these debates never seriously threatened to undermine agreement. The participants were fully aware of the need to make the treaty sufficiently flexible, and they worked assiduously to find a mutually acceptable solution. At most, overcoming entrapment concerns serves as an additional explanation for why these negotiations ended in agreement, not an alternative explanation.

My account is consistent with the 1980s shift in the historiography of NATO's creation (Folly 1988). Specifically, while the early research portrayed NATO's creation as a U.S. initiative (Osgood 1970; Feis 1970; Bohlen 1969), by the 1980s scholars recognized the Europeans, especially the British, as playing the lead role in the alliance's creation.[1] This shift was enabled by the opening of several European archives and the 1974 appearance of key documents in the *Foreign Relations of the United States* series (Wiebes and Zeeman 1983; Folly 1988, 59; MacKenzie 2004, 91). Particular emphasis is now given to March 22 to April 1, 1948, negotiations between representatives of the United States, Britain, and Canada (referred to as the ABC talks). These negotiations produced a draft treaty that was eventually presented to the Western Europeans and became, through further negotiations from mid-1948 to early 1949, the North Atlantic Treaty. I do not aim to offer an alternative history of NATO's creation, as my account also draws largely on the *Foreign Relations of the United States* series, a well-regarded source of material on these negotiations.[2] But the theory I offered in chapter 1, by placing joint war planning at the heart of alliance treaty negotiations, leads one to consider this source material from a new perspective.

The next section elaborates on why the 1948–49 North Atlantic Treaty negotiations are an appropriate case for evaluating my argument. I then begin my narrative of the negotiation of this treaty. The narrative starts with the collapse of the 1947 London foreign ministers conference. This failure induced the British to seek a transatlantic security arrangement. I then describe U.S. alternatives to an agreement and the lack of attractive alternatives for Britain and France. Next, I discuss how the signing of the Brussels pact in the spring of 1948 addressed U.S. concerns about the willingness and ability of the Europeans to provide for their own defense. These reliability concerns having been ameliorated, the Americans were ready to begin transatlantic security talks. These began with the American-

British-Canadian talks in the spring of 1948 and continued with the Washington Exploratory Talks starting in June 1948. The Washington talks, which culminated in the signing of the North Atlantic Treaty on April 4, 1949, are the heart of this chapter. My analysis of these talks will consider the role of entrapment concerns (driving disputes over the language used in the treaty text), strategic plan incompatibilities, and operational plan incompatibilities. I will show the degree to which each of these concerns created conditions that could have undermined agreement (but ultimately did not). To guide the reader through the case, table 5.1 lists the key participants in the negotiations. Given the negotiation's length and number of participating states, the list is quite lengthy. As in chapter 4's discussion of the Anglo-German negotiations, this table should help the reader keep track of who is speaking to whom.

TABLE 5.1.   Key participants of North Atlantic Treaty negotiation

NAME	OFFICE HELD DURING THE NEGOTIATION
Dean Acheson	U.S. Secretary of State (starting in January 1949)
Theodore C. Achilles	U.S. State Department Director for Western European Affairs
Ernest Bevin	British Foreign Minister
Georges Bidault	French Foreign Minister
Charles Bohlen	U.S. State Department Counselor
Henri Bonnet	French Ambassador to the United States
Thomas Connally	U.S. Senator and Chairman of the Senate Foreign Relations Committee (starting in January 1949)
Lewis Douglas	U.S. Ambassador to Britain
Oliver Franks	British Ambassador to the United States (starting in 1948)
John "Jack" Hickerson	U.S. State Department Director of the Office of European Affairs
Barn Inverchapel	British Ambassador to the United States (until 1948)
Gladwyn Jebb	British Deputy Foreign Secretary
George Kennan	U.S. Director of the Policy Planning Staff
E. N. Van Kleffens	Netherlands Ambassador to the US
Robert Lovett	U.S. Undersecretary of State
George Marshall	U.S. Secretary of State (until 1949)
Lester Pearson	Canadian Undersecretary of State for External Affairs
Escott Reid	Member of Canadian Delegation during Washington Exploratory Talks
Normal Robertson	Canadian High Commissioner to Britain
Harry S. Truman	President of the United States
Arthur H. Vandenberg	U.S. Senator and Chairman of Senate Foreign Relations Committee (until 1949)
James Webb	U.S. Undersecretary of State
Hume Wrong	Canadian Ambassador to the United States

Case Selection

Besides extending my analysis into the post-1945 period, there are two additional reasons to consider this case: it is a substantively important case, and it is not an easy case for my theory.

The first reason to consider the North Atlantic Treaty negotiation is that this is a substantively important case, meaning it is of special normative interest because of its major role in international politics (Mahoney and Goertz 2006, 242). NATO's role in deterring major war in Europe during the Cold War, its mission to stabilize and support newly democratic states following the Cold War, and its early-twenty-first-century role in combating such nontraditional threats as terrorism make it arguably the most significant post-1945 military alliance. Goertz (2012, 22) acknowledges the desire to explore important cases: "if it is a choice between the Bolivian and French revolutions, one might go for the historically important one."[3] Mahoney and Goertz (2006, 243) recognize the value of a theory being able to explain substantively important cases: "our view is that qualitative researchers almost instinctively understand the requirement of getting the 'big' cases right and worry when it is not met." For instance, Mahoney and Goertz (2006, 243) highlight how realist scholars invested much time and energy in rectifying realist theory with the end of the Cold War, while nonrealist scholars viewed the theory's inability to explain the end of the Cold War as "a major strike against the whole paradigm." In the field of alliance politics, the creation and operation of NATO is such a case: scholars are right to question a theory's utility if it cannot provide insights into this case. Bennett (2004, 41) cautions against using substantive importance as the sole criterion for case selection, especially when other cases (such as deviant or most likely cases) might be more useful for evaluating a theory. But I am not concerned about this critique given my second reason for selecting this case.

The second reason to consider the North Atlantic Treaty negotiation is that it is not an easy case for my theory.[4] There are three features of this negotiation that suggest, on the surface at least, that it fits the alternative explanations better than my joint-war-planning explanation.

First, this is a negotiation with low ideal war plan compatibility that ended in agreement. My theory allows for agreement to be reached when ideal war plan compatibility is low, but reaching agreement is not the most likely outcome. Following the coding rules described in chapter 2, the strategic compatibility score of the core seven participants in 1948 (the United States, Canada, Britain, France, the Netherlands, Belgium, and Luxembourg) was below the threshold for coding this negotiation as having high strategic compatibility. Indeed, the case study will show that the strategic incompatibilities were pronounced and largely driven by disagreement over the geographic area to be protected.[5] Key for me will be to determine if these concerns, rather than other concerns, brought the negotiations closest to collapse.

Second, there is much to suggest that the participants were primarily concerned with issues addressed by competing explanations, not with joint war planning. For instance, the conditions suggest high reliability concerns.[6] The negotiation was not asymmetric, with the British, French, and United States all identified as "major powers" according to the Correlates of War major power indicator.[7] The participants' past compliance with alliance treaties also raised reliability concerns.[8] Indeed, the evidence below shows that U.S. officials harbored reservations about the willingness and ability of the Europeans to cooperatively provide for their mutual defense. The key will be to determine if reliability concerns were largely addressed before the states entered the negotiations.

Third, previous accounts of these negotiations by international relations scholars stress entrapment concerns as the key issue. These accounts highlight the wording of the treaty's mutual defense clause (Article 5) as the critical point of contention during the negotiations. Lake (1999, 136–37) describes the compromises required to satisfy both the U.S. desire for the treaty text to convey freedom of action and the European desire for a strongly worded commitment. Central to Rathbun's (2011, 165) account is U.S. senators' fear of entrapment and how that fear fed numerous requests to change the treaty's language.[9] The evidence below will show that much time and effort were allocated to the task of finding acceptable wording. I will need to determine whether entrapment concerns or concerns over the compatibility of participants' ideal war plans brought the negotiations closer to collapse.

Proposing an Atlantic Pact

When discussing the negotiation of the North Atlantic Treaty, it is vital to set the stage. That stage is built on the postwar "German problem." From November 25 to December 16, 1947, the four postwar powers—Britain, France, the United States, and the Soviet Union—met in London to reach a final agreement on the political status of Germany. At that time, France, Britain, and the United States each occupied a segment of western Germany, while the Soviets occupied a large portion of eastern Germany. According to Secretary of State George Marshall, "The basic issue, as we saw it before the opening of the London conference, was whether or not the Allies could agree among themselves to reunite Germany."[10] Agreement was not reached. From the U.S. and British perspective, this was largely due to Soviet intransigence.

For example, in a humorous instance, John "Jack" Hickerson, the director of the Office of European Affairs of the U.S. State Department, describes how the Soviet foreign minister Vyacheslav Molotov informed the other participants, "I have the authority to say that we [the Soviets] will reduce our demand for reparations from Austria by 10 percent."[11] The British foreign minister Ernest Bevin immediately asked, "Ten percent? That's fine, but 10 percent from what?" Molotov replied, "I'm not in a position to tell you." While this response actually induced laughter from the participants, a more serious exchange took place when Molotov denounced British and U.S. efforts in the western German zones as directed toward "using one piece of German territory or another as a base for the development of a war industry."[12] Bevin remarked that "Mr. Molotov might at least have thanked us for listening to the end."[13] Marshall was less amused, as he no longer viewed the Soviet Union as a cooperative partner: "It finally became clear that we could make no progress at this time[,] that there was no apparent will to reach a settlement but only an interest in making more and more speeches intended for another audience. So I suggested that we adjourn. No real ground was lost or gained at the meeting, except that the outlines of the problems and the obstacles are much clearer. We cannot look forward to a unified Germany at this time. We must do the best we can in the area where our influence can be felt."[14]

The remainder of this section will explain how the collapse of the London conference spurred the parties to engage in early negotiations for an Atlantic security pact. I will begin by describing Bevin's initial proposal and the key participants' outside alternatives (or lack thereof) to a pact. I will then focus on the initial reluctance of the United States to pursue negotiations, at least until its concerns over the reliability of the European partners had been resolved. This leads directly to the first round of formal negotiations, the spring 1948 ABC talks. The plan coming out of these talks served as the basis for the Washington Exploratory Talks to finalize a North Atlantic Treaty.

The Bevin Proposal and Outside Options

Bevin immediately seized the opportunity accorded by the failure of the London talks to push for a transatlantic security apparatus.[15] On December 17, he met first with the French minister of foreign affairs, Georges Bidault, and then with the Canadian high commissioner in London, Norman Robertson, and finally with Secretary Marshall.[16] In all three meetings, Bevin shared his vision for responding to the breakdown of the talks: a transatlantic security community. Bevin described what this entailed in his evening meeting with Marshall: "We must devise some western democratic system comprising the Americans, ourselves, France, Italy, etc., and of course the Dominions. This would not be a formal alliance, but an understanding backed by power, money, and resolute action. It would be a sort of spiritual federation of the west. . . . The essential task was to create confidence in Western Europe that further Communist inroads would be stopped."[17]

Following this meeting, Marshall returned to his hotel, saw Hickerson, and said, "You'd better go down to the [British] foreign office and see some of your friends."[18] Marshall elaborated, "I just went down to say goodbye [before returning to Washington, DC] and Bevin started talking to me about some future arrangements. He mentioned two circles. I wasn't prepared for it. If I had known he was going to talk about this I would have taken you down. You've got to go down and see what the guy has in mind."[19]

Understanding how the Americans and French responded to Bevin's proposal and how firmly the British would stick to pursuing this proposal requires describing their outside alternatives to Western security cooperation. For the British, Bevin felt that U.S. financial assistance via the European Recovery Program (i.e., the Marshall Plan) was not enough.[20] Western European unification backed by the Americans and the British dominions was essential. In a telegram, Bevin wrote: "One of my great anxieties in this business is whether, if trouble did come, we should be left waiting as in 1940 in a state of uncertainty. In view of our experience then it would be very difficult to be able to stand up to it again unless there was a definite worked out arrangement for the Western area, together with other assistance, on the basis of collective security to resist the aggressor."[21]

The Communist takeover of Czechoslovakia in late February 1948 provided impetus for creating some arrangement in line with Bevin's vision.[22] Václav Nosek, the Czech minister of the interior and a member of the Czech Communist Party, had purged non-Communists from the Czech police forces (which were overseen by the Interior Department). This action was supported by Klement Gottwald, the prime minister and head of the Czech Communist Party, and eventually led to the resignation of the non-Communist members of the Czech cabinet on February 25. This enabled the Communists to gain full control of the government.[23] Reflecting on this event years later, Hickerson remarked, "The Soviet takeover of the Czech Government . . . scared the living bejesus out of everybody in Western Europe."[24]

Immediately following the coup, Bevin told U.S. undersecretary of state (and eventual secretary of defense) Robert Lovett, "We are now in the critical period of 6–8 weeks which . . . would decide the future of Europe."[25] Bevin was especially concerned that similar events would unfold in France and Italy.[26] This fear was shared by the French, though they were not necessarily worried that the events would transpire in France itself. In a March 4 letter to Marshall, Bidault wrote, "Everything must be done to prevent a repetition in Austria, in Italy or elsewhere of what has just taken place in Prague."[27] For Bidault, this meant that the United

States must supplement the Marshall Plan with a military alliance. Bidault deemed the alliance essential because, even though France was working with Britain to "organize the common defence in conjunction with all the European democratic powers," the reality was that such efforts required active U.S. military support: "The hour is too dire, the danger is too urgent, Soviet power is too mighty for France, just recovering from the wounds of war, to assume alone, even with the support of the allies which it is trying to organize, the role of defender of the Western territories."[28] The U.S. ambassador to France, Jefferson Caffery, who delivered the note to Marshall, had informed Marshall two days earlier that "[Bidault] is vitally interested in the 'contenu' of the treaties. In other words, what he really wants more than anything else, is a concrete military alliance (against Soviet attack) with definite promises to do definite things under certain circumstances."[29] In short, the British and French had no attractive outside options. As the historian Lawrence Kaplan (2013, 5) observed, from Bidault and Bevin's perspective only "once America participated in a European defense arrangement, the confidence Western Europe needed to promote integration and rebuild their economic and social systems would be in place."

The United States did not share the sense that an alliance treaty was the best solution. Unilateral action presented itself as an attractive alternative policy. Indeed, the United States had already shown itself capable of taking unilateral action. The 1947 Truman Doctrine was aimed at supporting nations under communist threat, and the goal of the Marshall Plan's economic assistance was to rebuild and strengthen Europe. Moreover, the United States already had military assets in Europe (Kaplan 2013, 4). Though three years removed from the end of the Second World War, U.S. troops were stationed in western Germany, and the U.S. retained airbases in Germany and Britain following the war (Harkavy 2007, 105).[30] Furthermore, regular U.S. Strategic Air Command deployments of B-29s in Britain had begun the previous year.

The United States' ability to act unilaterally was the basis of the recommendation made to Marshall by George Kennan, then U.S. director of the policy planning staff. Kennan recommended that the United States not go beyond "a unilateral guarantee, in partnership with the Canadians if the Canadians were willing, of the security of those Western European nations that chose to associate themselves with the Brussels Union."[31] Indeed, a "Points for Discussion" memorandum to guide U.S. officials during the ABC talks (see below) identifies the National Security Council (NSC) position as "recommends a unilateral assurance by the United States to the nations in [the] Western Union that the United States will consider armed attack by the USSR or its satellites against any one of these nations to constitute armed attack against the United States."[32]

U.S. Hesitation and Reliability Concerns

This brief outline of the outside options available to the key parties helps explain each party's initial response to Bevin's proposal. Bidault was immediately receptive. He and Bevin wasted little time putting Bevin's plan in motion. By January 22, Bevin and Bidault had extended invitations to the Netherlands, Belgium, and Luxembourg to create a mutual defense treaty "along the lines of the Anglo-French Treaty of Dunkirk."[33] The March 1947 Treaty of Dunkirk was a simple bilateral treaty of mutual defense in case of renewed German aggression.[34] Extending it to include the Benelux countries would create the first part of what Bevin envisioned as a "two-circle arrangement," with the second circle being an arrangement, perhaps less formal, between those countries, the United States, and Canada (Cook 1989, 111).[35]

Marshall responded cautiously. He was not opposed to the idea. Indeed, Marshall told the British ambassador that he was "already turning over in my mind the question of participation of the United States in the defense of Europe" (Cook 1989, 116). But the concept required more definite provisions (Cook 1989, 110). This was consistent with Kennan's advice. Despite advising unilateral action, Kennan also suggested that the British ambassador to the United States, Baron Inverchapel, "might be pressed for further details on [Bevin's proposal]."[36] So Marshall wrote to Inverchapel, stating that the proposal required "continuing study."[37]

On January 21, Hickerson met with Inverchapel to gain a "pick and shovel" understanding of the British proposal.[38] Hickerson remarked to Inverchapel that while the United States was immensely sympathetic to Bevin's proposal, "it is not clear whether Mr. Bevin envisages the direct participation of the United States in the security treaty arrangements [being conducted by the British, French, and Benelux countries]."[39] But Hickerson made clear that the United States was willing to consider participating in a defensive arrangement: "If it should be felt in western Europe that the direct participation of the United States in a defense arrangement, established in full harmony with the Charter of the United Nations, would be necessary to its success, the United States government would be no doubt prepared, very carefully to consider this question."[40]

Six days later, Inverchapel met with Lovett.[41] He told Lovett about Bevin's suggestion that the United States and Britain meet to conclude an agreement on how "to provide against aggression which could reinforce the defense project Mr. Bevin had proposed for Western Europe."[42] Bevin wanted the meeting to be similar to the meeting held in Washington between the British and Americans in July through September 1947. At those meetings, the two countries addressed a host of issues about the defense of the Middle East.[43] Most importantly, the impetus for and primary focus of those talks was the military logistics of maintaining troops and naval and air facilities in the Middle East, North Africa, and the Mediterranean. Hence, Bevin was requesting a British-U.S. meeting to discuss the logistics of maintaining U.S. troops and air and naval facilities in and near Western Europe. Lovett told Inverchapel that this would mean a military alliance between the United States and Britain, a possibility to which the United States was not then prepared to give a definite response: "What Mr. Bevin was now suggesting would in fact mean consideration of a military alliance between the United States and Great Britain. Before any reply could be made even to the suggestion for holding conversations, Mr. Bevin's proposal would require most careful consideration by the National Security Council for the purpose of formulating recommendations to the President and would then undoubtedly involve consultation with Congressional leaders."[44]

A key component of U.S. "careful consideration" was the status of cooperative arrangements between the Western Europeans themselves. Such arrangements were essential for the United States to consider developing its own security arrangements with the Europeans. In his January meeting with Inverchapel, Hickerson had made clear that U.S. participation ultimately depended on the shape of the expanded Treaty of Dunkirk being negotiated between Britain, France, and the Benelux countries. If the Europeans "created such an organization and made it work," the United States would be more inclined to assist it.[45] Similarly, Lovett told Caffery to tell Bidault that the "more tightly Five Power Treaty can be implemented [the] better we will like it."[46] This echoed the sentiment expressed by Marshall: "The deliberations in which representatives of France, Great Britain, Belgium, the Netherlands, and Luxembourg are now engaged at Brussels will, I hope, result in comprehensive arrangements for the common defense of the participating nations. Such a result would appear to be an essential prerequisite to any wider arrangement in which other countries including the United States might play a part."[47]

The successful completion of an expanded Treaty of Dunkirk was deemed critical by U.S. officials for two reasons. First, its completion would signal European willingness and ability to pool resources for common defense (Kaplan 2013, 5). As Marshall remarked to President Truman on March 12, "the outcome of the present Anglo-French-Benelux security talks in Brussels should indicate the extent to which the participating governments are prepared to go in mutual defense and should provide a starting point for our consultations with them."[48] Second, a European pact would enable the United States to identify exactly which assets were needed in Europe. The United States could know if the resources of the five powers were to be pooled if the types of equipment of the five powers were to be standardized, and if the five powers would have a plan of action until U.S. help is available.[49] As Lovett remarked to Inverchapel, negotiating a transatlantic pact prior to the completion of the Brussels negotiations meant "in effect asking us to pour concrete before we see the blueprints."[50]

Planning at the ABC Talks

An expanded Treaty of Dunkirk was signed in Brussels on March 17 between Belgium, France, Luxembourg, the Netherlands, and the United Kingdom. The signing of the Brussels pact immediately set in motion a flurry of U.S. diplomatic activity. On March 22, officials from Canada, Britain, and the United States met in Washington to discuss the possible relationship between the two North American countries and the Brussels pact signatories. The primary participants were Hickerson, Lester Pearson (Canada's undersecretary of state for external affairs), and Gladwyn Jebb (British deputy foreign secretary). As Hickerson later explained, these initial meetings excluded the French largely because the participants wanted secrecy: "The reason the French were not invited was that their codes were not secure and everything that they reported got into the wrong hands."[51]

At the first meeting of the American-British-Canadian (ABC) talks, the parties laid out four options for a transatlantic defense arrangement: (1) a verbal declaration of support by the president of the United States, (2) U.S. accession to the Brussels pact, (3) a new Atlantic pact, or (4) a worldwide collective security treaty.[52] At the second meeting, held on March 23, the parties hashed out the pros and cons of the options. Three of the four options were dropped.[53] Option 4 would be "too cumbersome," while option 2 would remove the Brussels pact as the "hard core" for the development of a "United States of Western Europe."[54] This narrowed the possibilities to two, as captured in the U.S. minutes of the meeting:

> Presidential declaration or defense pact are the two choices open to the US in giving assurances of military support to free nations menaced by Soviet Communism. The point was raised that while the US might in an emergency situation extend assurances of armed support against aggression on the basis of a declaration of intent, sooner or later the US would have to require reciprocal guarantees from others. Were reciprocal guarantees offered, the result would, in effect, be a mutual defense agreement. The objective, therefore, should from the outset include a pact of mutual defense against aggression to which the US (and Canada) would finally adhere.[55]

In essence option 1 was viewed as being subsumed by option 3, since it was felt that a verbal declaration would eventually require reciprocal guarantees. This account in the U.S. minutes differs slightly from the Canadian report of the meeting. According to the Canadian report, the U.S. representatives were concerned that domestic and international audiences would view a presidential declaration as "too one sided," and, therefore, the United States would experience resistance "in North America and among the European states."[56]

Regardless of the nuances of their motivations, the parties agreed to focus on exploring the idea of a "Western mutual defense pact." To assist in that exploration, they agreed to reconvene the next morning (March 24) with draft papers addressing the "pattern and procedure" for such a treaty.[57] These drafts would then be used to craft a joint paper that could be taken back to the respective capitals for consultation. The "March 24 paper" outlined six steps for the parties to take:[58]

1. The United States government should approach the members of the Brussels Pact about the conclusion of a North Atlantic pact;
2. Britain and France should approach Norway, Sweden, Denmark, and Iceland about acceding to the Brussels Treaty;
3. Britain and France should approach Italy about acceding to the Brussels Treaty;
4. The U.S. president should publicly declare an intention to consider "an armed attack against a signatory of the Brussels Pact as an armed attack against the United States to be dealt with by the United States in accordance with Article 51 of the United Nations Charter";
5. The president should make a similar statement regarding Greece, Turkey, and Iran; and
6. The United States would then formally invite Britain, France, Canada, Norway, Sweden, Denmark, Iceland, the Netherlands, Belgium, Luxembourg, Ireland, Switzerland, Italy, and Portugal to take part in a conference aimed at creating a North Atlantic pact.

These recommended steps are essentially identical to the ones that would be approved by representatives of the United States, Canada, and Britain and embodied in the April 1 "Pentagon Paper." There were three differences between the March 24 paper and the final Pentagon Paper. Two of the differences pertained to matters of procedure. First, the final draft stipulated that "when circumstances permit," the three western German zones, the three western Austrian zones, and Spain should be invited to join the pact. Second, once the pact was signed, political and military conversations should immediately be held "with a view to coordinating their military and other efforts and strengthening their collective security."[59]

The third difference between the March 24 paper and the final Pentagon Paper pertained to changes in the proposed treaty provisions (see table 5.2).[60]

The first major change is the reference to the Rio pact in the preamble. According to the Canadian memorandum of the meetings, this was included largely because "the Americans were anxious not to give the impression that this particular North Atlantic Pact was to be the nucleus for a general security arrangement, but rather that there would be a number of such pacts."[61] The second major change pertains to the concept of "mutual defense." Notice that Article 1 of the final draft contains more flexible and qualified language. The final draft no longer calls on each party to use "all" forms of aid "in its power." Instead, the provision now calls for each party to "undertake to assist."

The third major change in the treaty was additional provisions. Article 6 in table 5.2 makes explicit that the determination of the appropriate measures is in the hands of each individual party, at least until the parties agree on a joint response. It was included on the prompting of Lewis Douglas, the U.S. ambassador to Britain. According to the Canadian memorandum, Douglas was concerned that the initial phrasing of the provision "meant that the military forces of all the signatories would have to be moved at once to the actual point of attack."[62] The British and Canadian officials made clear that this was not the intention of the article and that "each state would judge how it would implement its obligation for the provision of military, economic, and other aid."[63] They apparently outlined the following scenario to Douglas: "If, for instance, there were an attack on Belgium, Canada's assistance to Belgium might conceivably take the form of moving troops to Fort Churchill in the first instance, and, in the long run, might take the form of concentrating on industrial production."[64] A similar concern about language revolved around Article 7 of the revised draft. This article delineated the geographic scope of the treaty's mutual defense guarantee.[65] Douglas had raised the concern that "when you begin to define, you play into the hands of the aggressor by telling him what to avoid." However, Douglas was also concerned that "a vague and general statement of this kind might worry Congress because of the all-embracing nature of the obligation."[66] In response to this concern, the British and Canadian officials "pointed out that each signatory of the Pact would itself determine whether an armed attack had taken place."[67]

While the treaty drafts had differences, a notable similarity between the two drafts is Article 3, which called for establishing "such agencies as may be necessary for effective implementation of the treaty," specifically highlighting the need to craft plans for mutual defense. In other words, the treaty should create an international body to address the logistics of executing war plans.[68] These agencies would essentially import the Consultative Council and the permanent military committee of the Brussels pact into the transatlantic pact.[69] Those bodies were added to the Brussels pact through a British initiative and were modeled on the Combined Chiefs of Staff used by the British and Americans during the Second

World War.[70] These bodies were to deal with "problems of production and pro-curement of equipment . . . [and] will study the tactical and technical problems of Western European defense."[71]

A proposed treaty having been drafted, one step remained before the U.S. of-ficials could pursue comprehensive negotiations: the Senate's blessing. If the final document was to be a treaty of alliance, it would require the approval of two-thirds of the Senate. To gain this approval, U.S. State Department officials would have to work with Senator Arthur H. Vandenberg, the chairman of the Senate Foreign Relations Committee. While Vandenberg was an internationalist who wanted engagement with Europe, he knew it was important for any treaty to guard U.S. sovereignty. Hence, when he reviewed the initial draft of the Pentagon Paper on April 11, he remarked: "[A military guarantee could] let [the Europeans] get a sense of false security which might result in their taking so firm an attitude as to become provocative and give the impression of having a chip on their shoul-ders. . . . [Therefore,] its form must in all event leave the determination to this country as to the circumstances under which we would aid, the type of aid, etc. . . . We must always have the right to determine for ourselves when we will act."[72]

This led to a series of back-and-forth meetings between Lovett, Hickerson, and Vandenberg. The goal was to draft a resolution by which the Senate would ap-prove the negotiation of a security arrangement with the European states. As de-scribed by Hickerson, "[Vandenberg] asked us to do a draft [of the resolution] for him, which we did. I mean, he gave us his ideas and we wrote them up."[73] According to Hickerson, it was vital that the resolution be short: "[Vandenberg] called me and said, 'Too damn long, got to get this on one page.' And we got it on one page."[74] By May 11, the resolution had been approved by the other mem-bers of the Foreign Relations Committee. In approving the resolution, the com-mittee report emphasized that "the lessons of World Wars I and II show that the best deterrent to aggression is the certainty that immediate and effective counter-measures will be taken and that the United States would, by making clear in ad-vance that any such attack would meet immediate American reaction," have taken an important step toward removing "uncertainties that might mislead potential aggressors."[75] On June 11, the resolution was put before the full Senate for a vote and passed, 83 to 14. Its core provision advised the president to pursue "such re-gional and other collective arrangements as are based on continuous and effective self-help and mutual aid, and as affect its national security."[76] With the Senate's pas-sage of the Vandenberg resolution in June 1948, the way was open for the United States to take an active role in European security.

TABLE 5.2. Comparison of draft treaty in the initial and final Pentagon Paper drafts

INITIAL DRAFT TREATY TEXT	FINAL TREATY DRAFT TEXT IN PENTAGON PAPER
Preamble A Preamble combining some of the features of the preamble to the Treaty of Brussels.	Preamble combining some of the features of the preambles to the Rio and Five-Power Treaties.
Article 1 A provision that an armed attack by any state against any party to the Pact is an attack against all the parties; that in accordance with Article 51 of the Charter each party undertakes to give immediately to any other party which is attacked by any State, all the military, economic, and other aid and assistance in its power.	Provision that each Party shall regard any action in the area covered by the agreement, which it considers an armed attack against any other Party, as an armed attack against itself and that each Party accordingly undertakes to assist in meeting the attack in the exercise of the inherent right of individual or collective self-defense recognized by Article 51 of the Charter.
Article 2 Arrangements for consultation between all the parties in the event of any party considering that its political independence or territorial integrity is threatened.	Provision for consultation between all the Parties in the event of any Party considering that its territorial integrity or political independence is threatened by armed attack or indirect aggression in any part of the world.
Article 3 Authority to establish such agencies as may be necessary for effective implementation of the treaty including the working out of plans for prompt and effective action under [Art 1] above.	Provisions for the establishment of such agencies as may be necessary for effective implementation of the agreement including the working out of plans for prompt and effective action under [Art 1] and [Art 2] above.
Article 4 Duration of ten years, with automatic renewal for five-year periods unless denounced.	Duration of ten years, with automatic renewal for five-year periods unless denounced.
Article 5 [NO EQUIVALENT ARTICLE]	Provision to the effect that action taken under the agreement shall, as provided in Article 51 of the Charter, be promptly reported to the Security Council and cease when the Security Council shall have taken the necessary steps to maintain or restore peace and security.
Article 6 [NO EQUIVALENT ARTICLE]	Provision following the lines of Article III, paragraph 2 of the Rio Treaty to the effect that, at the request of the State or States directly attacked, and until coordinated measures have been agreed upon, each one of the Parties shall determine the immediate measures which it will individually take in fulfillment of the obligation contained in [Art 1] and in accordance with the principle of mutual solidarity.
Article 7 [NO EQUIVALENT ARTICLE]	Delineation of the area covered by the agreement to include the continental territory in Europe and North America of any Party and the islands in the North Atlantic whether sovereign or belonging to any Part—This would include Spitzbergen and other Norwegian Islands, Iceland, Greenland, Newfoundland, and Alaska.

Source: Memorandum from Undersecretary of State for External Affairs to Prime Minister, March 29, 1948, *Documents on Canadian External Relations* 14, no. 322, chap. 6; and Minutes of the Sixth Meeting of the United States-United Kingdom-Canada Security Conversations, April 1, 1948, *Foreign Relations of the United States* 2:71–75.

The Washington Exploratory Talks

After the crafting of the Pentagon Paper and the passage of the Vandenberg resolution, it was time to involve the remaining Brussels pact members in the negotiations: the Netherlands, Belgium, Luxembourg, and France.[77] Invitations were extended, and the parties convened the Washington Exploratory Talks on July 6, 1948. Though the meeting was officially between acting secretary of state Lovett and the ambassadors of the other countries, the actual negotiations were conducted by a "working group" of the secretary and ambassadors' assistants (Achilles 1985, 34). Hickerson headed up the working group.[78] As Theodore C. Achilles, who as U.S. State Department director for Western European affairs was directly involved in the negotiations, recounted, "meetings of the Ambassadors with the Acting Secretary were held occasionally to review the progress of the Working Group, particularly when it was necessary to get an obstinate government to modify its position" (Achilles 1985, 34).

The talks were conducted in three phases: July 6 to September 9, 1948; December 10 to 24, 1948; and January 3 to March 18, 1949. Each phase had a goal. The first phase focused on using the ABC report to craft an initial seven-power pact. The initial pact was then taken to the respective governments for review. The second phase focused on hashing out differences between the parties based on these reviews. The third phase focused on addressing the last remaining issues and incorporating more countries identified as essential for the functioning of the pact.[79]

A draft treaty was produced at the end of each phase of the negotiations. The first phase produced a memorandum (subsequently referred to as "the Washington Paper") summarizing the proceedings and outlining an eventual treaty (which was literally called an "Outline of Provisions Which Might be Suitable for Inclusion in a North Atlantic Security Pact").[80] The second phase offered an updated draft treaty. This updated draft was largely reflected in the final treaty text, which was approved at the conclusion of the third phase and officially signed on April 4, 1949.

Overall, the negotiations were quite cordial. Referring to the first phase of negotiations, Achilles (1985, 34–35) recalls, "Derick Hoyer Millar, then Minister in the British Embassy and now Lord Inchyra, started what became known as 'the NATO spirit.' One day, he made a proposal which the rest of us criticized severely but constructively. Derick replied: 'Very well. Those were my instructions. I'll tell the Foreign Office I've made my pitch and been shot down, and ask for instructions along the lines we've agreed.'"

But disagreements did arise. The parties debated the treaty's duration (i.e., should it be ninety-nine years, fifty, or ten?) and the extent to which it would mention cooperation in nonmilitary affairs (as eventually embodied in Article 2 of the treaty). But as the account below should make clear, the most contentious disagreements arose over a key aspect of the joint war plan's strategic component: its geographic scope. The negotiations were marked by prolonged disputes over how to define the "North Atlantic" region and, related to this, which countries must necessarily be included in the pact.

Given the centrality of geography in these negotiations, it is useful to consider a map before delving into the details of the negotiations. Figure 5.1 shows a political map of Europe in 1948 with four groups of countries highlighted. The Soviet Union is black, with other communist countries in dark gray.[81] The members of the Brussels pact (Britain, France, and the Benelux countries) are shown in gray. Of key interest are the countries shown in light gray. It was debate over the possible inclusion of any or all of these five countries—Italy, Denmark, Norway, Iceland, and Portugal—that proved most contentious. Some countries were obviously critical from a logistical standpoint, such as the air and military installations offered by Portugal and Denmark (Kaplan 2013, 7). Iceland was included not just because it served as a "stepping-stone" from North America to Europe,[82] but to emphasize, as described by Kaplan (2013, 7), "the 'Atlantic' as opposed to the 'European' character of NATO."[83] But the possible inclusion of Italy stretched

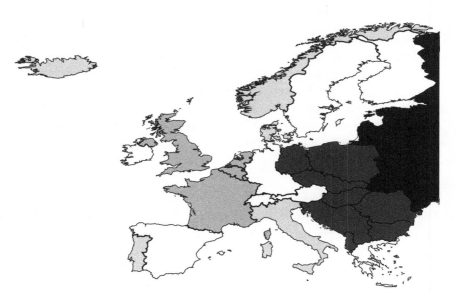

FIGURE 5.1. Europe in 1948

Note: Brussels pact members (in gray), possible NATO members (in light gray), Soviet Union (in black), non-Soviet Communist countries (in dark gray). Map created using Cshapes shapefile (Weidmann, Kuse, and Gleditsch 2010) and the spmap and shp2dta commands in Stata version 14.0. See the replication materials for more details.

the definition of "North Atlantic." Indeed, despite Italy being mentioned in the Pentagon Paper as a potential member state, debates over Italy were the most contentious and threatened at one point to undermine the negotiations. In the end, agreement was reached, and all five countries were invited to be initial members of the North Atlantic pact.

I have organized the narrative that follows in three parts. Each part focuses on a point of debate during the negotiations: entrapment concerns (which led to debate over the wording of the treaty's text), strategic compatibility concerns (which centered on defining the alliance's geographic scope), and operational compatibility concerns (which focused on creating a supranational body to define the general approach and logistics for engaging a threat). One should note that these mirror core parts of my theoretical claims (strategic and operational compatibility) and a key competing explanation for outcomes of alliance treaty negotiation (entrapment concerns). All of these concerns arose during the negotiations. I seek to consider the relative importance of each. Besides offering an explanation for how the North Atlantic Treaty came about, this will enable me to determine whether entrapment concerns are best considered an alternative or an additional explanation for alliance treaty negotiation outcomes.

Addressing Entrapment Concerns

The wording of the mutual defense clause generated much debate during the Washington talks. In his recollection of the negotiations, Achilles says that writing "the commitment to respond to armed attack" was "naturally the most controversial" portion of the treaty and negotiations (Achilles 1985, 35). Finding a mutually satisfactory formulation of the North Atlantic Treaty's mutual defense clause (Article 5 of the final treaty) "took many sessions of the Working Group, much consultation with Foreign Offices (and with the Senate Foreign Relations Committee)."

RIO OR BRUSSELS?

The parties considered two models for crafting the clause: the Rio pact and the Brussels pact. More precisely, the "models" are the wording of the mutual defense clauses in the 1947 Rio pact and the 1948 Brussels pact. The former was favored by the United States, while the latter was favored by the Europeans. The mutual defense clause of the Rio pact is found in Article 3. The first two paragraphs of Article 3 read as follows:[84]

1. The High Contracting Parties agree that an armed attack by any State against an American State shall be considered as an attack against all the

American States and, consequently, each one of the said Contracting Parties undertakes to assist in meeting the attack in the exercise of the inherent right of individual or collective self-defense recognized by Article 51 of the Charter of the United Nations.

2. On the request of the State or States directly attacked and until the decision of the Organ of Consultation of the Inter-American System, each one of the Contracting Parties may determine the immediate measures which it may individually take in fulfillment of the obligation contained in the preceding paragraph and in accordance with the principle of continental solidarity. The Organ of Consultation shall meet without delay for the purpose of examining those measures and agreeing upon the measures of a collective character that should be taken.[85]

The mutual defense clause of the Brussels pact is found in Article 4, which reads, "If any of the High Contracting Parties should be the object of an armed attack in Europe, the other High Contracting Parties will, in accordance with the provisions of Article 51 of the Charter of the United Nations, afford the Party so attacked all the military and other aid and assistance in their power."[86]

In comparing the two mutual defense clauses, three points stand out. First, Article 4 of the Brussels pact is simple and sparse in comparison to Article 3 of the Rio pact. Second, while Article 3 of the Rio pact contains the strong wording "considered an attack against all the American states," it specifies a relatively weak response. The treaty calls on the parties to simply "assist in meeting the attack," while paragraph 2 makes explicit that each member "may determine the immediate measures which it may individually take in fulfillment of the obligation contained in the preceding paragraph." In other words, a member promises to respond to an attack in a manner that seems appropriate, including not deploying military assets (and perhaps instead issuing diplomatic condemnation). Third, the Brussels pact explicitly calls on the parties to use "all the military and other aid and assistance in their power." This would seem to convey a stronger commitment than the Rio pact. However, the phrase "in their power" is admittedly vague; a state could claim that it is not presently in its power to provide any assets. Be that as it may, the Europeans considered the Brussels pact to carry greater "automaticity" than the Rio pact (English 2001, 338). The United States was instrumental in placing the more equivocal wording in the Rio pact, and it sought a similar wording for the North Atlantic Treaty (Kaplan 2013, 7). Doing so would be essential for gaining Senate ratification of the treaty (English 2001, 338). Dean Acheson, the U.S. secretary of state during the final phase of the talks, observed that the mutual defense clause essentially pitted continental European ambassadors against the U.S. senators (Acheson 1969, 280). As he writes, "the [Continental]

Europeans were naturally the most fervent advocates of strong and unequivo-
cal commitments for aid in case of attack. The British characteristically wished
an opportunity to appraise an emergency before plunging in, and the Americans and Canadians were most wary of what came to be known as automatic
involvement."

While the discussions of wording were contentious, did they ever threaten to
undermine the talks? Consider the September 9 Washington Paper produced at
the conclusion of the first round of the talks.[87] At the time of the report, final
agreement had not been reached on the mutual defense clause's wording. Indeed, the "Outline of Provisions Which Might Be Suitable for Inclusion in a
North Atlantic Security Pact" included with the report offered three phrasings of
the mutual defense provision: a U.S.-favored Rio pact–based provision, a
European-favored Brussels pact–based provision, and a compromise provision
offered by the Canadians.[88] The report states that the U.S. representatives had
suggested wording from the Rio pact as a basis for the provision, since such
wording "had been approved by the US Senate."[89] However, the report also states
that the U.S. representatives "fully recognized the relevance of provisions of the
Brussels treaty."[90] Moreover, the report emphasizes that "all representatives
stressed that their respective constitutional processes must be observed and
agreed that, as in any similar treaty, the question of fact as to whether or not an
armed attack had occurred would be a matter for individual determination."[91]
In other words, the report shows that while the parties were still in the midst of
extensive discussions about the appropriate wording, the essential meaning of
the clause was not really under dispute: the parties recognized that alliance treaties
carried no "automaticity."

AMBASSADORS VERSUS SENATORS

The events of February 1949 offer perhaps the most insight into the extent to
which entrapment concerns drove disputes over the treaty's language and whether
they threatened to undermine overall agreement. This month was critical, as it
was when Acheson was involved in separate discussions with the foreign ambassadors and U.S. senators over the treaty (Henderson 1983, 90).[92] It is useful to
first consider Acheson's conversations with the ambassadors and then his conversations with the senators.

Acheson met with the ambassadors on February 8 to assure them that he (and
the senators) agreed that Article 5 must "make it perfectly clear that an attack on
an area or upon a country which involved the security of the United States would
be met with force."[93] At the same time, however, Acheson admitted that "what
gave [the senators] pause at this moment was the detail of the draft text: What
was armed attack? Who would determine what was done?"[94] Acheson thought the

first question was "not really important enough to cause anybody any concern" since "if there was any doubt about whether there had been an armed attack, there would be no need to bring the armed might of all the nations into play."[95] But he acknowledged that the second question required more discussion. He said the senators knew that for the alliance to function "there would be preliminary talks, there would be plans."[96] This was only sensible. But they wanted to "avoid overstatement" and find "more neutral language" making clear that "the ultimate action would depend upon the decision of each member country."[97]

The ambassadors completely understood the senators' views, but they thought the wording was already sufficiently weak. As Henri Bonnet, the French ambassador to the United States, remarked, "the text did not really go very far . . . [It] was extremely prudent and modest."[98] At the same time, it was important that the wording not be too vague. A definite commitment clause would, as explained by the Canadian ambassador Hume Wrong in December, "achieve as exact a definition as possible of the nature of the obligation" and, perhaps more importantly, "prevent the Soviet countries from belittling the importance of the undertaking in the Pact."[99] As Oliver Franks, the British ambassador to the United States, remarked upon hearing Acheson's report on the senators, "the substance of the Treaty was what mattered and the words were of secondary importance."[100] But words still mattered, which is why Acheson explained to Bonnet that it was essential to limit the amount of information given to the public about the actual words being considered: "[I] suggested the wisdom of not rendering more difficult the task with the Senate, which must make the final decision as to whether the Treaty could be concluded or not. Unwise public discussion at this time might well make it impossible to conclude any treaty."[101]

Acheson then met with the two key members of the Senate Foreign Relations Committee: Vandenberg and Tom Connally. Recall that there was a long pause in the negotiations during the autumn of 1948. This was intended to give the participants time to consult with their respective governments and, perhaps more importantly, await the outcome of the November elections in the United States. President Truman was not expected to be reelected, and the U.S. State Department did not want to submit the treaty to a lame duck Senate.[102]

Truman did win, but control of the Senate changed hands from the Republican Party to the Democratic Party. Consequently, Vandenberg was no longer chairman of the Senate Foreign Relations Committee (though he remained on the committee). Connally, a Democrat, was the new chairman. While Connally had been a member of the committee when it unanimously approved the Vandenberg resolution, the State Department still had to work with him to ensure that the new Democratic members of the Senate (and of the committee) were supportive of the treaty. Moreover, it was far from guaranteed that Connally would continue to support the treaty. Fortunately, according to Hickerson, Truman saw to it that Connally would follow through:

> Mr. Truman took care of that for us. He called him up and said in effect, "Now look Tom, I want you and Lucille to come down and have supper with Bess and me, just the four of us. I'll tell you what I want to talk about. We've got to get moving on this North Atlantic Treaty thing, and these damn Republicans—Vandenberg is a hell of a nice fellow, he's fine, he's fine, but now I want you to take this thing over and I want to bring you up to date on anything you may have missed along the line, and you just take charge on this thing." And Tom just ate it up. He was wonderful.[103]

Truman's efforts appeared to pay off, but not without Connally offering push-back on the wording of the treaty. In a February 14 meeting, Connally and Vandenberg immediately began picking away at Article 5.[104] Connally took issue with the phrase "an attack on one was an attack on all," preferring instead "an attack on one would be regarded as a threat to the peace of all." Vandenberg thought the "attack on all" wording was acceptable since it was also used in the Rio pact,[105] but he insisted on removing the word "military" from the description of responses. Vandenberg also agreed with Connally that the treaty should include the phrase "as it may deem necessary," because it would make plain that what action to take was a matter for individual states to determine.[106]

To find wording that would be acceptable to both the senators and the ambassadors, Acheson, with the assistance of Undersecretary James Webb and State Department counselor Charles Bohlen, devised a clever diplomatic maneuver. First, based on the feedback from the first meetings with Vandenberg and Connally, Bohlen met with Hickerson and Achilles to devise a "minimally acceptable" draft of Article 5.[107] This draft read: "The Parties agree that an armed attack against one or more of them in Europe or North America shall be considered an attack against them all; and consequently that, if such an armed attack occurs, each of them, in exercise of the right of individual or collective self-defense recognized by Article 51 of the Charter of the United Nations, will take, forthwith, individually, and in concert with the other Parties, the measures it deems necessary to restore and maintain the security of the North Atlantic area."[108]

Next, Bohlen met privately with Ambassador Franks to gain his opinion on whether the ambassadors would accept this draft Article 5. Franks suggested holding it "in reserve" when meeting with the senators. Acheson should instead offer a variant of Article 5, called variant A, which replaced "will take" with the phrase "will assist the Party or Parties so attacked by taking" and replaced "the measures" with "such military or other action."[109] If this variant was unacceptable, Frank then proposed that Acheson show variant B, which replaced the phrase "the mea-sures" with "such military or other action."[110] If this variant was also unaccept-able, then Acheson could offer variant C. This third variant replaced "will take" with the phrase "will assist the Party or Parties so attacked by taking" and replaced "the measures" with "the actions." If all three of these variants failed, then Ache-son could offer the minimally acceptable Article 5.

Equipped with these variants of Article 5, Acheson and President Truman met with Senator Connally. The goal was to gain Connally's support for the draft article and ask Connally if he thought it necessary to meet with the other Demo-cratic leaders of the Senate. Acheson never had to resort to variant B. Connally was willing to accept Article 5 provided that the phrase "military and other action" was changed to "action including the use of armed force."[111] Acheson made this change and then presented the revised Article 5 to Vandenberg. Vandenberg was the last to see and approve the article, since he was already in favor of the treaty. With Van-denberg's agreement, Acheson then presented the new Article 5 to the ambassa-dors. As Franks expected, the ambassadors approved (Henderson 1983, 93).[112]

In his later reflections, Acheson (1969, 282) called all of this a "ridiculous epi-sode" that despite not having great importance does illustrate "the difficulty of negotiating when one is operating through an executive-legislative soviet." This is not to say that the United States would have signed the treaty without accept-able wording. They likely would not have, which is why the parties exerted great effort in finding acceptable wording. The parties had to find acceptable language, but that was not the only concern. Nor was the choice of words the most conten-tious issue. This distinction belongs to strategic compatibility issues, to which I will now turn.

Addressing Strategic Incompatibilities

The negotiation's most contentious debates pertained to the strategic component of a war plan. In this case, the incompatibilities were not about the identification of the threat. Instead, debate arose over the territory to guarantee protection to and, related to this, over alliance membership. In other words, the debate wasn't over whom to attack but over whom to protect. As remarked by the Dutch ambassador E. N. Van Kleffens, defining the "security area" was a "delicate problem."[113] Simi-larly, Lovett referred to "the difficult points relating to the area to be covered, the inclusion of Italy, and the nature of the assurances to be given to countries not signatories to the pact" (the last point referring to Greece and Turkey).[114]

Broadly, the debate was over defining the southern boundary of the treaty area. Lovett feared that defining the area to include parts of Africa "would open up a limitless field."[115] He favored excluding southern European countries, such as

Greece and Italy. His view was supported by Wrong (Canada) and Van Kleffens (the Netherlands).[116] Bonnet (France) favored a more expansive definition. Franks (Britain) did not have a rigid position (though he expressed sympathy for the French view).[117] The parties eventually agreed to define the southern boundary of the treaty as areas "north of the Tropic of Cancer" that were under the parties' jurisdiction (Article 6 of the final treaty). Getting to this point required addressing two highly contentious issues: Italian membership and the inclusion of French Algeria.

INITIAL DISAGREEMENT ON ITALY

Incompatibilities over this issue were evident as early as July.[118] During the first round of talks, the participants took an extensive list of countries that were not present at the talks and then proceeded to discuss, country by country, the merits and feasibility of including each in the pact. While many countries were quickly dismissed as possible members (e.g., Brazil), Italy required careful consideration. Hickerson held that "Italy was an integral part of Western European security," though it could also be included in a separate Mediterranean-focused arrangement.[119] Van Kleffens remarked that it could be "a mistake to refer to Italy in their final report as a 'necessary' member of the pact."[120] He recognized that Italy could not be isolated but suggested that it could be part of "some sort of umbrella arrangement" rather than granted full membership.[121] For Kennan, since Italy was "close to the Soviet orbit" and "contribute[d] little in the way of military power," there were "certain advantages with Italy excluded from the arrangement."[122] Discussions over Italy continued until the September 2 session. At that meeting, Hickerson bluntly stated that the Europeans needed to take the initiative in "solving the problem of Italy's relationship to a North Atlantic arrangement."[123] Lovett reiterated Hickerson's view during the ambassador-level meeting the next day, stating that "Italy presented a problem on which he believed the Brussels Pact signatories would want to express a very definite view one way or the other."[124]

The Washington Paper produced in September 1948 singles out the dispute over Italy: "The case of Italy presents a particular problem."[125] The report summarizes the debate as boiling down to two points. On the one hand, Italy "is not a North Atlantic country and it is subject to the military limitations imposed by the [World War II] Peace Treaty."[126] On the other hand, "[Italy's] territory is of strategic importance to the nations here represented and its Western orientation must be maintained and strengthened."[127] A decision about Italy's status was postponed until December.

Much was achieved at the December meetings. The Working Group report summarizing the December talks opens by stating, "The Working Group have reached agreement on practically all the articles of a possible Pact."[128] The parties crafted what would, by and large, be the final text of the North Atlantic Treaty. But the end of the report also lists three items on which the parties had not been able to reach agreement: the area to be covered, conciliation procedures for disputes between members, and treaty duration. Disagreement over the first of those items was primarily due to continued debate over Italy. As Acheson wrote in a memorandum a month later, Italy's status was the "principal outstanding question and satisfactory solution would materially expedite conclusion of negotiations."[129] So important was the Italian issue that the Working Group's December report included an annex dedicated solely to outlining the arguments for and against Italian membership (annex C).[130] Annex C was the only report annex focused on a sole negotiation item. The other annexes dealt with overarching aspects of the negotiations, such as a draft of the entire treaty (annex A), comments on the provisions of the draft treaty (annex B), and recommended procedures for carrying out the remaining negotiations (annex D).

According to annex C, France favored Italy's inclusion, while Britain and Canada were strictly opposed. French support was based on a host of reasons ranging from geography (Italy's position on the "southern flank" and southern supply routes, along with being geographically contiguous with France) to its culture (its civilization and maritime traditions were "Western"). Britain and Canada opposed including Italy in the Atlantic pact for three reasons: (1) Italy was not in the "North Atlantic," (2) Italy's postwar arms limitations meant it would not be able to contribute to the alliance,[131] and (3) adding Italy could beg the question of how much further the territorial protection offered by the pact should be stretched (e.g., should Greece and Turkey also be included?).

The United States, along with the Benelux countries, opted for an ambiguous position. The U.S. representatives wanted some "association" for Italy with the Brussels and Atlantic pacts but didn't specify that this must include full membership. In a January memorandum, Acheson stated that the U.S. preference was for what had been labeled argument (g) in annex C: "If one of the objectives of the Pact is to tighten cultural and political ties between North Atlantic and Western European countries, Italy, by reason of her civilization and her mercantile and maritime traditions, would appear to be an appropriate member."[132] But Acheson later acknowledged that Italy was a "perplexing problem."[133] Including Italy made little sense geographically: "She was most decidedly not a North Atlantic state in any geography."[134] But leaving Italy out risked creating a renewed threat and abetting the spread of communism in Europe:

> From a political point of view an unattached Italy was a source of danger. A former enemy state, with the connection with the United States such as Greece and Turkey had had since 1947 through our economic

and military programs, without connections to Western Europe, except for the late, unlamented one made between Mussolini and Franco, Italy might suffer from an isolation complex and, with its large communist party, fall victim to seduction from the East. We had expressed these ideas to Bevin at the end of January, stressing the importance of strengthening Italian resistance to Russian domination.[135]

The Brussels pact members tried to reach a consensus view. In late-January meetings of the Brussels Pact Permanent Commission and the Brussels Pact Consultative Council, the parties failed to arrive at a common view (Henderson 1983, 80), but they agreed that if the Americans wanted Italy in the pact, they would not object.[136] This view was shared by Belgium's prime minister Paul-Henri Spaak. On January 22, the Belgian ambassador told Acheson, "If [U.S. officials] feel strongly that Italian inclusion is essential," the Europeans would not oppose it.[137]

This placed Italy's fate in the hands of the Americans, but the United States delayed a decision. When Italian membership was raised during the February 8 meeting of the Washington Exploratory Talks, Acheson and Franks simply asserted that "no conclusions had been reached about Italy."[138] The reason for delay was expressed well by Bevin in a February 24 memo to the British ambassador in Paris, Sir Oliver Harvey.[139] Inviting Italy to participate in the negotiations would "bedevil them" because Italian officials would insist on "bringing up the colonial question and the Peace Treaty."[140] The latter point was in reference to the arms limitations placed on Italy by its post–World War II treaty of peace with the Western Allies, while the former referred to the concern that Italy might insist on including colonial possessions under Article 5 protection. Bevin feared that, as a result of these complications, "we might end by getting no pact at all."[141]

THE FRENCH ITALIAN TACTIC

Unfortunately, Italy's status was brought to a head by the French. Fearing that the Americans would opt to leave Italy out, Bonnet threatened to block Norway's admission if Italy was not also included (English 2001, 339).[142] Acheson described Bonnet's proposal as an "extraordinary exhibition" since "Norwegian and Italian participation had never previously been linked."[143] Acheson felt that Bonnet "appeared ready, in order to get Italy in, to run extreme risks over Norway, risks to which he was not entitled to subject all of us and that if French government insisted on this position I would not take responsibility for consequences."[144] Franks wrote to Bevin that the Americans, notably Acheson, "are resentful of [the French] tactics which they regard as near blackmail."[145] But the French position was that Italian inclusion was as essential to French security, given their shared border, as Norwegian inclusion was to the security of the northern European

states.[146] Moreover, the French government had grown tired of the other participants delaying a decision on Italy and, therefore, decided to press the issue: "The
question of Italy's inclusion had been pushed to and fro between the Brussels Powers and the United States and Canada—so far without result—and the French
Government felt that the time had come when they must know how we all stood
in this matter."[147] Bevin viewed the whole matter as a ploy by the French to gain
Article 5 protection for French Algeria: "We are now very close to final agreement
on the Pact and I cannot believe that the French Government are prepared to sacrifice the progress made in order to obtain the immediate inclusion of Italy . . .
[If the] French Government are obstinate over Italy they will lose whatever chance
there may now be of getting Algeria covered under Article 5 of the Pact, which
seems to be their real purpose in pressing for the inclusion of Italy."[148]

Despite these protestations, the French government decided to double down
on its demand. At the March 1 meetings of the Washington Exploratory Talks,
Bonnet informed the other participants that France was prepared not to participate in the pact if Italy was not invited: "if [the French] government had to present to the public and the Parliament a pact including Norway and to which Italy
would not be a party, not mentioning the question of the Algerian Departments
in addition, then the French Government would have to reconsider its position
as far as its own participation was concerned. . . . [We] hope that conclusions
would not be reached which, by including Norway, would exclude France."[149]

Bonnet then rebutted the claim that Italy was not "North Atlantic" by assert-
ing that, with Norway in the treaty, it would actually be more of an Arctic treaty,
not Atlantic: "much of the territory covered by the Pact was not North Atlantic
but Arctic territory. Italy and France had a common frontier and from the point
of view of strategy as well as politics, [the French] Government thought it better
to include Italy if countries in the North of Europe were to be included."[150]

A formula for addressing the situation was reached at the next meeting.[151] According to Bonnet, the Italian government informed him that "its representative
would not raise the question of Italian colonies or of the disarmament clauses of
the Peace Treaty or any other clauses of the kind if she was admitted to the discussions."[152] Acheson confirmed Bonnet's claim: "[I] confirm the view of the Italian
Government reported by the French Ambassador that the Italians would not raise
any difficult points if they were admitted to the discussions."[153] Acheson added
that this new information meant that differentiating between Norwegian and Italian membership was now "an academic question" so long as "it was agreed that all
countries [the original seven and the additional five] should sign at the same
time."[154] Franks and Wrong asked for time to consult with their governments.

Acheson also consulted with Truman after the meeting. When describing the
state of the negotiations to Truman, Acheson conveyed that the United States had

no strong views on the Italian issue: "There had never been a well thought out United States position on the inclusion or exclusion of Italy from the Atlantic Pact.... Nevertheless, in the course of the negotiations, the United States negotiators had drifted into the position that the European nations must take a position upon Italy."[155] Acheson now recommended that the U.S. support Italian inclusion because he feared France really would walk away from the negotiations: "France was so emphatically in favor of Italian participation that she had stated, and we believed she meant it, that she would have to reconsider her whole relation to the Pact if Italy was not to be included."[156] To Acheson, it now appeared that the Canadians and European participants were ready to accept Italian inclusion. If the United States drew a hard line on Italy, "we might still have a treaty but we would get it in a rather damaged condition."[157] Acheson's ultimate request was that the president "authorize me to agree to the inclusion of Italy in the Pact" under the formula agreed on at the March 1 meeting.[158] Admitting that he "would have preferred, certainly at this time, a pact without Italy," Truman nevertheless gave Acheson approval to admit Italy into the pact.[159] The ambassadors and Acheson then met again on March 7, at which time it was agreed to invite Italy and the other additional states.[160]

ALGERIA

Debate over Italy was contentious and threatened to prevent an agreement. But Italy was not the only geographic component to spark debate. French officials also wanted "North Atlantic" defined in such a way as to include the French départments of Algeria, in northern Africa. During the January 14 meeting, Bonnet remarked, "France did not see how a Pact could include part of the Arctic regions and the northern part of Canada without including the three departments of Algeria which were a part of France."[161] Indeed, during the December 22 meeting, Bonnet argued that Algeria's relationship to France was the same "as Alaska or Florida to the United States."[162]

However, Acheson made clear at the February 8 ambassadors' meeting that the United States favored leaving explicit mention of Algeria out of the treaty.[163] His reasoning was that he could not foresee a circumstance where external forces would attack French Algeria and not European France: "[I] would much prefer to avoid a reference in the Treaty to Algeria. The United States Government did not see how there could be an attack on Algeria without there being also an attack on European France, unless it was a local scrimmage which would not be within the scope of the Treaty. The U.S. would much prefer merely referring to an attack 'in Europe and North America' rather than having a definition of area in the Treaty."[164] Bonnet retorted that the words "in Europe and North America" did constitute a definition of area and "to use them alone would amount to leaving out a part of French national territory."[165] Acheson responded that "the United States attitude was pretty strong and that the question would have to be postponed."[166]

A resolution was reached during the March 1 meeting. Acheson informed Bonnet that he had explained the importance of Algeria to France to the Senate Foreign Relations Committee. The senators understood his explanation and agreed to include Algeria in the treaty. According to the minutes, Acheson described the situation with the senators as follows:

> [Upon coming into the negotiations, I] had been disturbed to find that the discussions with the [U.S.] Senators had not progressed as far as [I] had been led to believe. In particular, the Senators did not know that the problem of Algeria entered into the Treaty and was part of the French position; [I] had had a difficult time with them on the matter and it had been a problem of explaining to them the political problems of the French Government, the structure of the French State, and the Relation of Algeria to France. They had gradually come to see the matter in a different light, and [I] was happy to report that it was now agreeable to include in the Treaty the Algerian Departments of France.[167]

With this, Article 6 of the final treaty, which defines the geographic scope of the protective commitment, read, "The territory of any of the Parties in Europe or North America, or the Algerian Departments of France."[168]

Why did the U.S. officials eventually concede to France on this issue? According to Escott Reid of the Canadian delegation, U.S. officials had actually made the decision to concede on Algeria in January but wanted to delay revealing that decision to France. The hope was that doing so would make the French more willing to concede on other issues: "By January 24 the [U.S.] State Department had also moved to this position [of reluctantly accepting the inclusion of French Algeria]. Achilles told [the Canadian diplomat Thomas] Stone on that day 'for his own very private ear that the United States will swallow Algeria' . . . [but] for various reasons they wanted to let this question hang in the balance for as long as possible."[169] Reid acknowledges that the U.S. motivation for leaving the issue unresolved was unclear (Reid 1977, 217). One possibility was that Acheson, who had just become secretary of state, did not agree with the U.S. position. Another is that he simply knew it would take more time to convince the senators that Algeria was important to France. Given Acheson's description of the efforts he made to explain Algeria to the senators, this was likely the case. Another possibility, not mentioned by Reid, is that the United States wanted to keep Algeria in its back pocket in case it was needed to bring Norway into the treaty. This is implied by Acheson in his memoir: "At the end of February the Norwegian

Government made application to join. At once the French attempted to condition Norwegian membership upon acceptance of Italy also.... [Truman] and the two senators [Connally and Vandenberg] lost patience with this haggling. I reported to the ambassadors at our meeting on March 1 that our Government, while open-minded about Italy, was united in requesting that we accept Norway at that meeting. We would also agree to extend the treaty to cover Algeria. Norway was accepted."[170]

Addressing Operational Incompatibilities

While there was much debate over the treaty's wording and the strategic scope of the alliance, the participants in the negotiation largely set aside detailed discussions about a war plan's operational component. The treaty itself says little about the operational component of the plan. This is not because the participants deemed the operational component unimportant. Quite the contrary. Instead, the participants, based on recent experience, chose to have the treaty establish an intergovernmental body to devise such plans. In other words, the operational component of the treaty was, in a sense, a plan to plan a body to conduct planning.

Delegating operational joint war planning to a yet-to-be-established international organization was sensible for the participants for two reasons: recent experience with intergovernmental military cooperation institutions and that the Soviet threat was not imminent. I will now discuss each.

First, all of the participants, including and perhaps most notably the United States and Britain, had recent experience with institutions for intergovernmental military cooperation. During the 1940s, they had established a number of intergovernmental bodies designed to facilitate joint military planning. These included the Combined Chiefs of Staff utilized by the United States and Britain during World War II, the Permanent Joint Board on Defence between the United States and Canada, and the Military Staff Committee of the United Nations (Bland 1991, 114). Additionally, the recently signed 1947 Rio pact and 1948 Brussels pact had provisions calling for the establishment of "organs" to help implement their security arrangements. Even the Pentagon Paper from the ABC talks explicitly called for creating agencies for implementing the security arrangement. Stated simply, by the time of the North Atlantic Treaty's negotiation, creating international organizations to facilitate military cooperation had become normal.

Second, the participants did not consider the Soviet threat to be imminent. The near-term possibility of major military operations by the Soviet Union against Western Europe was viewed as remote. The Soviets were still recovering from World War II, so there was time to devise an appropriate plan for countering an eventual Soviet offensive. However, longer-term problems could arise if the Western states failed to eventually devise plans or failed to signal to the Soviets their efforts to organize defensive measures. Bevin made this view clear to Lovett in April 1949: "We believe that a real effort at organisation of collective security by the western powers now is more likely to cause an eventual reorientation of policy on the part of the Soviet Union, whereas if we proceed with half measures which are purely economic and financial and do not carry them to their logical conclusion, the Soviet Government might think that that is all we are likely to do. This would consequently weaken our position and so might precipitate the conflict we desire to avoid."[171]

While the necessity of establishing an intergovernmental institution to govern the alliance was not really in question, the participants predictably had differing views on the shape of the institution. This question, however, was largely set aside during the treaty negotiations. As early as the July 9 meeting of the Washington Exploratory Talks, Lester Pearson remarked that the Canadian government thought "the actual machinery for implementing a [North Atlantic] pact would probably have to be worked out later."[172] The participants agreed on this point and inserted a provision calling for the eventual creation of appropriate machinery. But it is worth noting that the language used in this provision was subject to much discussion. Throughout the negotiations the participants tweaked and modified the language used to describe the future international body.

Consider the September 9 Washington Paper. It simply states that "the military and other measures to be taken immediately by each participating country should be planned and decided beforehand by the agencies established for effective implementation of the treaty."[173] Article 12 of the draft treaty attached to the September 9 report only calls for "provision for establishment of agencies necessary for the effective implementation of the Treaty."[174] This article then cites Articles 11 and 21 of the 1947 Rio pact and Article 7 of the Brussels pact, both of which called for creating supranational bodies for implementing the respective treaties.[175] Next, the draft treaty attached to the December 24 report moved the provision for establishing such an organization from Article 12 to Article 8.[176] It also referred to the body as a "Council" (echoing similar wording found in the Brussels pact), and granted the council the ability to establish subsidiary bodies "as may be necessary," notably a "defense committee" to "recommend measures" for mutual defense.[177]

During the final round of negotiations, the French requested that the phrase "and prepare plans" be added after "recommend measures."[178] As explained by Bonnet, "the insertion of these words would make acceptance of the Treaty easier in the French Parliament" because they would "add strength and substance to Article 8."[179] But Acheson objected. After discussing the French proposal with U.S.

military authorities and U.S. secretary of defense James Forrestal, Acheson "thought it much better to leave the text permissive in the sense that the defense committee could recommend measures which might include the preparation of plans."[180] The Americans did not want the final treaty to convey that the defense committee "was the only place in which plans were prepared."[181] Doing so might suggest that U.S. sovereign military control was being given to the alliance "machinery."[182] Bonnet conceded on this point, apparently because the inclusion of Algeria in the geographic scope of the treaty was a higher priority.[183]

The French had another request regarding the provision.[184] Bonnet wanted the body to be a "tripartite Chiefs of Staff" based in Washington. He was convinced that the Anglo-American Combined Chiefs of Staff had continued to exist following World War II, and he wanted the French to be viewed as equal to the British in military planning.[185] Achilles (and before him Marshall) assured Bonnet that the Combined Chiefs had been defunct for more than two years and "existed on paper only."[186] Bonnett replied, "[Nevertheless,] there were close relations between the US Joint Chiefs of Staff and the important British military mission here [in Washington] and that France considered itself of sufficient military importance to be included in such discussion."[187] Achilles informed Bonnet that, at that time, a French proposal to make Article 8 more specific would complicate matters. He suggested that a ranking French general could discuss the matter with U.S. military authorities who were studying the matter.[188]

As the text of Article 8 was being finalized, military officials from the participating states, in separate negotiations, were already discussing organizational charts for the article bodies. Between January and March 1949, British, Canadian, and U.S. military officials met and individually put forward schematics for the eventual structure of NATO. The U.S. plan, proposed on January 3, 1949, called for a U.S.-British Combined Chiefs of Staff under the governing council composed of the foreign ministers (Bland 1991, 115). This body would then oversee a set of regional and service subcommittees. Overall, the U.S. plan offered a rather streamlined and sparsely specified structure. The Canadian plan, put forward in March 1949, had a council of defense ministers overseeing four subregional groups: a Western European group, a Scandinavian group, a North American group, and a "Strategic Reserve" group run by the United States, the United Kingdom, and Canada (Bland 1991, 118–19). The suggestion of a "Strategic Reserve" group meant that the Canadian plan essentially viewed Western European defense as a matter of self-help, backed by a U.S.-Canadian-British expeditionary force. In other words, the Canadian plan would minimize (or even eliminate) the stationing of Canadian and U.S. forces in Europe. These forces would instead play the role of "distant guarantors" (Bland 1991, 119). The British plan, also introduced at the January 3 meeting, fell between these two proposals. It outlined several subregional units but assigned each unit to a committee of countries. There would also be an "Atlantic Pact Chiefs of Staff Committee" that would set higher-level policy (Bland 1991, 117). This supracommittee would serve as the military planning organ of the alliance, be chaired by the United States, and have four other members, one representing each of the subregions.

All three plans had some influence on the thinking of the military and diplomatic representatives. But it was the British plan that the U.S. Joint Chiefs of Staff modified when putting forward their own recommendation for the NATO governing bodies in June 1949 (Bland 1991, 119). The British scheme also served as the initial basis for discussions that took place during the summer and fall of 1949 regarding the final structure of the body.[189] But it should be stressed that these plans were not finalized by the time of the North Atlantic Treaty's signing in April 1949.

Historians love the irony on display during the April 4, 1949, North Atlantic Treaty signing ceremony. To open the ceremony, the Marine Corps band performed "I've Got Plenty of Nothin'" and "It Ain't Necessarily So" from the musical *Porgy and Bess*.[190] But the treaty signed that day was the product of hard negotiating and represented more than "plenty of nothin'." The parties secured a pact and laid the foundation for an international security organization that would continually create, refine, and administer joint war planning among its members.

From the standpoint of my theory, the North Atlantic Treaty negotiations illustrate a number of points. First, they show the influence of a participant having an attractive outside option (namely, the U.S. ability to take unilateral action). On almost all issues of importance to the United States, the Americans prevailed. The French did achieve their desired outcome with respect to Italy and Algeria despite the United States preferring to exclude both from the treaty. However, neither Italy nor Algeria was a core component of the U.S. strategic objectives for the treaty: as Acheson admitted to Truman, the United States had not bothered developing a solid position on either.

Second, the negotiations show the importance of the participants having similar, if not identical, visions for the strategic and operational components of a joint war plan. The parties agreed on the core membership of the alliance and that a supranational body should be created to handle operational planning. But the parties had key differences regarding peripheral members, largely because they disagreed on the geographic locus of the threat. The French were more concerned about the Soviets threatening southern Europe, namely, Italy. The British and Americans were more concerned about the Soviets threatening northern Europe, namely, Norway. While the parties were ultimately able to overcome this apparent strategic incompatibility in their ideal plans for joint action, this issue at one point threatened to undermine the negotiations and lead to nonagreement.

Third, the negotiations show that participants took the treaty's wording seriously. Much time and effort were spent finding the right words to express the treaty's mutual defense clause. Though the ultimate wording did not matter for how the parties understood the treaty, one cannot deny that entrapment concerns can lead to disputes over a treaty's wording, especially when actors face the need for legislative ratification. But the negotiations show that entrapment concerns, driven by domestic political considerations, appear to be, at most, an important additional explanation in this case, not an alternative explanation. Even once agreement was reached on the treaty's wording, incompatibilities in the strategic component of the participants' ideal plans threatened to delay (or even undermine) agreement. That the negotiations ended in concessions and agreement, not in collapse and nonagreement, speaks highly of the negotiating creativity of the participants.

NEGOTIATIONS AND THE FUTURE OF ALLIANCE STUDIES

Winston Churchill had a way with words. Of the many quotes attributed to him, perhaps the most famous conveys a reluctant appreciation for Britain's role in the "Grand Alliance" against Nazi Germany: "There is only one thing worse than fighting with allies, and that is fighting without them!"[1] Much is conveyed by this quote, not least a recognition that allies should not be taken for granted. Gaining allies is not easy.

When states sit down to negotiate an alliance treaty, what determines whether the negotiation ends in agreement and a signed treaty or instead in nonagreement with the parties leaving the table empty-handed? Answering that question is the focus of this book. In what follows, I will summarize the book's main claims and empirical findings. I will then conclude the book with a brief discussion of implications of my findings and directions for future research.

Summary of Claims and Findings

At their heart, alliance treaties are about using military force. Even if the hope is to deter a threat, the allies must be ready to use force if necessary. This is why I conceptualize war planning as the core of alliance treaty negotiations. Equipped with this premise, I argued that the key variable determining whether conditions are conducive to agreement is the compatibility of the participants' ideal war plans. These plans must be both operationally and strategically compatible. Strategic compatibility means the participants have highly similar initial ideas about the target(s) and geographic scope of the alliance's commitments. Operational compatibility means the participants have similar ideas about the application of force against the target, as captured in their military doctrines. If the states have highly compatible ideal war plans, agreement is likely. But agreement is still possible even in the face of low compatibility. When war plan compatibility is low, the second key explanatory variable comes into play: the number of negotiation participants that have attractive outside options. Such outside options include unilateral action, an alternative alliance, or a willingness to pass the buck in terms of countering a threat. How attractive each participant finds these outside options is private information.

I showed how the compatibility of ideal war plans and the number of participants with attractive outside options interact to produce four negotiation types: Same Page negotiations, Pleasant Surprise negotiations, Standard Bargaining negotiations, and Revealed Deadlock negotiations. Same Page and Pleasant Surprise negotiations are likely to end in agreement because the states find that they have highly compatible ideal plans. In contrast, Standard Bargaining and Revealed Deadlock negotiations are the most prone to nonagreement because plan compatibility is relatively low. Whether these negotiations actually end in nonagreement depends on how many of the participants have attractive outside options. All participants have attractive outside options in Revealed Deadlock negotiations. This is not the case in Standard Bargaining negotiations: only some of the participants have attractive outside options. This results in a mixture of expected outcomes for Standard Bargaining negotiations. Standard Bargaining negotiations could end in capitulation (i.e., one party fully adopts another party's ideal war plan), compromise (i.e., all the parties modify their plans in order to reach agreement), or collapse (i.e., none of the participants capitulate or make concessions and one party eventually leaves the negotiations to pursue an outside option). The outcome depends on each participant's beliefs about the attractiveness of the others' outside options: if state I does not have an attractive outside option and believes that state J does have an attractive outside option, state I will likely capitulate by adopting state J's plan.

I then evaluated this theory's empirical claims, beginning with large-n analysis of data on alliance treaty negotiations. After explaining how I measured the outcome variable, negotiation agreement, and the primary explanatory variable, ideal war plan compatibility, I analyzed the data. I asked whether the data show that ideal war plan compatibility is positively associated with agreement and found that this is indeed the case. I then subjected the data to a host of additional analyses. These additional tests account for alternative explanations (via control variables) or complications in my data (such as the possibility of selection bias) or alter the assumptions I used in creating the variables. Having thoroughly evaluated the relationship between war plan compatibility and alliance treaty negotiation outcomes, I then used my measure of war plan compatibility in a test of how the existence of outside options influences the outcomes of alliance treaty negotiations. I discussed the challenges of such a test and how I measured the existence of outside options among the negotiation participants. Using matching techniques, I found some support for my theoretical claim that the existence of outside options reduces the probability of a negotiation ending in agreement but only when the participants have low ideal war plan compatibility.

While the large-n analysis lends much support to my theoretical claims, it also points to the data's limits, especially for clarifying the exact mechanisms leading to the association between war plan compatibility and alliance treaty negotiation outcomes. Therefore, I turned to case study analysis. I studied two of the most important alliance treaty negotiations since the turn of the twentieth century: the 1901 Anglo-German negotiations that ended in nonagreement and the 1948–49 negotiations that created the North Atlantic Treaty. The participants in both sets of negotiations had important incompatibilities in their plans, particularly with respect to the strategic component. Stated simply, they disagreed about the geographic scope of the respective proposed alliances. Outside options also played a role. In the 1901 Anglo-German negotiations, the British had the attractive outside options of "splendid isolation" in Europe and an alternative alliance with Japan in East Asia. For its part, Germany could always turn to its Triple Alliance partners in Europe. In 1948 and 1949, the United States had the fallback option of issuing a unilateral proclamation of an intent to protect Western Europe (a type of Monroe Doctrine for Western Europe). For this reason, the United States gained its preferred wording of Article 5, the North Atlantic Treaty's mutual defense clause. France drew a hard line on a couple of key strategic issues, namely, the inclusion of Italy and French Algeria in the region covered by the alliance. However, it was not clear that France truly perceived itself as having an attractive outside option. The other European participants in the negotiations, not wanting to risk deadlock over the issue, gave in to France's demands.

Overall, my analysis shows that discussions of joint war planning lie at the heart of alliance treaty negotiations. The ability of the participants to reach a mutually acceptable joint war plan is the key to an alliance treaty negotiation ending in agreement. Other considerations, such as concerns over the treaty language or fears that a prospective ally will be unreliable, could (and do) still play a role in alliance formation. However, such considerations either influence the decision to seek an alliance in the first place (as is the case for reliability concerns) or must be addressed alongside joint war planning considerations (as is the case for disagreement about the language of the treaty). Hence, these competing considerations are best conceived of as additional explanations for the origins of alliances, in addition to joint war planning, not alternative explanations to joint war planning. In short, when states are arguing about an alliance, they are arguing about joint war plans.

Future Research

This book is about negotiations to form an alliance treaty. My focus is on alliance formation. But by focusing on formation, I am leaving unexplored other key (and related) areas of keen interest to alliance scholars—namely, the maintenance and collapse of alliances. For instance, I do not evaluate whether an alliance treaty formed via Same Page negotiations is more effective at tying the hands of the ally in a future crisis. I do not consider whether a state that compromised during a Standard Bargaining negotiation will be entangled in an unwanted future conflict.

These are topics with extensive and venerable literatures.[2] Though I did not explore such issues, my argument and findings should offer fresh insights into these and other literatures. I will illustrate this point by highlighting how the argument and evidence in this book indicate new research directions in four areas related to alliances: alliance treaty design, alliance reliability, NATO expansion, and the formation of defense cooperation agreements.

Alliance Treaty Design

I focused on the negotiations leading to the signing of an alliance treaty. While I contend that war planning is a core component of these negotiations, I maintained that the plans need not be reflected in the actual treaty text—the discussions could be detailed, but the agreed-upon text can be vague. But this does not prevent elements of the plans from appearing in the treaty text. Therefore, it could prove insightful to consider the extent to which the plans discussed during the negotiations do appear in the treaty text and what this might say about the negotiations or the future performance of the alliance.

To be clear, details of war plans do appear in some alliance treaties. When war plans appear in treaties, they can be quite detailed. Consider Article 2 of the 1913 alliance treaty between Greece and Serbia. This article states, "In the beginning of the hostilities, at whatever moment they begin, Greece is bound to have an army of ninety thousand fighting men concentrated in the region between the Pangaion Mountain, Salonika, and Goumenitsa, and Serbia an army of one hundred and fifty thousand fighting men concentrated in the region of Ghevgheli, Veless

(Kioprulu), Koumanovo, Priot."[3] This provision identifies a precise number of troops and their exact placement. Some treaties go so far as to outline the timing of their mobilization. Article 1.2 of the 1920 Franco-Belgian alliance treaty states, "[To reinforce French and Belgian troops in the Rhineland], France will send nine divisions of infantry within the 8th to the 21st day and Belgium will send two divisions of infantry, latest on the 12th day. [If Germany attacks] France provides 55 divisions . . . Belgium provides 12 divisions."[4]

The strategic component of war plans offers a sense of the variation in the ways planning appears in alliance treaties. There are four ways the threat targeted by an alliance can be expressed in the treaty text. First, a treaty can be direct and explicit about the threat targeted by the alliance. For example, according to Article 1 of the 1912 alliance treaty between Bulgaria and Greece, the parties will take action if "one of the parties should be attacked by Turkey, either on its territory or through systematic disregard of its rights, based on treaties or on the fundamental principles of international law."[5] Second, a treaty could use a general designation rather than naming a specific state. This was the case with Articles 3 and 4 of the 1882 alliance treaty between Austria, Germany, and Italy. These articles referred only to the actions of a "Great Power nonsignatory."[6] Similarly, the 1921 treaty between Turkey and Afghanistan was aimed at "any imperialistic state" that was pursuing a "policy of invasion and exploitation of the east."[7]

Third, a treaty could express a general need to defend against aggression. Consider the 1833 treaty between Turkey and Russia.[8] Article 1 simply states, "This alliance, having solely for its purpose the common defense of their dominions against all attack." In many respects, the North Atlantic Treaty text echoes such language. However, both the North Atlantic Treaty and the 1833 Turkish-Russian treaty did explicitly define the geographic area protected by the treaty.[9] Fourth, a treaty can make explicit that the alliance is not targeting any particular state. For example, the 1934 pact between Greece, Romania, Turkey, and Yugoslavia explicitly states that it is "not directed against any power."[10]

The variation in whether the treaty text is explicit about the identity of the threat or the region covered appears to have a temporal element. From 1815 to 1945, over two-thirds (57 out of 84) of alliance treaties signed outside of active wars identified a specific target of the alliance or an area in which the treaty's obligations applied.[11] From 1946 to 2001, fewer than one-third (41 out of 141) of alliance treaties signed outside of active wars identified a specific target of the alliance or an area in which the treaty's obligations applied. Such variation across time and across treaties raises a host of questions regarding alliance treaty design. Why do some allies place operational details in the alliance treaty, while others are content to leave the details vague or omit them from the treaty entirely? What explains the post-1945 drop-off in the explicit mention of the strategic component of the joint war plan? What explains when states explicitly mention the alliance target and when treaties are more general? Future research should engage such questions.

Alliance Reliability

If alliance treaty negotiations are about formulating a joint war plan, this should have implications for how states interact with their allies after signing the treaty. One should expect states to begin taking actions that position them to execute the joint war plan. For instance, they could seek to enhance the interoperability of their forces. This, in turn, can influence how the allies (and third parties) perceive the reliability of the alliance. The key is that actions to improve interoperability also raise the costs of opportunism. Conybeare (1992; 1994) and Lake (1996, 14) discuss how treaties can lead to "asset specificity," meaning that a party to the treaty, rather than having internal military capabilities sufficient for fully equipping its armed forces, has limited capabilities and seeks to realize economies of scale and gains from trade associated with specialization. This makes the country more reliant on its alliance partners, which raises the costs of unreliability. In this sense, the treaty ties the allied states' hands by creating dependency.

Additionally, the adjustments necessary to execute a joint war plan provide litmus tests for gauging an ally's reliability. A defining feature of alliance treaties is that the core issue—attack by a foreign power—is an event that may never take place. Consequently, states can reside indefinitely in a condition of blissful ignorance about the true willingness of their allies to offer protection in a time of need. But by asking its allies to take a number of actions after signing a treaty, a state can acquire information about their willingness (and ability) to come to its aid. These actions can include incurring what Morrow (1994) described as "peacetime costs," such as basing troops on an ally's territory (or the ally allowing the basing of foreign troops on its territory). Such actions inject "normal time" (i.e., nonwar times) with small tests of reliability. This relates to alliance treaty negotiation because the required actions can be specified in the treaty text. Including a promise to engage in costly actions shortly after signing the treaty means the allied states do not have to wait and hope (fear?) that their allies will prove reliable during a future crisis. Instead, these promised costly activities provide an immediate test of each state's intent to uphold the alliance treaty. Since the promised action will be tested shortly after signing the treaty, only a state intent on carrying out these actions will agree to include such promises in the treaty text. In essence, the state is tying its own hands by making the promise.[12] Hence, such promises can reveal a state's intention to be a reliable ally.

Article 9 of the North Atlantic Treaty is a good example. If the United States had dragged its feet on building the machinery of a collective security organization (putting the "O" in "NATO"), the Europeans could reasonably have concluded that the United States was less than fully committed to the alliance. Peacetime basing is also a common means by which states have positioned themselves to support their allies (thereby signaling their intent to follow the treaty plan). From the 1702 and 1703 Methuen Treaties, which made Lisbon a wintering base for the British Navy, to the 1951 Security Treaty between Japan and the United States, foreign basing provisions in alliance treaties are a long-established practice.[13] Admittedly, basing creates the possibility of political "hold-up" (Cooley and Spruyt 2009; Carnegie 2015, 13). The host country could strategically use its ultimate sovereign control over the base's territory to periodically demand a renegotiation of the terms for allowing the base (Cooley and Spruyt 2009, 17).[14] A similar dilemma could arise for a state promising territorial access rights to an alliance partner: the host state could later threaten to defect from the promise if the protecting state does not sweeten the deal. While this possibility can and has occurred, exploring when and how states include and use such litmus test provisions is another potentially fruitful avenue for future research.

NATO Expansion

While I focused on negotiations to create a new alliance, my argument has implications for the addition of members to an existing alliance. NATO added new members within a few years of its creation, with Greece and Turkey joining in 1952 and West Germany entering in 1955. Subsequent additions included Spain in 1982, East Germany (through German reunification) in 1990, and then the series of multistate expansions into Eastern Europe after the Cold War. Each of these additions was preceded by lengthy negotiations between the current NATO members and the candidate countries. These are not dissimilar to the negotiations to create a treaty in the first place, as it is necessary for the candidate to agree with NATO's strategic objective and to integrate with existing NATO members at an operational level. Therefore, understanding how and when a state gained NATO membership can be facilitated by considering the compatibility of the ideal war plans held by the candidate and the existing NATO members, as well as the outside options available to both sides.

Take the process leading to the NATO accession of the Baltic states.[15] Among the existing NATO members, the key participant was the United States. From the U.S. perspective, it had an attractive outside option: maintain the status quo by leaving out the Baltic states. Because Russian president Boris Yeltsin had made clear publicly that Russia would not tolerate new NATO members on the border of Russia, in 1994 U.S. president Clinton remarked, "We're trying to promote security and stability in Europe. We don't want to do anything that increases tensions."[16] The Baltic states, in contrast, had little choice but to seek NATO membership. As Audrius Butkevicius, the first Lithuanian minister of defense, recalled, "We were searching for a possibility to 'go through the wall.' I looked for different ways to start cooperation with NATO. In 1991–1992 such a thing as international cooperation with NATO without being a member of NATO was impossible. What we needed was a vision for the impossible."[17]

As for the compatibility of their ideal war plans, there were some fundamental differences in what the two sides—the existing NATO members and the Baltic states—viewed as the appropriate use of Baltic forces. Given their location on the border of Russia and a history of Russian occupation and control, defense ministers in the Baltic states wanted to establish "hard defense" units that would focus on territorial protection (Ito 2013, 247). But this went against NATO plans. Establishing a traditional territorial defense force was not immediately beneficial to NATO, and it ran the risk of antagonizing Russia. This is a major reason why, as Chris Donnelly, the special advisor for Central and Eastern Europe to the NATO secretary-general, remarked, the Baltic states "did not get an enthusiastic response" from NATO members to the idea of establishing a more traditional territorial defense force (Ito 2013, 247). Instead, the existing NATO members wanted the Baltic states to focus on contributing peace-keeping forces, which NATO needed to help stabilize the Balkans. With incompatibilities in their ideal plans and only one of the participants having an attractive outside option, the NATO-Baltic membership deliberations can be classified as Standard Bargaining negotiations. The Baltic states eventually capitulated. They abandoned plans for a territorial-defense-based force and began developing peace-keeping forces, with the assistance of the Nordic states (Poast and Urpelainen 2018). This allowed agreement to be reached, with the Baltic states joining NATO in 2004.

Could a combination of ideal war plan incompatibility and attractive outside options help explain the inability of Ukraine and Georgia to become full members of NATO? In many ways, they are facing extreme versions of the issues that faced the Baltic states. Given that both states have experienced (or are presently experiencing) direct military incursions by Russian forces, Ukraine and Georgia have an interest in prioritizing territorial defense. Do Ukraine, Georgia, and the existing NATO members have similar visions for how best to accomplish this defense? Given ongoing hostilities, do the existing NATO members view the current arrangement as a sufficiently attractive outside option? Such questions are active areas of policy analysis and scholarly research.

Defense Cooperation Agreements

If the theoretical framework is to be used to understand modern challenges of negotiating a security cooperation treaty, one will need to relax the requirement that the document being negotiated require "active military force to a nonsignatory's aggression," which is how I defined an alliance treaty at the beginning of the book. Such a relaxation is necessary because the most common form of negotiated security cooperation in the late twentieth and early twenty-first centuries is the defense cooperation agreement (DCA) (Kinne 2016; Kinne 2018; Kinne and Bunte forthcoming). Unlike alliance treaties, DCAs are about the terms of military cooperation during peacetime.[18] They are framework agreements and are commonly limited to a very specific day-to-day aspect of military cooperation, such as intelligence sharing, the scheduling or organization of joint military exercises, the terms of basing foreign troops, joint research and development, or even weapons sales. Importantly, DCAs usually deal with a single issue, so the same pair of countries could have multiple DCAs. Indeed, DCAs can be signed by existing allies as a means of adding an additional dimension of defense cooperation, such as the 2014 Enhanced Defense Cooperation Agreement between the United States and the Philippines (which signed a mutual defense treaty in 1951).[19]

Given the lower stakes, it is unsurprising that these agreements have proliferated and that some states will sign multiple DCAs with one another. Nevertheless, negotiations to form a DCA can still fail to end in agreement. Most famous were the initial negotiations between Japan and South Korea to form a military-intelligence-sharing DCA, called a General Security of Military Information Agreement (GSOMIA). After over a year of negotiations, an agreement was ready for signing in June 2012. South Korea then walked away, allowing the negotiations to fail (Sheen and Kim 2012). The decision was made in literally the last hour and framed rather innocuously: "With regards to the South Korea-Japan General Security of Military Information Agreement (GSOMIA), which was due to be signed at 4 p.m., (the government) decided to discuss the matter with the 19th National Assembly and then push ahead with the signing."[20] The delay was largely attributed to domestic opposition within South Korea to signing an agreement with Japan, a country with which South Korea has a long history of animosity. But another factor was divergences in the strategic component of the parties' ideal war plans: they have different perceptions of China. Japan wanted the agreement to cover information relevant to North Korea and China, while South Korea wanted to limit cooperation to North Korea (Sheen and Kim 2012).[21] Moreover, both parties have a viable outside option: their alliance commitments to the United States. Indeed, a stopgap agreement was reached in 2014, in which the two parties agreed to share information but only by first giving the information to the United States.[22] While this paved the way for the parties to return to the issue and agree to a GSOMIA in 2016,[23] the episode highlights how the negotiations to create such lower-level agreements should, like military alliances, be systematically explored and that the conceptual framework presented in this book can offer insights into the outcome of these negotiations.

Failures and Counterfactuals in International Politics

Delving into the intricacies of alliance treaty negotiations unveils a fact that might be uncomfortable to many scholars of international politics: the influence of contingency. It's possible to presume that the United States chose to embrace its role as a European power following World War II and, in that capacity, bestowed upon a war-weary Western Europe a "blanket of protection" in the form of the North Atlantic Treaty. But carefully exploring the negotiations leading to the treaty's signing suggests that, absent the efforts of Canadian and British officials, the United States could well have been content to remain a distant (and highly reluctant) offshore balancer.

Or consider the onset of World War I. Chapter 4 showed how the 1901 Anglo-German alliance negotiations are viewed as the great "missed opportunity." But there were other "missed opportunities" that might have blocked the march to World War I. Most notably are the 1905 Russo-German negotiations that, for a fleeting moment, culminated in the signing of the Treaty of Björkö. Germany's Kaiser Wilhelm II and Russia's Tsar Nicholas II met off the coast of modern-day Finland and signed a mutual defense treaty that promised to aid "with all his land and sea forces" in the event that "one of the two Empires is attacked by a European Power."[24] But the effort, in the words of the esteemed historian John C. G. Röhl (2014, 554), "ran miserably into the sand." Wilhelm's chancellor Count von Bülow, whose signature was required and who had not been consulted on changes the kaiser made to the treaty text, refused to sign the treaty and threatened to resign (Röhl 2014, 575–76). With the tsar facing similar backlash from his ministers, attempts to find a satisfactory treaty text were abandoned. If either of these treaties had been secured, to what extent would it have altered the course of history? Could World War I have been completely prevented, simply delayed, have still been fought but between different blocs, or none of the above? Such a counterfactual is obviously difficult to answer, but the contingency of apparently critical events brings these questions to the fore.

On the one hand, one might see the plausibility of history having gone down "roads not taken" as suggesting that international politics is highly unpredictable. On the other hand, these alternative roads are ideal for leveraging the historical record to test our explanations for international politics (Capoccia and Kelemen 2007, 356). After all, thinking through counterfactuals is the core of inference (King, Keohane, and Verba 1994, 77). For example, theories claiming that alliances deter will benefit from further exploring the book's opening example of the 1939 Triple Alliance negotiations: Would a unified British-French-Soviet front have deterred Hitler?

The history of international politics is replete with such what-if moments where it is possible to see subsequent events unfolding in an entirely new direction.[25] What happens in a world where the United States declares its intent to defend Europe but signs no treaty? What happens in a world where Germany and Britain enter July 1914 with an alliance treaty? Or a world where India accepts an offer to replace China on the UN Security Council (Harder 2015)? Or what about the times when the U.S. Congress failed to ratify a signed treaty, be it the Treaty of Versailles to form the League of Nations or the Havana Charter to form the International Trade Organization? With any of these events, it is possible to imagine the course of history being dramatically altered. With others, this seems less likely. But scholars should continue to study international politics in light of the many possible "dogs that failed to bark."

Notes

INTRODUCTION. THE FRAGILITITY OF ALLIANCE DIPLOMACY

1. While the Soviets, British, and French did eventually form an alliance two years later (in 1941), this was only after all three incurred devastation wrought by the Germany military machine.

2. Data introduced in chapter 2.

3. See, for example, Hoover Memorandum, August 25, 1956, *Foreign Relations of the United States*, 1955–57, vol. 22, ed. Robert J. McMahon, Harriet D. Schwar, and Louis J. Smith (Washington, DC: Government Printing Office, 1989), 82.

4. See Ambassador in France (Dunn) to the Department of State, February 3, 1953, *Foreign Relations of the United States*, 1952–54, vol. 5, part 2, ed. David H. Stauffer, Ralph R. Goodwin, Marvin W. Kranz, Howard McGaw Smyth, Frederick Aandahl, and Charles S. Sampson (Washington, DC: Government Printing Office), 1557–58.

5. Memorandum in appendix 2 of Kennan 1984, 265–66; Kennan 1984, 48.

6. See Bueno de Mesquita and Singer 1973, 241; Morrow 1994, 273; Leeds 2003a, 802. Wallace (2008) considers how coordinating the military strategies of allies is enhanced once the allies are part of highly institutionalized alliances, such as NATO and the Warsaw pact. (In contrast, I claim that such coordination must begin before the states even become formal allies.)

7. Subsequent work uses the signaling property of alliances to understand their effect (e.g., Leeds 2003; Johnson and Leeds 2011; Poast 2013; Fuhrmann and Sescher 2014; Johnson, Leeds, and Wu 2015).

8. This is not unrelated to the signaling provided by "peacetime costs" (Morrow 1994). But Morrow's argument focuses on actions taken by states after the signing of the alliance treaty. My evidence is on the plan coordination that happens prior to signing the treaty.

9. Other recent work, namely, Wolford (2015) and Henke (2019), develop how they become ad hoc coalition members.

10. Part 1 of Snyder is titled "Alliance Formation," but it is largely a formalization of the motivations for seeking allies (as found in such work as Walt), not a discussion of the process by which the alliance is secured.

11. A few studies conceptualize alliance formation as a bargaining process, but they do not use bargaining to explain agreement or nonagreement (Snyder 1997, 75, 174; Benson, Meirowitz, and Ramsay 2014).

12. See also Leeds 2005, 4. This definition avoids the vagueness in some other definitions of alliance treaties (see Gibler 2009, xlix; Morrow 2000, 63; Benson 2012, 17; and Wolford 2015, 7). Requiring active military force differentiates alliance treaties from nonaggression pacts or neutrality pacts (see Leeds 2005, 9).

13. Work such as Walt (1987) and Wolford (2015) could more properly be labeled as dealing with the broader category of "alignments," in which the states cooperate but do not have a signed treaty.

14. Eighty alliance treaties in ATOP have offensive provisions, but only fourteen do not also include a defensive provision. These fourteen treaties are major powers writing promises to protect a minor power nonsignatory. This can be observed by reading the primary

obligation recorded by the ATOP project for each of the fourteen treaties (question 18 on the codesheet).

15. From the answer to question 18 of ATOP Codesheet for Alliance #1145.

16. See ATOP Codesheet for Alliance #1055 and Benson (2012, 28).

17. Not all of these are strictly treaties, meaning they require ratification. Instead, they are "formal agreements" that are legal documents ostensibly binding upon states (Toscano 1966, 22).

18. See also Odell 2000, 10. Some scholars speak of "pre-negotiation," which is when the parties consider negotiation as a potential policy option (McKibben 2015, 24n46; Gross Stein 1989). But it is unclear in alliance treaty negotiations where to draw a line between prenegotiation and negotiation (see chapter 2).

19. Another motivation is to restrain an ally from initiating a conflict with a third state (Fang, Johnson, and Leeds 2014). Deterring violence and restraining behavior also includes forming alliances to reduce conflict between any of the alliance members (Weitsman 2004; Schroeder 2004; Pressman 2008).

20. This tendency is especially notable in the empirical literature on alliances (Lai and Reiter 2000; Leeds et al. 2002; Gibler and Sarkees 2004; Gibler and Wolford 2006; Gibler 2008; Moaz 2007; Warren 2010; Cranmer, Desmarais, and Menninga 2012; Crescenzi et al. 2012). A few studies mention individual cases of nonagreement, namely the 1901 Anglo-German negotiation (Miller 2012; Cresenzi et al. 2012).

21. There is also "internal balancing" via arms production. I emphasize a "balance of threat" approach, but it is not essential for my theory to make a distinction between "balance of power" and "balance of threat."

22. Emphasis in the original.

23. This phenomenon is more generally referred to as "underbalancing" (Schweller 2004).

24. This fear can be of abandonment or free riding. The former is where an ally completely fails to honor its promise (Snyder 1984a). The latter is where an ally underdelivers (but still delivers a positive amount) on its promise (Olson and Zeckhauser 1967; Sandler 1977; Sandler and Forbes 1980; Thies 1987; Sandler and Hartley 2001).

25. Jervis (2002, 296) suggests a way of alleviating reliability fears: observing behavior. See also Schelling 1966, 150; Jervis 1970, 26, 91; and Jervis 2002, 303.

26. Snyder (1997, 191) writes, "This possibility [of abandonment] is the primary source of bargaining power between allies in a multipolar system." However, it is not clear that the final clause—"in a multipolar system"—is required. Indeed, Snyder himself (Snyder 1984a) draws on the United States' concerns about its NATO allies during the Cold War (a period of bipolarity) to illustrate abandonment fears.

27. See also Fearon's (1994) critique of Huth's (1988) claims regarding deterrence in crisis bargaining.

28. Entrapment combines moral hazard (risky behavior whose costs are born by another individual) and adverse selection (difficulty differentiating "high risk" types from "low risk" types). See Lake 1999, 53n62.

29. The constraining role of legislators is the core of "two-level game" theories of negotiation (Putnam 1988). More recently, see McManus and Yarhi-Milo 2017.

30. See Abbott and Snidal 2000, 435; Koremenos, Lipson, and Snidal 2001, 772; and Cooley and Spruyt 2009, 9.

31. One might question the need for flexibility in the treaty text, given the lack of an overarching enforcement authority in the international system (Goldstein 1995, 39). For the argument that flexibility is a rational response to uncertainty inherent in the international system, see Koremenos, Lipson, and Snidal 2001; Koremenos 2005.

32. Cha (2000, 265) refers to the interplay between abandonment and entrapment as the "abandonment/entrapment" complex: high fear of one usually means lower fears of the other.

33. The term "unprovoked" is an ambiguous phrase of the type highlighted by Benson (2012).

34. States "selecting out" of forming treaties that will not accord sufficient flexibility could be why numerous studies find entrapment to be nearly nonexistent (Kim 2011; Johnson and Leeds 2011; Beckley 2015).

35. The number of great powers varied over this period. For example, the United States did not reach great power status until, at the earliest, the late nineteenth century.

36. Scholars have claimed that multipolar systems, relative to bipolar systems, are marked by relative alliance instability, as states have more potentially viable alliance partners (Snyder 1984a; Gowa 1989; Christensen and Snyder 1990; Gowa and Mansfield 1993). Moreover, there is the need to account for the system-altering role of nuclear weapons.

37. Quote by U.S. secretary of state John Kerry in David Rhode, "How John Kerry Could End Up Outdoing Hillary Clinton," *The Atlantic*, December 2013.

38. United States and Donald J. Trump, *National Security Strategy of the United States* (Washington, DC: White House, 2017), 27.

39. See Nye 2012. In the same issue as the Nye article, William Wolhforth is also critical of the claim, made by Christopher Layne, of an end to U.S. unipolarity. But one of the components of his argument is to point out that Layne identified Britain as unipolar in 1870 despite China outstripping Britain on a GDP basis. In other words, nineteenth-century data, rather than mid- to late-twentieth-century data, is perhaps more useful for evaluating unipolarity claims. See Wolhforth 2012.

40. Quoted in Thom Shanker, "Defense Secretary Warns NATO of 'Dim' Future," *New York Times*, June 10, 2011.

41. Shayna Freisleben, "A Guide to Trump's Past Comments about NATO," CBS News, April 12, 2017, https://www.cbsnews.com/news/trump-nato-past-comments/ (accessed April 30, 2018).

1. A THEORY OF ALLIANCE TREATY NEGOTIATION OUTCOMES

1. Deterring violence by a threat can also include instances where states form alliances out of collective security motivations, namely, when the alliance seeks to reduce conflict between any of the alliance members (Weitsman 2004; Pressman 2008).

2. Record of the Meeting of the Military Missions of the USSR, Britain, and France, August 12, 1939, in *Soviet Peace Efforts on the Eve of World War II: Documents and Records*, ed. V. M. Falin, A. A. Gromyko, A. N. Grylev, M. A. Kharlamov, V. M. Khvostov, S. P. Kozyrev, V. Ya. Sipols, I. N. Zemskov, no. 314 (Moscow: Progress Publishers), 466–72. Emphasis added.

3. Memorandum in appendix 2 of Kennan 1984, 265–266; Kennan 1984, 48.

4. Odell (2000, 10) explicitly refrains from differentiating negotiation from bargaining, as doing so "is more trouble than it is worth" (see also Jönsson 2002, 218). For contrasting views, see Zartman 2010; Zartman 1987, 6; Fisher and Ury 1981, 3; and Underdal 1983, 184. Both bargaining theory and negotiation analysis take Schelling (1960), Luce and Raiffa (1957), Raiffa (1982; 1997), and Rubinstein (1982) as their intellectual foundation. See Sebenius 2009; Jönsson 2002, 224; Odell 2005, 381; Sebenius 2009, 458; and Pouliot and Cornut 2015, 303.

5. This is similar to how Odell emphasizes the market conditions that make economic agreement negotiators more likely to adopt value-claiming or value-creating strategies (see Odell 2000, chap. 4).

6. Leeds (2003a, 808) recognized that this process likely applies to alliance treaties: "Leaders limit their promises to the instances in which they expect to be willing to intervene on behalf of their allies and make clear the actions they expect their allies to provide in the event the alliance comes into effect."

7. I presume some semblance of military and diplomatic bureaucracy. Paul Kennedy (1980b, 3) discusses how general staffs emerged in the mid- to late nineteenth century in response to the success of the Prussian military system.

8. There is debate in the World War I historiography concerning whether it should instead be referred to as the Moltke plan rather than the Schlieffen plan (see Mombauer 2014).

9. Gartner (1997, 16). While Gartner provides his own definition of strategy, Newell's definition clearly distinguishes the strategic from the operational (while acknowledging overlap between the two).

10. The centrality of intentionality and violence for my conception of security echoes Kolodziej (2005, 23), who offers an extensive (and relatively recent) discussion of the meaning and purpose of security in the international system. Emphasizing "well-being" echoes Lake (1999, 21).

11. Quoted in Mombauer 2014, 46.

12. In a recent review on perceptions and threat in international relations, Stein (2013) identifies Walt as providing the initial work that focused on intentions as independent of capabilities.

13. Walt mentions offensive weapons, but these are indistinguishable from defensive weapons (Levy 1984).

14. Wendt (1992, 407–8) emphasizes how the origin of those intentions (and perceptions of intentions) is exogenous and comes from a host of sources.

15. Walt also highlights this example.

16. Memorandum by Mr. Eyre Crowe, "Memorandum on the Present State of British Relations with France and Germany," January 1, 1907, in *British Documents*, vol. 3, ed. G. P. Gooch and H. Temperly, appendix A (London: H. M. Stationary Office), 397–420. To dispel any notion that Eyre's memo had little influence on British policy, see "Minutes" in *British Documents* 3:420 (appendix A).

17. Memorandum by Mr. Eyre Crowe.

18. Levy's statement is largely summarizing the major claim from Jervis (1976), who sought, among other objectives, to explain the misperceptions among the European powers prior to the onset of World War I.

19. Note of M. Ribot, November 21, 1891, *Documents Diplomatiques: L'Alliance Franco-Russe. Ministére des Affaires Etrangeres. 1918*, no. 21 (1891): 20. Translation in Michon 1929, 37.

20. Note of M. Ribot.

21. In nuclear war planning, the operational component includes the usage doctrine—first strike or second strike—as well as the logistical procedures for developing, maintaining, and stationing the weapons.

22. For details of the German war plan, see Ehler, Gross, and Epkenhans 2014.

23. Millet, Murray, and Watman seem to move between several conceptions of doctrine, ranging from the high-level conception of how to deploy force to what they call "tactical doctrines," meaning how best to use particular weapons in a given battle. The former usage is consistent with my definition of doctrine.

24. Newel (1991, 79) describes how the operational component can have "strategic aims which link it to the strategic perspective of war" and "tactical objectives to be attained by the tactical forces, which links the operational perspective to the tactical perspective of war."

25. For excellent discussions on the logistical aspects of war fighting, see Thompson 1991 and Creveld 2004.

26. See Stevenson 1999.

27. According to Jackson (2013, 1), doctrine "determines the way a military fights."

28. Emphasis in the original. Posen (1984, 13) formally defines doctrine as "the sub-component of grand strategy that deals explicitly with military means," where "grand strategy" is the state's decision makers' political-military plan for creating security for itself.

29. Taylor (2001, 35) describes doctrine as "a framework within which to prepare, plan, and conduct operations." Levy (1986, 215) writes of "military plans and the military doctrine from which they derive."

30. The word "guides" is key for how doctrine links to actual war fighting. Newell stresses the need for flexibility in doctrine; doctrine and peacetime plans are more effective if they serve as general guidelines rather than rigid regulations.

31. This is essentially Posen's (1984, 14–15) definition of offensive doctrine and is similar to how Biddle (2004, 6) defines "offensive" military capability. See also Levy 1986, 215n42.

32. Quoted in Posen 1984, 21.

33. This as similar to how Biddle (2004, 6) defines "defensive" military capability. This also essentially combines what Posen (1984) labels as defensive and deterrent military doctrines (since neither is based on a first strike).

34. At the outbreak of World War I, Plan XVII called on French forces to capture Alsace-Lorraine. French forces launched an initial attack on August 7, 1914, followed by a full attack on August 14.

35. Quoted in Mombauer 2014, 47.

36. Levy and Gochal (2001) label this as one of the rare instances in which a democracy fought a preventive war.

37. Reiter (1995, 6) classifies the 1967 war as one of the few instances of preemptive war. Preemptive war is different than preventive war. Preventive war is used to stop a yet-unrealized future shift in power, while preemptive attack is used to seize the initiative upon receiving strategic warning that the enemy is preparing an attack of its own. See Levy 2011 and Poast 2015, 507n17.

38. According to the Stam (1996) data (see chapter 2), Israel is coded as using an offensive doctrine in both wars.

39. Formally, the number of participants with attractive outside options shapes the "zone of agreement," a conceptual region populated by joint war plans deemed acceptable to the participants (Odell 2000; Poast 2004). Bargaining theorists commonly use the term "bargaining range" (Fearon 1995).

40. This is related to the issue of delay in counteroffers and how these can lead to negotiation breakdown (Leventŏglu and Tarar 2008, 534, 536). As Posen (1984, 30) writes, "changing doctrines takes time; it disorients a military organization. A war during such a period of transition can be very dangerous."

41. The notion of rigidity in the executability of war plans should be familiar to anyone who has studied the 1914 July crisis and the need to adhere to strict mobilization schedules. See Taylor 1966 and Stevenson 1999.

42. Suspecting an ally's plans and then having that suspicion revealed to be wrong is similar to the concept of "misplaced certainty" (Mitzen and Schweller 2011). Also, Smith and Stam (2004, 784) write of how failure to reach a peaceful settlement in prewar crisis bargaining depends on the states having different assessments of the probability that state A (or B) is strong.

43. An example is European observers during the American Civil War (see Luvaas 1959). Many European nations observed military exercises during the 1930s. See Neilson 1993, 209; Murray 2000, 88.

44. See the seminal work of Tversky and Kahneman (1975). More relevant to military assessment and planning, see Snyder 1989, esp. chap. 1; and Smith and Stam 2004, 786.

There is also the possibility of civil-military disputes preventing accurate learning: military officials might want to change plans but face opposition from civilian officials (or vice versa). See Kier 1997, 56–65; and Posen 1984, 26. Overall, Jervis (1976, 241–42) is dubious about the quality of information that can be gained by war observers: "[It is rare that] an event made more of an impression on bystanders than on the actor. . . . The amount one learns from another's experience is slight even when the incentives for learning are high and the two actors have much in common and face the same situation." See also Ferris 1993, 226.

45. Pownall diary quoted in Mearsheimer 1983, 82. Quote is in reference to a March 1939 meeting.

46. John Slessor, *The Central Blue: Recollections and Reflections by Marshal of the Royal Air Force Sir John Slessor* (London: Cassell and Company), 231.

47. Even if I treat compatibility as continuous, I would still dichotomize the concept by talking of ideal war plans as being more similar or less similar.

48. The British historian Norman Michon (1929, 49), in his evaluation of the negotiations, felt that by August 1892 debate over this point meant the "negotiations seemed bound to end in a deadlock." It is not clear that this is the case. In an August 9 letter to the French foreign minister Ribot, the French ambassador to Russia Gustave Lannes de Montebello acknowledged disagreement over the response to Austrian mobilization and that the French viewed an Austrian-only mobilization as unlikely, but he also wrote that this detail could be worked out and that the parties were in agreement over the main principles of the treaty: "I think everything should be easy; the arrangement can be easily submitted to M. de Giers, who has also already approved the main principles" (Montebello to Ribot, August 9, 1892, *Documents Diplomatiques Français* 9, no. 440 [1892]: 638–39 [translation by author]). It is unclear whether this was Montebello's sincere opinion or just words meant to reassure Ribot.

49. In a May 1892 memorandum from the Russian war minister Pyotr Vannovski to the Russian foreign minister Nikolai Giers, Vannovski writes how "the occasion for mobilization itself" is an attack by any member of the Triple Alliance (the alliance between Germany, Austria, and Italy). See Memorandum in appendix 2 of Kennan 1984, 267.

50. Report by Boisdeffre, August 10, 1892, *Documents Diplomatiques: L'Alliance Franco-Russe. Ministére des Affaires Etrangeres. 1918*, no. 53 (1892): 72–73 (translation by author).

51. Report by Boisdeffre.

52. This is not inconceivable, as a state's military officials may want to control the majority (or all) of ground operations. Auerswald and Saideman (2009, 227–35) address this point regarding U.S. operations in Afghanistan in the early 2000s. From the perspective of U.S. officials, it was easier for the United States to conduct the major combat operations on its own and then use its NATO allies to perform secondary tasks.

53. Report by Boisdeffre, *Documents Diplomatiques: L'Alliance Franco-Russe. Ministére des Affaires Etrangeres. 1918*, no. 71 (August 18, 1892): 95–96 (translation by author). Boisdeffre writes the emperor's response in quotes as "C'est bien comme cela que je le comprends."

54. Report by Boisdeffre.

55. Such a view of mobilization helps one to understand why early and quick mobilization was deemed so important to the parties during the July crisis of 1914: the party that could bring its troops to the battlefield the soonest, regardless of the number of troops available in reserve, could score a quick victory. This fed the "Cult of the Offensive" beliefs prevalent in military circles prior to World War I (Van Evra 1984).

56. The notion of an outside option (sometimes called an "exit option") is standard in the bargaining and negotiation literatures. Rather than the term "outside option," the

negotiation analysis literature uses the term "BATNA," meaning the "best alternative to a negotiated agreement" (Odell 2000; Poast 2004).

57. The first and third outside options are two outside options that Voeten (2001) considers when evaluating the motivation of a superpower (read, the United States) to pursue agreement on a UN Security Council resolution to authorize force against a threat.

58. Christensen and Snyder go on to argue that this behavior is explained by considering the perceived offensive-defensive balance in weaponry—namely, that defensive weapons contribute to buck-passing. Mearsheimer (2001, 271–73) emphasizes geographic distance as an incentive to pass the buck. Buck-passing is one variant of a broader phenomenon that Schweller (2004) calls "underbalancing."

59. This will be especially evident in the 1901 Anglo-German negotiations discussed in chapter 4.

60. These alternative allies could be acquired by the initiative of the state or by the alternative allies approaching the state. The latter is indicative of the "wedge strategies" discussed by Crawford (2008; 2011).

61. On the possibility of "insincere" negotiations, much debate remains about whether the Soviets were simply playing the British and French for a better deal with the Germans in 1939 (see Miner 2015). Roberts (1992, 58–66) describes and critiques the various views of historians regarding when the Soviets initiated talks with Germany and the extent to which an agreement with Germany was pursued as a true alternative to a pact with the British and French.

62. Bensahel (2007, 197) highlights how intelligence sharing is a perennial problem in alliance operations. See also Auerswald and Saideman 2014, 46.

63. This is an example of what Ramsay (2011) calls adverse inference.

64. The importance of participants perceiving themselves as having attractive outside options echoes a claim made by Snyder (1997, 75). Snyder writes that states' bargaining power in alliance formation is largely a function of "the comparative availability and attractiveness of other alliance alternatives, valued similarly, and of nonalliance alternatives, such as increased armament or concessions to the opponent."

65. As Poast (2004, 284), drawing on Odell (2000, 26n3), writes, "Naturally, 'best' need not mean the best achieved through maximisation, but rather the perceived best, or approximately best alternative that can be found with average effort."

66. When describing the concept of BATNAs, Odell (2000, 27–28) uses the words "attractive" and "satisfactory" interchangeably.

67. See Odell (2000, 28) for how perceptions of outside options are in the negotiator's mind.

68. A host of works make the point that uncertainty over intentions can lead to nonagreement. See Olekalns and Smith 2009, 347–48; Fearon 1995; Morrow 1992; Powell 1999; Wagner 2007; Underdal 1983; Odell 2000; and Koremenos 2005. For general bargaining models on this point, see Rubinstein 1982; Fudenberg and Tirole 1991, 114; and Powell 2002.

69. Even if one conceives of the negotiation as the pursuit of a joint solution to a common problem (Zartman 1987), each participant would prefer, all things being equal, to have the agreed-upon joint plan be as close as possible to its ideal plan.

70. Some realists maintain that this initial distribution of beliefs cannot be updated (Parent and Rosato 2015) or updating is unlikely (Snyder 1997, 181).

71. For more on beliefs being subjective within a rational choice framework, see Osborne and Rubinstein 1994, 5; Al-Najjar and Weinstein 2009; and Fundenbuerg and Tirole 1991, 211.

72. The negotiation could resemble a war of attrition (where each side waits for the other side to concede) (Fearon 1998, 277). The possibility of ending the negotiation in

nonagreement is not technically found in basic attrition models, such as Fearon (1998). Instead, the standard models only allow for attractive outside options to delay agreement. Voeten (2001, 854) offers a model with negotiation breakdown.

73. ABC simply stands for "American-British Conversations."

74. The Declaration of the United Nations is found in the ATOP data set as ATOP ID #2550. It followed the British-American ARCADIA conference of December 1941 (following the Japanese attack on Pearl Harbor). "ABC-1" established Anglo-American military missions for sharing information and to continue the efforts of war planning. This prompted the creation of the British Joint Staff Mission in Washington and the U.S. Special Observer Group in London, which provided the basis for the Combined Chiefs of Staff established during the ARCADIA conference (Baylis 1984, 5).

75. See, for example, Office of the Chief of Naval Operations to the Naval Staff, British Joint Staff Mission, December 16, 1941, *Foreign Relations of the United States*, The Conferences at Washington, 1941–42, and Casablanca, 1943, ed. Fredrick Aandahl, William M. Franklin, William Slany (Washington, DC: Government Printing Office, 1958), 16. See also Watson 1950, 375.

76. January 14, 1941, Memorandum of the Joint Planning Committee. Quoted in Watson 1950, 371.

77. See, for example, Johnsen 2016, 81–104.

78. Quoted in Reynolds 1993, 249. As an interesting and relevant aside, this is the same Lord Ismay who would become the first secretary-general of NATO.

79. Churchill to Roosevelt, December 7, 1940, in Kimball (1984, 103).

80. The participants were key U.S. and British military officials. No political officials were present, though they helped craft and approve the initial statement of policy offered by both sides (see Watson 1950, 373).

81. However, complete and total overlap in plans is unlikely. In this case, the disagreement between the two parties was over the status of Singapore. This was addressed in trilateral talks between the United States, Britain, and the Netherlands (Watson 1950, 374, 394–95). These talks produced the ADB (American-Dutch-British) report of April 27, 1941 (reproduced as exhibit no. 50, in Congress of the United States, Seventy-Ninth Congress, 1946, *Pearl Harbor Attack: Hearings before the Joint Committee on the Investigation of the Pearl Harbor Attack*, part 15 [Washington, DC: Government Printing Office], 1551–84).

82. Reported in Matloff and Snell 1953, 34.

83. Reported in Matloff and Snell.

84. Watson 1950, 372–73.

85. Quoted in Watson 1950, 374.

86. The talks ended March 27, but a statement on air policy collaboration was added on March 29.

87. The full report is reproduced as exhibit no. 49, in Congress of the United States, Seventy-Ninth Congress, 1946, *Pearl Harbor Attack: Hearings before the Joint Committee on the Investigation of the Pearl Harbor Attack*, part 15 (Washington, DC: Government Printing Office), 1485–550. The report also contained five annexes—covering the organization of the military missions (annex 1), the areas in which the Americans or the British assume responsibility of command (annex 2), the geographic regions of operation and force deployments in those regions (annex 3), naval communication (annex 4), control and protection of shipping (annex 5)—and an additional statement on air policy collaboration.

88. Like the "ABC-1" document produced by the 1941 Anglo-American negotiations, the St. Petersburg protocol set the foundation for continued planning. This continued planning culminated in the July 1827 Treaty of London (between Britain, Russia, and France) and the subsequent Battle of Navarino (October 1827) between a joint Anglo-French-Russian naval force and the Ottoman navy.

89. The Greek revolutionaries sought independence from the Ottoman Empire. See Temperley 1925, 342–43.

90. The message was sent through Dorothea Lieven, the wife of the Russian ambassador to London Khristofor Andreyevich Lieven.

91. Quoted in Temperley 1925, 346. The message was verbally delivered by Nesselroade to Lieven. Alexander did not want the instructions given in writing. Instead, Lieven was to be "a living dispatch" (quoted in Temperley 1925, 347).

92. Alexander died in December 1825. Historians conclude that Canning was provided with this message (or at least aware of Russian interest in negotiation) sometime between late October and early December of 1825 (Temperley 1925, 348).

93. Canning had inquired with the British Admiralty to determine if the British Mediterranean force was sufficient to enforce a possible armistice between Turkey and Greece and, if not, how quickly it could be made ready (Temperly 1925, 350; Cowles 1990, 704).

94. As Canning instructed Wellington, "every effort must, however, be made to induce the Emperor of Russia to forgo, or at least to suspend, an appeal to arms." Canning to Wellington, February 10, 1826, in *1868: Despatches, Correspondence, and Memoranda of Field Marshal Arthur Duke of Wellington*, vol. 3, ed. K. G. Wellington (London: John Murray), 85–93.

95. Canning to Wellington, 88.

96. Nesselrode memorandum for Nicholas I, February 16/28, 1826. Quoted in Saunders 1992, 174.

97. Nesselrode memorandum for Nicholas I, February 16/28, 1826. Quoted in Jelavich 2004, 79. See also Cowles 1990, 707.

98. Wellington to Canning, April, 4, 1826, in *1868: Despatches, Correspondence, and Memoranda of Field Marchal Arthur Duke of Wellington*, vol. 3, ed. K. G. Wellington (London: John Murray), 224–50.

99. Quoted in Wellington to Canning, April, 4, 1826, in *1868: Despatches, Correspondence, and Memoranda of Field Marchal Arthur Duke of Wellington*, vol. 3, ed. K. G. Wellington (London: John Murray), 226. In an April 4 dispatch, Wellington informed Canning that Nicholas had sent a note of demands to the Porte, with many of the demands related to the Ottoman failure to fulfill the terms of the 1812 Treaty of Bucharest that ended the 1806–12 Russo-Turkish War (Cowles 1990, 700). See Wellington to Canning, April, 4, 1826, in *1868: Despatches, Correspondence, and Memoranda of Field Marchal Arthur Duke of Wellington*, vol. 3, ed. K. G. Wellington (London: John Murray), 224–31.

100. Wellington to Canning, April, 4, 1826, in *1868: Despatches, Correspondence, and Memoranda of Field Marchal Arthur Duke of Wellington*, vol. 3, ed. K. G. Wellington (London: John Murray), 224–31.

101. Wellington to Canning, 227–30.

102. Text of the April 4, 1826, Protocol in Holland 1885, 5–6.

103. Plan in Bastide to Beaumont, August 29, 1848, in Taylor 1934, 157.

104. Quoted in Taylor 1934, 157.

105. Quoted in Taylor 1934, 157.

106. In a note to the French prime minister Louis-Eugéne Cavaignac, Beaumont states the advantages of having an alliance with England but acknowledged that the Parliament and cabinet would likely block it (Beaumont to Cavaignac, August 22, 1848, in Taylor 1934, 153).

107. Bastide to Beaumont, August 29, 1848, in Taylor 1934, 157.

108. Beaumont to Palmerston, August 26, 1848. Quoted in Taylor 1934, 153.

109. Palmerston to Russell, August 30, 1848. Quoted in Taylor 1934, 154.

110. Though it appears Beaumont took Palmerston's remarks about the onset of war potentially altering the British position seriously. See Beaumont to Bastide, August 7, 1848. Quoted in Taylor 1934, 158.

111. Fearon (1998, 278n32) mentions that if both states choose "quit" at the same time in a war-of-attrition model, then a deal is chosen by a fair lottery between the two proposals.

112. For work on the relationship between verbal communication and information, see Crawford and Sobel 1982; Schelling 1966, 150; Slantchev 2011, 43; Farrell and Gibbons 1989, 1217; Trager 2010, 348; and Sartori 2005. See also work on how verbal messages sent outside the internal deliberations can influence the negotiation outcome: Guisinger and Smith 2002; Schultz 2001; Schultz 2012; Slantchev 2006; Smith 1998; Tomz 2007; Weeks 2008; Levendusky and Horowitz 2012; Levy, McKoy, Wallace, and Poast 2015; and Brutger and Kertzer 2016.

113. This is a costly signaling, meaning engaging in a difficult activity that enables an agent to prove itself to a principal (Schelling 1966, 150; Jervis 1970; Spence 1973; Fearon 1995; Jervis 2002, 303; Slantchev 2011).

114. The literature on issue linkages is massive. See, for example, Wallace 1976; Tollison and Willet 1979; Stein 1980; Sebenius 1983; Axelrod and Keohane 1985; Putnam 1988; Haas 1990, 76; Hoekman 1989; Bernheim and Whinston 1990; Oye 1992; Mayer 1992; Morrow 1992; Eichengreen and Frieden 1993; Lohmann 1997; Aggarwal 1998; Odel 2000; Spagnolo 2001; Poast 2012; 2013.

115. In a memorandum, Colonel Robert Home of the British War Office Intelligence Department systematically explained why Cyprus would be the ideal acquisition for the British in terms of protecting Turkey and maintaining open passage through the Dardanelles and Bosporus (reprinted in Lee 1931, 237–41).

116. Beginning of the May 10 letter is in Temperley 1931, 277. The actual conditions are in Cecil 1921, 269.

117. Layard to Salisbury, May 19, 1878, Secret Telegram. Quoted in Seton-Watson 1935, 425.

118. Layard to Salisbury. See also Lee 1934, 83–84.

119. The treaty annex shows that Britain did make a token financial concession, by paying the sultan the "excess of revenue over expenditure" from controlling Cyprus (see Saville 1878, 25–26).

120. Quoted in Lee 1934, 83. See also Cecil 1921, 271; Kuneralp 2009, 397.

121. They agreed on May 29 (Lee 1934, 85n82). The treaty itself (the "Cyprus Convention") was signed on June 4. Treaty is ATOP ID #1330. Full text of the treaty and annex available in Hakki 2007, 3–5.

122. Austria-Hungary would accede to the agreement in March 1887.

123. Original French version of memorandum is attachment 2 of January 26, 1887 letter from the Italian foreign minister, Count Robilant, to Corti, in *Grosse Politik*, vol. 4, no. 887. Translation in Buben 1999, 135–36.

124. Salisbury to Queen Victoria, February 2, 1887. Quoted in Buben 1999, 137. See also Corti to Robliant, February 5, 1887, in Buben 1999, 139–40.

125. Buben quotes Bismarck advising Italy to seek an alliance with England to assist with North Africa and to recover Nice from France (Burden 1999, 138). See also *Grosse Politik* 4, no. 883.

126. While foreign minister in 1885, Salisbury described Britain's isolation as "an abyss" (see Benians, Butler, and Carrington 1959, 255; Medicott 1926, 70).

127. The two parties officially exchanged notes on February 12. The agreement was an "exchange of notes" and kept secret so that it would not be subjected to parliamentary approval (Buben 1999, 142).

128. Salisbury had advised to either delete the article or, at minimum, modify the language (Buben 1999, 140). See also Roubliant to Corti, February 6, 1887, quoted in Buben 1999, 141–42.

129. The treaty stipulated that Italy was to take the subordinate role behind Britain in Egypt, while Britain accepted a subordinate role in North Africa.

130. The British and French delegations agreed to negotiate with the Soviets as one. (See Instructions to the British Military Mission to Moscow, August 1939, in *Documents on British Foreign Policy, 1919–1939*, series 3, vol. 6, appendix 5, 762.)

131. As Geoffrey Roberts (in Miner 2015) writes, "Long-standing Soviet war plans envisaged an advance through Poland and Romania to engage the Germans. Originally, the Soviets feared they might have to fight their way through countries that would be at best neutral and at worst German allies."

132. Telegram from the Soviet ambassador in Britain to the People's Commissariat for Foreign Affairs of the USSR, April 6, 1939, in *Soviet Peace Efforts on the Eve of World War II: Documents and Records*, ed. V. M. Falin, A. A. Gromyko, A. N. Grylev, M. A. Kharlamov, V. M. Khvostov, S. P. Kozyrev, V. Ya. Sipols, I. N. Zemskov, no. 149 (Moscow: Progress Publishers), 248–50. Additionally, Poland thought participating in a military arrangement with the Soviet Union would "run counter to the basic line of Polish policy, which was to take a 'neutral' stand between Germany and the USSR" (248–50).

133. Following the Soviet invasion of Poland, the Polish territory was never officially annexed.

134. Minutes of the Anglo-French-Soviet Military Delegations held in Moscow at 11 a.m. on August 21, 1939, *Documents on British Foreign Policy, 1919–1939*, series 3, vol. 7, appendix 2, 589–93.

2. MEASURING WAR PLANNING AND NEGOTIATION OUTCOMES

1. In essence, eminent historians will serve as my research assistants.

2. Historians' accounts might also be susceptible to not identifying the dogs that didn't bark, but I expect their microscopes to identify most of what is important.

3. Indeed, Small was a diplomatic historian.

4. The source for each identified failed alliance treaty negotiation is included in the online replication materials.

5. This treaty appears in the ATOP data set as ATOP ID #1420. See also Michael Hurst, ed., *Key Treaties for the Great Powers 1814–1914*, vol. 2 (New York: St. Martin's Press, 1972), 735–38.

6. Andrassy sent the note to the five other major powers (Russia, France, England, Germany, and Italy) and the Turkish government. All of the governments immediately accepted the terms laid out in the note (though the note ultimately failed due to the insurgents within Turkey not accepting the concessions specified in the note to be made by the Turkish government). See Langer 1966, 75–76.

7. To ensure transparency, in Poast (2012) I produced a full data set that includes sources for each negotiation failure and conducted an intercoder reliability check. Available in the online replication materials.

8. Taylor 1954, 214–15.

9. Schroeder 1994, 735.

10. I did identify a few pre-1945 alliance treaty negotiations that had more than five participants. In the ATOP data set, there are only four pre-1945 offensive or defensive alliance treaties involving European states with more than five members. These are ATOP ID #1005 (formed in 1815 by six states), ATOP ID #1020 (formed in 1820 by ten states), ATOP ID #2420 (formed in 1937 by seven states), and ATOP ID #2550 (formed in 1942 by eleven states). With only one event of each size, Poast (2010, 415) discourages analysts from including those events in the statistical analysis, since they are not just "rare" but "unusual."

11. Levy (1981, 597) makes a similar observation based on more systematic data than used by Langer.

12. One could also count the North Atlantic Treaty Organization (NATO) as a famous peacetime alliance, as Langer's statement did not count "cold" wars. Regardless, both NATO and the Franco-Russian pact faced obvious external threats (the Soviet Union and Germany, respectively).

13. In addition to these approaches, some studies use the existence of territorial disputes to identify the set of potentially threatening states, but territorial disputes are not a necessary condition for one state to perceive another as a threat (Johnson 2017).

14. Goertz, Diehl, and Balas (2016) used an approach based on the Klein, Goertz, and Diehl (2006) coding of rivals.

15. For example, this removed the United States–Cambodia pair. (While the two states engaged one another in five MIDs between 1964 and 1975, all five were associated with the Vietnam War.) See table 2.1 of Colaresi, Rasler, and Thompson 2007, 47, for a useful side-by-side comparison of the Diehl and Goertz (2000) and Klein, Goertz, and Diehl (2006) lists of rivalries.

16. This limit also affected earlier dispute density approaches (Bennett 1996; 1997a; 1997b; 1998; Goertz and Diehl 1993; Diehl and Goertz 2000).

17. PRIE draws on the notion of "politically relevant dyads" by identifying as potential threats all contiguous states and major power states, such as Britain during the nineteenth century and the first half of the twentieth (Most and Starr 1989; Siverson and Starr 1991; Maoz and Russett 1993).

18. Subsequent studies have modified the notion of PRIE to account for the fact that "within the political relevant international environment some states have friendly relations, and others do not" (Leeds and Savun 2007, 1127). Leeds and Savun (2007) eliminate from consideration allies of the state and states that have an above-population-median s-score of foreign policy similarity (Signorino and Ritter 1999). S-scores use the alliance relations of states to determine which states have similar alliance partners. I do not assume that alliance ties automatically eliminate the perception of threat between two states.

19. Correlates of War Project, Direct Contiguity Data, 1816–2006, version 3.1, http://correlatesofwar.org.

20. But bodies of water larger than rivers create complications for classifying states as contiguous. For this reason, COW offers a four-category coding for contiguity, based on the miles of separation created by a body of water: up to 12 miles (category 1), between 13 and 24 miles (category 2), between 25 and 150 miles (category 3), and between 151 and 400 miles (category 4). Two states separated by 150 miles of water or less can reasonably be classified as contiguous. This would classify such state-to-state pairs as the United States and Cuba (90 miles of water separation), Britain and France (21 miles of water separation), and Spain and Morocco (9 miles of water separation) as contiguous.

21. Levy (1982, 16) provides perhaps the most widely applied definition of major power, while Drezner (2009, 36) defines major powers with respect to economic issues, not military ones. Daina Chiba, Carla Martinez Machain, and William Reed (2014, 994–95) find that the key characteristics of a major power—being large and the desire to project power—are tightly linked. It is beyond the scope of this study to explain why states pursue power projection, but the reasons include securing external economic resources (Fordham 1998, 360), protecting strategically important areas (Desch 1989, 100–108), and imperial control (Gilpin 1971, 405).

22. The initial survey asked historians which states other states considered to be major powers. The COW project (www.correlatesofwar.org) has subsequently refined and updated the results of that survey.

23. Japan (1895 to 1945) and the United States (1899 to 1945) became major powers after 1816 and were still major powers in 1945. Scholars have recently attempted to classify major powers using a more transparent and quantitative approach, but such approaches, at least for the pre-1945 period, have not offered insights different from the COW approach. These attempts include Fordham (2011) and Cline et al. (2011). They offer quantitative classifications of major powers on a host of characteristics. Fordham (2011) uses military size, economic size, and the diplomatic reach of a state (as measured by the number of diplomatic missions the country has in other countries). Cline et al. (2011) uses economic size, military size, and trade volumes.

24. Recent alliance work uses "strategic rivalries" to identify when states are threats (Maoz et al. 2007; Lupu and Poast 2016). Surprisingly, none of this literature is mentioned by Janice Gross Stein (2013) in her review of perceptions and threats, despite the fact that perception is core to the notion of rivalry.

25. The difficulty of identifying the existence of a rivalry in the historic record, due to not having direct access to the decision makers' actual perceptions, is acknowledged by Thompson (2001, 563).

26. The rivalry is coded as ending in 1904 with the signing of the Entente Cordial.

27. An example is the United States–Haiti. This dyad is not in the Thompson data, but some MID density data sets code the United States and Haiti as rivals between 1891 and 1915 (see Bennett 1998). Interestingly, Klein, Goertz, and Diehl (2006, 340) also mentions the U.S. rivalry with Mexico as an asymmetric case that Thompson would consider "doubtful," but this rivalry does in fact appear in the Thompson data set (1821 to 1848).

28. I use model 1 in table 3.3 in chapter 3 to evaluate the sensitivity of choosing the median as a cut point. I consider two alternative values for coding the cut point for when *high strategic compatibility* = 1: the mean and a half standard deviation above the mean. The findings are not dependent on choosing the median as the cut point, as the other two cut points actually increase the coefficient on the *high strategic compatibility* variable and the *both strategic and operational compatibility* variable. Cut points of one or two standard deviations above the mean value cause *both strategic and operational compatibility* to perfectly predict agreement when the variable equals 1.

29. This figure specifically plots the weighted global s-score. Signorino and Ritter (1999, 124) write that it is useful to use the scores that weight states by their capabilities "in order to avoid exaggerating the importance of small states." The global scores are also useful since these two states are major powers with colonial possessions.

30. Because the s-score uses the active alliance memberships of the two states, it is one level removed from my compatibility measures: s-scores capture similarities in the outcomes (i.e., alliance formation decisions) that are influenced by similarities in strategic and operational compatibility. While a scholar's theory might focus on similarities in two states' alliance portfolios, this similarity is not the core theoretical concept in my theory. My theory focuses on the similarity of threats and military doctrines between states.

31. The collections by military historians include Dupuy and Dupuy 1986; Holsti 1991; Clodfelter 1993.

32. Stam (1996, 81) defines military doctrine as the state's military goals and plans for attaining them. But inspection of the data suggests that it more closely captures the latter rather than the former. Stam's actual "offensive/defensive" empirical coding of military doctrine is more similar to Posen's (1984, 13) definition of military doctrine than Posen's definition of grand strategy.

33. Relatedly, if more than one country fought on a side in a war, the strategy of each state on a given side is the strategy used by the largest state (Bennet and Stam 1996, 247).

34. In a footnote, Bennet and Stam (1996, 246n7) state that when states did switch strategies, they tended to do so soon after the beginning of a war.

35. In the case of the United States, I use the War of 1812. However, this hardly matters since the United States is not involved in alliance treaty negotiations in my data set until much later (the twentieth century).

36. Also referred to as the CBD90 data or the CAA (U.S. Army Concepts Analysis Agency) data.

37. Mearsheimer (1989, 66) and Desch (2002, 39) point to the findings of four groups of historians who reviewed eight randomly chosen battles from an early version of the HERO data set. These historians disagreed with many of the HERO analysts' coding decisions (Ramsay 2008, 856). My reading of the reviews and the responses offered by HERO (Dupuy et al. 1984) suggests the "errors" resemble the typical arguments among military and diplomatic historians rather than incompetence on the part of the HERO team. The HERO team did subsequently revise the data in 1986 and 1987 (Biddle and Long 2004, 534n15).

38. Desch (2002, 39–40) is concerned with the "soft" variables capturing leadership and initiative (see also Brooks 2003, 181–82) and with measurement error in hard variables, such as number of troops and battle deaths. However, I am not using these variables from the HERO data.

39. The most recent application of the HERO data set in prominent academic work is Weisiger 2016, where he discusses the limits of the HERO data (Weisiger 2016, 357). All of these critiques apply to the use of the data to analyze individual battles rather than analyzing the overall war strategy of the participants.

40. The HERO data do not contain naval battles (Ramsay 2008, 856), but Stam (1996) and Bennett and Stam (1996, 247) use naval engagements, where appropriate, to code doctrines and strategies. Additionally, naval engagements do not influence my coding of overall military doctrine from the later stages of the Napoleonic Wars, as the only major naval battle was Trafalgar in 1805 (Modelski and Thompson 1988, 21; Kennedy 1976, 124). The major battles were on land (Hall 1992, 90).

41. I use the *pri1* variable, which codes the first primary tactical strategy of an army during a battle.

42. HERO codebook information from Arnold (2014).

43. To translate strategies to doctrines, I looked at the wars in the Bennett and Stam data set that had only one HERO battle. The FF coding is based on comparing the U.S. HERO codings for the Mexican-American War to the Bennett and Stam codings for that war; the DD coding is based on comparing the Mexico HERO codings for the Mexican-American War to the Bennett and Stam codings for the Mexican-American War. The DO coding is based on comparing the Turkey HERO codings for the First Balkan War to the Bennett and Stam codings for that war; the EE coding is based on comparing the HERO codings for Serbia for the First Balkan War to the Bennett and Stam codings for the First Balkan War. The EE coding is a bit difficult, as Serbia is coded by Bennett and Stam as using an attrition substrategy, while other battles suggest that it was a maneuver substrategy. Regardless, in the case of Serbia and the French at Leipzig, EE strategies were part of an offensive doctrine.

44. Troop allocations based on the *str* variable in HERO.

45. I also code wars associated with the Napoleonic Wars. For the War of 1812, the United States is coded as using an offensive strategy. (For Britain, the War of 1812 has no influence on its 1815 coding because its coding is based on the battles fought in Europe.) For the Russo-Turkish War, Turkey is coded as using a defensive strategy. (For Russia, the Russo-Turkish War has no influence on its 1815 coding because its coding is based on the battles Russia fought against French forces.)

46. With respect to the attrition, maneuver, and punishment substrategies, only EE is not an attrition substrategy. (It is best classified as a maneuver strategy.) However, focusing

only on the Napoleonic Wars, EE was last employed in 1811 at the Battle of Albuera (by the French army). This appears to be an accurate coding of the French strategy in this particular battle, as the French general Soult planed a flanking attack to divide the British-led forces rather than engage in a frontal assault (see Dempsey 2008). EE strategies are coded by HERO as having been used as a second primary tactical strategy in later battles.

47. For instance, Posen (1993, 88, 109) expects that states will adopt mass armies if they have been beaten by a mass army. Jervis (1976, 241–42) claims that states rarely implement lessons from observing others.

48. Both studies code direct experience with maneuver strategies and find that a positive direct experience with maneuver makes a state likely to adopt or maintain use of that strategy (see also Wallace 2008).

49. I also code wars associated with the Napoleonic Wars. The War of 1812 is coded as a draw between the United States and Britain, while the Russo-Turkish War is coded as a Russian victory (and, hence, a defeat for Turkey).

50. This also included the use of blitzkrieg, meaning the use of a tank to effect a deep penetration into enemy forces (focused on one or two points) (Mearsheimer 1983, 36).

51. This is also acknowledged by Bennett and Stam (1996, 247). In their own coding of peacetime strategies between 1903 and 1994, Reiter and Meek (1999, 374) find that maneuver strategies were selected only 12 percent of the time.

52. Such a question lies at the heart of measurement validity, or the idea that "scores (including the results of qualitative classification) meaningfully capture the ideas contained in the corresponding concept" (Adcock and Collier 2001, 530). See also King, Keohane, and Verba 1994, 25; Sechrest 2005.

53. The phrase appears to have originated with a French captain de Thomasson, who in 1920 wrote of the "passionate cult of the offensive," though French general Joseph Joffre used the phrase "the cult of the offense" in his 1932 memoir. See Van Evera 1999, 196.

54. Quoted in Van Evera 1984, 60.

55. Quoted in Van Evera.

56. For new countries with no doctrines already specified, compatibility is determined by the countries with doctrines. This means that if only one member of the negotiation has an established doctrine, then the negotiation is coded as compatible. For example, in 1816, Austria formed alliances with the Kingdom of the Two Sicilies (ATOP ID #1025) and with Tuscany (ATOP ID #1030). Since the latter two states were established in 1815 by the Congress of Vienna, neither, as of 1816, had a military doctrine available through the HERO data set. Hence, both observations are coded as compatible, since neither had a doctrine that was in opposition to Austria's (which, at the time, was a defensive doctrine).

3. ANALYZING ALLIANCE TREATY NEGOTIATION OUTCOMES

1. A t-test finds the difference between the 77 percent agreement rate and the 53 percent agreement rate to have a p-value of 0.016 for a two-sided test. A t-test finds the difference between the 77 percent agreement rate and the 46 percent agreement rate to have a p-value of 0.001 for a two-sided test. See note 23 for description of a p-value.

2. A third complication, reverse causality, is of less concern. Reverse causality would imply that plan agreement (or perhaps the expectation of plan agreement) leads to war plan compatibility. This concern would not refute the pattern shown in table 3.1. Instead, it would lead one to reconsider the directionality of the relationship between war plan compatibility and negotiation agreement. But my variables capturing war plan compatibility draw on data based on past events (doctrines during wars in the case of operational compatibility and history of rivalry in the case of strategic compatibility). These factors are not unrelated to alliance negotiation outcomes, but it is difficult to envision how the

outcomes of a negotiation at time T could have influenced the values of variables determined by factors from time periods prior to T.

3. See Ellenberg 1994, 557–58.

4. Bushway et al. (2007, 157) refer to selection leading to a truncated sample as "explicit" selection.

5. Freedman and Sekhon (2010, 138) distinguish this form of "incidental" selection from selection into the sample.

6. This is what Bushway et al. (2007, 158) refer to as "incidental selection," as opposed to "explicit selection," and highlight as a "slightly more complicated type of selection" (see also Berk 1983, 392).

7. Because this "something" is typically unobservable, Heckman (1979) claims selection bias can be treated as a form of omitted variable bias (see also Cameron and Trivedi 2005, 549).

8. More precisely, the errors between the "selection model" and the "outcome model" will be correlated to such an extent that I will not be able to identify the effect of the variable of interest.

9. One could think of this as an application of Mill's method. As John Stuart Mill (1843) wrote in *System of Logic*, "If an instance in which the phenomenon under investigation occurs, and an instance in which it does not occur, have every circumstance save one in common, that one occurring only in the former; the circumstance in which alone the two instances differ, is the effect, or cause, or a necessary part of the cause, of the phenomenon" (455).

10. It is too restrictive to limit the conflict to the first day of the conflict. It is indeed the case that most multilateral wars witness third-party involvement rather quickly, usually within a few days of the war's onset (Vasquez and Valeriano 2010, 564n3). More importantly, Uzonyi and Poast (n.d.) show that even in the cases where the third parties did not intervene on the first day, the initial belligerents knew of (or at least anticipated) their eventual participation. Therefore, I code participants involved since the beginning of the conflict as those that entered the conflict in the same year as the conflict's onset. However, similar results are obtained if I limit the sample to states that entered the conflict on the first day.

11. This determination was made using the ATOP version 3.0 alliance level data set. If multiple members of a coalition each had a bilateral alliance with a single member of the alliance (e.g., the small Germanic states each having an alliance with Prussia), this was not sufficient to consider the states an alliance rather than a coalition. An alliance required that all of the coalition members were linked through the same alliance treaty.

12. See the description of MIDs when I describe the identification of rivals in chapter 2.

13. A simple t-test finds that the differences between all of these percentages are statistically indistinguishable from zero.

14. While Heckman offered a two-step approach, Bushway et al. (2007) and Feeman and Sekhon (2010) offer a thorough discussion of maximum likelihood approaches for simultaneously estimating both models (which is necessary when the dependent variable in the outcome equation is binary).

15. This allows for identification, which means that there is not more than one set of parameters that will generate a given distribution of observations. Absent an exclusion restriction, the model suffers from severe problems of multicollinearity (Wooldridge 2002, 570).

16. Similarly, contiguous states likely wish to protect the same region. Poast (2016) identifies contiguity as the most robust predictor of whether states ally with one another. Contiguity likely influences entering alliance negotiations and whether the states reach an agreement.

17. Hübler and Frohm (2007, 207), citing Puhani (2000, 64–65), explain that absent exclusion restrictions, selection models are identified only by assumptions about functional form and error distributions. The researcher could have theoretical reasons to believe that the error terms in the selection and outcome equations are nearly identical for a given observation (Sartori 2003, 117). This is likely to be the case when the selection and the outcome of interest "represent similar decisions, have the same causes, and are close together in time and space" (Sartori 2003, 117). See also Clayton and Gleditsch 2014, 270. But distributional assumptions alone are not a solid foundation for identification (Berk 1983, 392).

18. Technically, Heckman (1979) treats selection as a form of omitted variable bias: one is leaving out a variable, λ, capturing how the states entered the sample.

19. Ray (2003) usefully distinguishes confounding from complementary control variables.

20. I must account for factors that are meaningfully correlated with the participants having compatible plans, are meaningfully correlated with the states reaching agreement, and are not part of the process leading from plan compatibility to negotiation agreement (see Ray 2003; Oneal and Russett 2005).

21. This second approach is done more out of a sense of custom than out of a sound application of statistical analysis best practices (Sartori 2005, 88). Achen (2005, 330–34) refers to this as the "First Pseudo-Theorem" and then goes on to argue that this pseudo-theorem is wrong. This point is elaborated upon by Clarke (2005).

22. The likelihood is the probability of the data given the model. Formally, maximum likelihood asks for $Pr(D|\theta)$, where D is the data and θ is the parameter values from the model.

23. The p-value essentially tells the researcher the probability that the results are consistent with random chance. It does not tell the researcher whether the results are due to chance.

24. Achen (2003; 2005) advocates using no more than three variables in a model. The spirit of the advice is to stress simplicity: do not jump immediately to the most complicated and variable-laden model.

25. Morrow (1991), building on Morrow (1987), uses the terms "security" and "autonomy." Palmer and Morgan (2006) refer to security as "maintenance" and autonomy as "change."

26. Mattes (2012b, 688–89) echoes this view.

27. I am deliberate in not using the word "reputation" because it is rather vague (Tang 2005, 34). Some scholars view reputation as synonymous with past behavior (Miller 2003; Leeds and Savun 2007; Gibler 2008; Leeds, Mattes, and Vogel 2009; Crescenzi et al. 2012; Mattes 2012b), some with learning (Jervis 1976; Reiter 1996), and some as being determined by actions taken concurrent with the bargaining situation (Slantchev 2011).

28. Leeds and Savun (2007) and Leeds, Mattes, and Vogel (2009) measure past violation using this variable. The primary difference between the two studies is that Leeds, Mattes, and Vogel assign reputation to leaders, while Leeds and Savun assign reputation to states. The Leeds, Mattes, and Vogel measure is only available since 1919.

29. The rate of decay is exponential: it increases with the amount of time that has passed since the last event, but this decay slows with the number of events that have accumulated over time (e.g., if a state pair has a lot of events, the behavior information remains more informative for longer).

30. Each J to K alliance history is weighted by the foreign policy similarity s-score between states J and K (Ritter and Signorino 1999). Notice that I to J alliance reputation does not include the direct history of interactions between I and J.

31. The mean value for the sample is approximately zero.

32. Each of these six components has its own coding procedures, the details of which can be found in Marshall and Jaggers (2002).

33. Of course, this requires the public to recognize when a particular ally is strategically important. How the public makes such a determination is left unclear by Clare, but it would likely be a function of the leader's own statements regarding the ally.

34. This result is confirmed by Levy et al. 2015.

35. See the Correlates of War National Military Capabilities Codebook for more details on the coding of these variables (available at http://www.correlatesofwar.org/).

36. Military expenditure data are more accurate following World War II. For an analysis of military expenditure levels after World War II, see DiGiuseppe and Poast (2018).

37. This difference in means is statistically significant at the 0.95 confidence level (p-value of 0.04).

38. Moreover, it is not a priori clear in which direction a state would want to obscure its capabilities. A state may wish to underreport its capabilities or even hide that it is in possession of a particular weapon. Alternatively, a state may seek to give the false impression that it has more capabilities or that it is in possession of a particular weapon. Additionally, it is not clear whether such overreporting or underreporting would make agreement more or less likely in a negotiation. Other participants might be seeking a weaker ally (for it to grant basing rights) or a stronger ally (for it to project power).

39. The random element captures how my theory is probabilistic, not deterministic.

40. Binary choice data estimators are commonly motivated using random utility models (Greene 2011, 684).

41. The assumed distribution of the random element determines the estimator being employed: probit estimators assume a normal distribution; logit estimators assume an extreme value distribution. In most applications, the logit and probit estimators produce nearly identical results (Achen 2002, 438). Both probit and logit impose the assumption that agents with a probability of 0.5 of choosing either of two alternatives are most sensitive to changes in the independent variables (see Nagler 1994 for a critique of this assumption).

42. All analyses conducted using Stata version 14 software.

43. If 0 falls inside the confidence interval, then an estimated effect of 0 is consistent with the model and data.

44. This is related to broader concerns about models with a large number of controls (Achen 2005).

45. In Stata version 14, this is done using the mfx command.

46. To include control variables in the substantive effect calculation, I multiply all of the coefficients for all of the control variables by either the mean value of that variable (for continuous or ordinal variables, such as the number of negotiation participants) or by the proportion of observations that are coded with a 1 (for the dichotomous variables, which are most of the variables in the model).

47. Computed using the mfx command in Stata version 14.

48. See Caroll and Kenkel (2016) for a summary of studies since the year 2000 that use CINC scores.

49. Comparing the substantive effect of the *asymmetric negotiation* variable is difficult because the substantive effect is computed differently when using the ratio in equation 1 than when using the binary measure in the main analysis. When using the binary asymmetry measure from the main analysis, the substantive effect is the difference between the probability of agreement when *asymmetric negotiation* = 0 and when *asymmetric negotiation* = 1. In contrast, for both of the ratio-based measures of *asymmetric negotiation*, the substantive effect is the difference between the probability of agreement when *asymmetric negotiation* is set to some reference value (such as its mean) and the probability of agreement when *asymmetric negotiation* is set to a new value (such as one standard deviation above the mean).

50. 0 is the lowest score and 121 is the highest.

51. Conscripts have advantages for states defending broad borders. A giant poorly trained conscript army (e.g., the French in the 1790s) can force neighbors with small professional armies to try to defend their entire borders.

52. Indeed, this is consistent with the statement I make to my graduate students (only partly in jest) that "the entire study of international security is driven by Russia."

53. The average value of years since war is 33.7, with a median of 26, a minimum of 0, and a maximum of 100. If the number of years since the last war is greater than 100, the value of probability of no doctrine change will be set to 0.

54. The maximum effect identified using this procedure is 0.443, while the minimum effect is 0.146. The maximum 0.95 upper bound is 0.572, while the minimum 0.95 upper bound is 0.323. The maximum 0.95 lower bound is 0.313, while the minimum 0.95 lower bound is −0.032. While the minimum is below 0, a negative lower bound was produced in only eleven iterations. In other words, only 1.1 percent of the iterations produced statistically insignificant results.

55. See Abadie, Diamond, and Hainmuller (2015) for an application of the technique for evaluating the economic cost of the 1990 German reunification.

56. In addition to the variables listed in the text, I also include a lagged dependent variable. This means I use the ATOP data set to code whether the k-ad is already in an alliance in year T.

57. I use capital-to-capital distance, treating contiguous states as having a distance of 0 (Singer and Small 1982). I also conduct my analysis using the minimum distance metric developed by Weidmann, Kuse, and Gleditsch (2010). Minimum distance is measured by the smallest distance between the borders of the two states (represented by polygons).

58. The Leeds and Savun measure of threats facing state I is created in three steps. Begin with the set of all major powers and the set of states contiguous to state I. Second, members of this "politically relevant international environment" that had no alliance with state I and had an s-score with state I lower than the median for all politically relevant dyadic relations in the international system during the 1816–2000 period are considered potential threats. Third, add the CINC scores of all potential threats facing state I. Having created this measure for all states in the system, I convert it into a k-adic measure of threat using the average score of all the states in a k-ad. This average increases as more members of the potential coalition face greater threats and fewer potential members face relatively little threat.

59. The coefficient on *both strategic and operational compatibility* was 0.83 (z-score of 2.50 and a p-value of 0.012). I evaluate the sensitivity of using the ninetieth-percentile threshold by creating my "failed alliance attempt" sample using the eighty-ninth percentile and the ninety-first percentile. These alternative thresholds yield coefficients on *both strategic and operational compatibility* of 0.74 (z-score of 2.27 and p-value of 0.023) and 0.99 (z-score of 2.85 and p-value of 0.004), respectively.

60. Harada's procedure builds on the approach outlined by Imbens (2003).

61. I must leave out *strategic compatibility only* and *operational compatibility only* because they are dropped out of the treatment model due to collinearity with *both strategic and operational compatibility*.

62. Lipscy cites an earlier study by Edward D. Mansfield and Eric Reinhardt (2000), who argue that forming a regional Preferential Trade Association accords a state leverage during GATT/WTO trade negotiations. This is because the PTA serves as a viable outside option to reaching an agreement within the multilateral institution. Unfortunately, Mansfield and Reinhardt test how being involved in bargaining within the GATT/WTO leads to PTA formation rather than the reverse: how the presence of the outside option—PTA membership—influences outcomes of GATT negotiations.

63. This is not dissimilar to how Christina Davis (2004) attempted to measure the influence of issue linkage offers. Rather than measure the effect directly, Davis posited (not unreasonably) that more linkage offers would be available in multilateral trade negotiations (such as those taking place within the GATT) than in bilateral negotiations (such as between the United States and Japan).

64. The Serbia-Bulgaria 1904 negotiation ended in an alliance pact (ATOP ID #1425), as did the Serbia-Bulgaria 1912 negotiation (ATOP ID #1470).

65. Serbia's two alliances were ATOP ID #1480 and #1490, the Triple Alliance was ATOP ID #1350, and the Romanian alliance was ATOP ID #1355. This negotiation ended in non-agreement (see Taylor 1954, 516).

66. The Serbian-Bulgarian alliance was ATOP ID #1470, while the Greek-Bulgarian alliance was ATOP #1475. Talks between Serbia and Greece began in January 1913, with an agreement reached and a treaty signed on May 4, 1913 (ATOP ID #1490). Serbia would terminate its alliance with Bulgaria at the onset of the Second Balkan War at the end of June 1913. See Dakin 1962, 362.

67. Not all of the 135 negotiations in this cell are Revealed Deadlock negotiations. All of the negotiation participants had an attractive outside option in 71 of these 135 negotiations (53 percent). In this subset of the negotiations, the agreement rate was 41 percent.

68. Not all of the negotiations in this cell will be Pleasant Surprise negotiations. In 23 of the 41 negotiations in this cell (56 percent) all of the negotiation participants had an attractive outside option. In this subset of 23 negotiations, the agreement rate was 78 percent.

69. The p-value is 0.12.

70. The difference is actually statistically significant at the 0.99 confidence level (p-value of 0.0017).

71. These are similar to the concerns raised by Poast (2012) to motivate the use of matching analysis.

72. Indeed, if I run a logit model with control variables and the sample limited to negotiations with high war plan compatibility, the model fails to converge. Similarly, if I estimate an interaction model, with an interaction between the *outside options exist* and *both operational and strategic compatibility* variables, the coefficient on the interaction is extremely large (over 10), indicating near-perfect separation in the data and near failure of the logit model to converge.

73. A fully nonparametric approach is to compute bounds around the effect as suggested by Manski (1995; 2007) or, in the case of missing data, Molinari (2010) and Membane and Poast (2013).

74. My description of matching borrows extensively from Poast (2012, 297–98).

75. See also Morgan and Winship 2007; Ho et al. 2007.

76. Example drawn from Rubin 2006, 12.

77. Though, as discussed below, I could still have selection on unobservables.

78. Compared to matching without replacement, matching with replacement generally lowers the bias but increases the variance (Abadie and Imbens 2006; Abadie et al. 2004, 1).

79. When using matching, it is important to evaluate the balance of the observable covariates, that is, the extent to which the control and treated groups are similar. There is no standard practice for evaluating balance in observational tests (Imai, King, and Stuart 2008; Diamond and Sekhon 2013), but the Kimogorov-Smirnov (KS) test, which assesses the similarity in all moments of the distributions, is an especially strict test since it is sensitive to the location and shape of the cumulative distribution functions of the populations (Lyall 2010, 182). Higher p-values in the test results suggest that the samples are similar to one another. When using matching on the set of 149 negotiations with low plan compatibility, all but one of the covariates, *Number of Participants in the Negotiation*, were

balanced. Balance is achieved when the sample is restricted to negotiations with two or three participants, which reduces the sample to 135 observations.

4. A KEY NONAGREEMENT

1. See also Lieberman 2005.

2. For instance, if there is no variation in the value of the dependent variable, it is impossible to know whether the presence of variable X raises the likelihood of an outcome.

3. A negotiation is considered correctly predicted when the predicted probability of a negotiation that did end in agreement is greater than or equal to 50 percent and the predicted probability of a negotiation that did not end in nonagreement is less than 50 percent.

4. Hence, the percent of correct predictions is $\dfrac{67+79}{197} = 0.741$.

5. This is in the fifth percentile (the lowest 5 percent of observations).

6. One could consider this an "extreme case," meaning that it has extreme values on the variables of interest. For a discussion of extreme cases, see Gerring and Seawright 2017; and Gerring 2017, 55–57.

7. This was based on the British strategy adopted during the Boxer Rebellion. One obtains the same coding using the Boer War to code the British doctrine. During the entirety of the Boer War, which was taking place simultaneous to the negotiations, the British used, according to the HERO database, a frontal attack (FF) strategy. According to my coding rules in chapter 2, this is an offensive strategy.

8. This is based on the strategy it adopted during the Franco-Prussian War (Germany is not coded as a belligerent during the Boxer Rebellion by the COW war data set used by Bennett and Stam [1998]). The determination that Germany used a defensive doctrine is largely based on France having been the party to declare war and first mobilize, though there is debate about whether France was actually provoked by Bismarck (see Agatha 1967, 308–13). The notion of Germany having a defensive doctrine after the Franco-Prussian War is consistent with Van Evera (1998, 29), who argues that during the period 1871–90, "the defense dominated because of Bismarck's new diplomacy. . . . In the military area the cult of the offensive had not yet taken hold." However, because some view the Prussian strategy as offensive during the Franco-Prussian War (Sagan 1986, 153), I conducted a robustness check where I changed, just for this observation, the coding of the *strategic-only* variable from 1 to 0, kept the coding if *operational-only* at 0, and changed the both *strategic* and *operational* variable to 1. Even with this change, the predicted probability of agreement for this observation remained below 0.50.

9. Both are identified as such using the coding of threat discussed in chapter 2. Germany and Britain had almost nearly perfect overlap in the countries perceived as threats. The only difference is that Austria-Hungary is coded as a possible threat for Germany if I use the Thompson-plus coding of threat (as was done in a sensitivity analysis test). This coding might seem odd, given that Austria-Hungary was an ally of Germany. But given that I use a dichotomous measure of compatibility (where negotiations with participants that have an above-median ratio of common threats to total threats are coded with a 1), including Austria would not change how I code this observation (in either case, including or excluding Austria, the case would be coded as the parties having an above-median ratio of common threats to total threats).

10. Koch (1969, 378) highlights the early literature arguing for a "missed opportunity."

11. This view is echoed in a recent account of the negotiations found in Gardner 2015.

12. In fact, another reason the model from chapter 3 predicts this particular case well is that the case received low values on the various reliability indicators. It had a value of 0 on the *asymmetry* variable. The other two reliability measures, *highly reliable past behavior*

and *all participants are democracies*, were also both coded with a 0. With respect to the latter variable, Britain was a democracy, while Germany was autocratic (Germany's Polity IV score in 1901 was 4 on the −10 to 10 scale). This is below the standard democracy cutoff of 6 or 7. With regard to reputation, the Crescenzi et al. reputation score for the year 1900 was 0, which was equal to but not above the median score. Hence, across all three reliability variables, this case is coded with values indicating the presence of reliability concerns.

13. Memorandum by Mr. Bertie, November 9, 1901, in *British Documents* 2, no. 91.

14. The British had an alliance with Portugal, for example. Indeed, this was (and remains) the oldest active alliance.

15. Memorandum by Prime Minister Salisbury, May 29, 1901, in *British Documents* 2, no. 86. Emphasis in the original.

16. Salisbury also claimed that Parliament and, in particular, public opinion would prevent an alliance treaty. But many scholars have subsequently highlighted how this claim is disingenuous. Salisbury was skilled at building public support for policies, as during the Boer War (Porter 1980, 223–33). Early in his time as prime minister, Salisbury also went beyond public opinion by seeking ways to prevent the massacre of the Armenians in the Ottoman Empire (March 1972, 74–76). Hence, it would perhaps be more accurate to say, rather than public opinion preventing Salisbury from supporting an Anglo-German alliance treaty, Salisbury did not view the treaty as sufficiently beneficial to merit the effort of swaying public opinion. Otte (2007, 279) is dismissive of Salisbury's domestic constraints claims. Otte labels the claim that no treaty could bind the hands of any successor a "reiteration" of the "well-rehearsed constitutional argument" and that there is nothing novel about the claim that the domestic climate was one of public hostility.

17. Based on an April 2, 1898, report by the chief hydrographer at the Admiralty. See Davis and Gowen 2000, 92. Engineering measures, such as dredging, could have been taken to improve Weihaiwei's usability as a naval base (Davis and Gowen 2000, 92).

18. Langer 1951, 492–93. According to Marder (1940, 309) the cabinet voted to acquire Weihaiwei from the Japanese (who acquired it after the 1894–95 Sino-Japanese War) because otherwise the Germans would have seized it.

19. See the editor's note in chapter 11 of *British Documents* 2:89 (top of page).

20. See Hayashi 1915, 119–22. See also Eckardstein 1922, 209.

21. Landsdowne to MacDonald, April 17, 1901, in *British Documents* 2, no. 99.

22. After the April 17 letter from Lansdowne to MacDonald (vol. 2, no. 99), the next document on the Anglo-Japanese negotiations in the *British Documents* is a June 21 letter from Lansdowne to Whitehead. Hence, Hayashi's memoir is useful for filling the gap between April and June of 1901.

23. See Hayashi 1915, 125.

24. Hayashi.

25. These lessons would subsequently be reinforced by the Japanese victory over Russia in the 1904–05 Russo-Japanese War.

26. The German empire under Kaiser Wilhelm II was setting off on an expansion of Germany's overseas empire, as embodied in Weltpolitik, or "global policy." Weltpolitik was most forcefully expressed in a December 6, 1897, speech by then secretary of state for foreign affairs (later chancellor) Bernhard von Bülow: "We don't want to put anyone in the shadow, but we too demand our place in the sun." Quoted in Clark 2013, 151.

27. Lascelles to Salisbury, August 24, 1900, in *British Documents* 2, no. 9.

28. Only the German government referred to it as the "Yangtze agreement." See the extract from the Lord Sanderson 1907 Memorandum, in *British Documents* 2, no. 1, note 1.

29. "Germany and Great Britain—Agreement Relative to China," October 16, 1900, in *Treaties and Agreements with and Concerning China*, 1894–1919, vol. 1, ed. John V. MacMurray (New York: Oxford University Press, 1921), 263.

30. Indeed, the treaty is not considered a formal alliance treaty in either the ATOP data set or the COW data set.

31. In response to notification of the treaty, the Russian government issued a memorandum that stated, "As to the third point . . . the Imperial Government . . . can only renew the declaration that such an event would compel Russia to modify its attitude in accordance with the circumstances." Memorandum in *Treaties and Agreements with and Concerning China*, 1894–1919, vol. 1, ed. John V. MacMurray (New York: Oxford University Press, 1921), 265.

32. Salisbury to Curzon, October 17, 1900, quoted in Monger 1963, 17.

33. In the memorandum by Eyre Crowe, he details the events surrounding the Yangtze agreement as "manifestations of hostility" by Germany that "were again met though with perhaps increasing reluctance, by the old willingness to oblige" on the part of the British. See Memorandum by Mr. Eyre Crowe, "Memorandum on the Present State of British Relations with France and Germany," January 1, 1907, in *British Documents* 3:397–420, appendix A.

34. Extract from Speech by Count Bülow in Riechstag, March 15, 1901, in *British Documents* 2, no. 32.

35. For more on Holstein's influence, see Rich 1965. The historian Naill Ferguson (1999, 47) refers to Holstein as the German foreign office's "éminence grise."

36. Memorandum by Baron Von Holstein, German Foreign Office, October 31, 1901, in *German Documents* 3:146–47.

37. Quoted in Monger 1963, 24.

38. Quoted in Kennedy 1980, 243; Miller 2012, 67.

39. Hatzfeldt to Foreign Ministry, January 18, 1901, *Grosse Politik* 17, no. 4979. Author translation from original German.

40. Metternich to Bülow, January 22, 1901, in *Holstein Papers* 4:217–18.

41. Metternich to Bülow 4:217n7.

42. Metternich to Bülow.

43. Holstein to Eckardstein, January 21, 1901, *Grosse Politik* 17, no. 4985. In the memo, Holstein does not specify exactly what Germany would request of Britain.

44. Holstein to Hatzfeldt, February 14, 1901, in *Holstein Papers* 4:218–19. Footnote 2 describes the telegram advising to wait for a British proposal.

45. Holstein to Eckardstein, March 2, 1901, in *Holstein Papers* 4:219.

46. In his memoir, Eckardstein viewed these as "the most promising opportunity" to form an alliance (Eckardstein 1922, 198). He also identified the previous alliance attempts as "the overtures of Lord Salisbury to the Kaiser in the summer of 1895—those of Chamberlain to Count Hatzfeldt in the spring of 1898—and those of Chamberlain to myself in the autumn of 1899."

47. Hatzfeldt to Foreign Office, March 8, 1901, *Grosse Politik* 16, no. 4929.

48. Hatzfeldt to Foreign Office.

49. Hatzfeldt to Foreign Office.

50. Holstein to Eckardstein, March 9, 1901, in Eckardstein 1922, 204. Holstein referred to the Yangtze agreement as the "agreement of October 16."

51. Holstein to Eckardstein.

52. Holstein to Eckardstein.

53. Holstein to Eckardstein.

54. Holstein to Eckardstein.

55. Holstein to Eckardstein, March 17, 1901, in Eckardstein 1922, 206. Capitalization in the original.

56. Eckardstein to Holstein, March 19, 1901, in Eckardstein 1922, 207–8.

57. Eckardstein to Holstein.

58. Eckardstein to Holstein.

59. Eckardstein to Holstein.

60. Eckardstein to Holstein.

61. Eckardstein to Holstein.

62. Eckardstein 1922, 208.

63. Eckardstein.

64. Holstein to Eckardstein, March 20, 1901, in Eckardstein 1922, 208–9.

65. Holstein to Eckardstein.

66. Holstein to Eckardstein.

67. Memorandum by Hatzfeldt, German Foreign Office, March 23, 1901, in *German Documents* 3:142.

68. Memorandum by Baron Von Holstein, German Foreign Office, March 27, 1901, in *German Documents* 3:140–41.

69. Memorandum by Baron Von Holstein. He also mentions the possibility of Japan joining via an arrangement with England.

70. Memorandum by Baron Von Holstein.

71. Richthofen to Hatzfeldt, April 14, 1901, in *German Documents* 3:144.

72. Richthofen to Hatzfeldt.

73. Richthofen to Hatzfeldt.

74. Lansdowne to Lascelles, March 18, 1901, in *British Documents* 2, no. 77.

75. Lansdowne to Lascelles.

76. Lansdowne to Lascelles.

77. Lansdowne to Lascelles.

78. As a further illustration of the German view that England was overextended, consider the following comment by Eckardstein in a February 28, 1901, letter to Holstein: "As for England, it was regrettable that 200,000 men had still to be kept in the field in South Africa. Otherwise, England would long ago have struck a different note as to Russian encroachments." Eckardstein to Holstein, February 28, 1901, in Eckardstein 1922, 200.

79. Lansdowne to Lascelles, March 18, 1901, in *British Documents* 2, no. 77.

80. Lansdowne to Lascelles.

81. Lascelles to Lansdowne, March 23, 1901, in *British Documents* 2, no. 78.

82. Lansdowne to Lascelles.

83. Lascelles to Salisbury, December 21, 1901, in *British Documents* 1, no. 124.

84. Lascelles to Salisbury.

85. Hatzfeldt to Foreign Office, March 23, 1901, in *German Documents* 3:141–43.

86. Hatzfeldt to Foreign Office.

87. Hatzfeldt to Foreign Office.

88. Hatzfeldt to Foreign Office.

89. Eckardstein 1922, 211.

90. Hatzfeldt to Foreign Office, March 23, 1901, in *German Documents* 3:141–43.

91. Hatzfeldt to Foreign Office.

92. Hatzfeldt to Foreign Office.

93. Hatzfeldt to Foreign Office.

94. Bülow provides no elaboration in his formal response to Hatzfelt dated March 24,1901. He only writes, "The agreement must not be secret by parliamentary." See Bülow to Hatzfeldt, March 24, 1901, in *German Documents* 3:143–44.

95. Bülow to Hatzfeldt, March 24, 1901, in *German Documents* 3:143–44.

96. Lansdowne to Lascelles, March 29, 1901, in *British Documents* 2, no. 79.

97. Lansdowne to Lascelles, April 9, 1901, in *British Documents* 2, no. 78.

98. Lansdowne to Lascelles, April 13, 1901, in *British Documents* 2, no. 81.

99. Lansdowne to Lascelles.

100. Lansdowne to Lascelles.

101. Hatzfeldt to Holstein, April 20, 1901, in *Holstein Papers* 4:221–22.

102. Hatzfeldt to Holstein.

103. Hatzfeldt to Holstein.

104. Hatzfeldt to Holstein.

105. Hatzfeldt to Holstein.

106. Hatzfeldt to Holstein.

107. Hatzfeldt to Holstein, May 4, 1901, in *Holstein Papers* 4:222–23.

108. Hatzfeldt to Holstein.

109. Hatzfeldt to Holstein.

110. See Eckardstein to Holstein, March 31, 1901, in *Holstein Papers* 4:219–20n1. Details of German claims arising from the Boer War are found in *Grosse Politik* 17, no. 5025 (note **).

111. Hatzfeldt to Holstein, May 4, 1901, in *Holstein Papers* 4:222–23.

112. Hatzfeldt to Holstein.

113. Hatzfeldt to Holstein, note 3.

114. Bülow to Holstein, May 16, 1901, in *Holstein Papers* 4:224–25.

115. Hatzfeldt to Foreign Office, May 16, 1901, in *German Documents* 3:145–46; Hatzfeldt to Foreign Office, May 16, 1901, in *Grosse Politik* 17, no. 5005.

116. Hatzfeldt to Foreign Office. In the marginal notes, Bülow writes, "Naturally," to the portion stating that Salisbury has objections.

117. Hatzfeldt to Foreign Office.

118. Hatzfeldt to Foreign Office. Lansdowne thought it necessary to add that, in his second question, Spain still "technically" counted as a great power.

119. Hatzfeldt to Foreign Office, May 17, 1901, in *German Documents* 3:146; Hatzfeldt to Foreign Office, May 17, 1901, in *Grosse Politik* 17, no. 5006.

120. Hatzfeldt to German Foreign Office, May 18, 1901, in *Grosse Politik* 17, no. 5008.

121. Memorandum by Sir T. H. Sanderson, May 27, 1901, in *British Documents* 2, no. 85.

122. Memorandum by Sir T. H. Sanderson.

123. Hatzfeldt to Holstein, May 26, 1901, in *Holstein Papers* 4:225–27.

124. Hatzfeldt to German Foreign Office, May 23, 1901, in *Grosse Politik* 17, no. 5010; Lansdowne to Salisbury, May 24, 1901, in *British Documents* 2, no. 82.

125. Hatzfeldt to German Foreign Office, May 23, 1901, in *Grosse Politik* 17, no. 5010.

126. Hatzfeldt to German Foreign Office.

127. Hatzfeldt to German Foreign Office.

128. Hatzfeldt to German Foreign Office.

129. Hatzfeldt to German Foreign Office.

130. Lansdowne to Salisbury, May 24, 1901, in *British Documents* 2, no. 82.

131. Lansdowne to Salisbury. As an aside, Lansdowne offered to "print and distribute" the memo to each member.

132. Lansdowne to Salisbury, May 24, 1901, in *British Documents* 2, no. 82 (enclosure).

133. Lansdowne to Salisbury.

134. Lansdowne to Salisbury. There subsequently arose a bit of debate about whether Eckardstein promised to write a memorandum outlining his position on an Anglo-German arrangement. See Hatzfeldt to Holstein, May 26, 1901, in *Holstein Papers* 4:225–26; and, in particular, *British Documents* 2, nos. 84, 87 (with enclosures), and no. 88.

135. Lansdowne to Salisbury, May 24, 1901, in *British Documents* 2, no. 82 (enclosure).

136. Lansdowne to Salisbury.

137. Lansdowne to Salisbury.

138. Lansdowne to Salisbury.

139. Lansdowne to Salisbury.
140. Lansdowne to Salisbury.
141. Lansdowne to Salisbury.
142. French in the original. In English translation: "It will cost you dearly."
143. Lansdowne to Salisbury.
144. Memorandum by Prime Minister Salisbury, May 29, 1901, in *British Documents* 2, no. 86.
145. Memorandum by Prime Minister Salisbury. Emphasis in the original.
146. Memorandum by Lansdowne, November 11, 1901, in *British Documents* 2, no. 92.
147. Hatzfeldt to Holstein, June 8, 1901, in *Holstein Papers* 4:229–30.
148. Memorandum by Lansdowne, November 11, 1901, in *British Documents* 2, no. 92.
149. Memorandum by Lansdowne.
150. Memorandum by Lansdowne.
151. Memorandum by Lansdowne.
152. Memorandum by Lansdowne.
153. Memorandum by Lansdowne.
154. Memorandum by Lansdowne.
155. Lascelles to Lansdowne, August 25, 1901, in *British Documents* 2, no. 90.
156. Lascelles to Lansdowne.
157. Lascelles to Lansdowne.
158. Record of Kaiser Wilhelm II, August 23, 1901, *Grosse Politik* 17, no. 5023.
159. Record of Kaiser Wilhelm II.

5. AN IMPORTANT AGREEMENT

1. Thies (2003, chap. 2) also provides an account consistent with this shift toward a European-initiated project.

2. Kaplan (2007, 255–60) offers a valuable bibliographic essay covering most of the important primary and secondary sources (to that point) on NATO's creation.

3. Goertz implies that the French revolution is the important one but does not make this explicit. This is more explicit in Mahoney and Goertz (2006, 243).

4. Though it would probably be too much to label it a "deviant" case (Levy 2008, 13).

5. For good measure, the coding rules in chapter 2 also indicate that the participants did not have operational compatibility: the British had a defensive doctrine in 1948, and the Americans had an offensive doctrine.

6. The conditions were also indicative of high uncertainty over capabilities. The maximum capability variance was well above the sample median value. Following the coding rules discussed in chapter 3 (which rely on military personnel data), the variance was well above the sample median value.

7. While the United States was substantially stronger than the other participants, this is not an unreasonable coding, as the British and French were still influential in Western Europe—particularly compared to the Benelux countries and Western German Occupation Zones—as well as globally through their colonial possessions.

8. Following the coding rules in chapter 3, the reliability score for the negotiation was 0, which is not above the sample's median. The British and French abandonment of Czechoslovakia in 1938 is the main event that lowers the score for the group.

9. Rathbun shows this by drawing extensively from the following source: U.S. Senate, *The Vandenberg Resolution and the North Atlantic Treaty: Hearings Held in Executive Session before the Committee on Foreign Relations*, 80th Congress, 2nd session on S. Res. 239 (Washington, DC: Government Printing Office, 1973). In particular, see "Informal Session, The North Atlantic Treaty, Tuesday, March 8, 1949," 129.

10. Fifth Meeting of the Council of Foreign Ministers, London, November 25–December 16, 1947, Report by Secretary Marshall, December 19, 1947, available through the Avalon Project, Yale Law School, http://avalon.law.yale.edu/20th_century/decade24.asp (accessed on December 23, 2016).

11. Transcript of Oral History Interview with John D. Hickerson, November 10, 1972, Truman Library and Museum, https://www.trumanlibrary.org/oralhist/hickrson.htm (accessed on January 15, 2018).

12. Quoted in Cook 1989, 107.

13. Quoted in Cook.

14. Fifth Meeting of the Council of Foreign Ministers, London, November 25–December 16, 1947, Report by Secretary Marshall, December 19, 1947, available through the Avalon Project, Yale Law School, http://avalon.law.yale.edu/20th_century/decade24.asp (accessed on December 23, 2016).

15. Several scholars recount Bevin's actions. See Cook 1989, 109; Shwabe 1992, 170; English 2001, 337; Kaplan 2013, 5. See also Hemmer and Katzenstein (2002) for discussion of how the "North Atlantic" was created as a new geographic category.

16. See Gallman to Secretary of State, December 22, 1947, *Foreign Relations of the United States*, 1948, vol. 3, ed. David H. Stauffer, Ralph R. Goodwin, Marvin W. Kranz, Howard McGaw Smyth, Frederick Aandahl, and Charles S. Sampson (Washington, DC: Government Printing Office, 1974), 1; Inverchapel to Secretary of State Marshall, January 13, 1948, *Foreign Relations of the United States* 3:3–6; Hickerson to Secretary of State Marshall, January 19, 1948, *Foreign Relations of the United States* 3:6–7; and Memorandum by Kennan to Secretary of State Marshall, January 20, 1948, *Foreign Relations of the United States* 3:7–8.

17. Quoted in Cook 1989, 109–10.

18. Transcript of Oral History Interview with John D. Hickerson, November 10, 1972, Truman Library and Museum, https://www.trumanlibrary.org/oralhist/hickrson.htm (accessed on January 15, 2018).

19. Transcript of Oral History Interview with John D. Hickerson.

20. While the Marshall Plan was not officially signed by U.S. President Harry Truman until April 3, 1948, the plan had been drafted by June 1947 (with the consultation of the European states).

21. Paraphrase of a Telegram from the British Secretary of State for Foreign Affairs of April 9 Regarding Recent Talks on North Atlantic Security Arrangements, April 9, 1948, *Foreign Relations of the United States* 3:79–81. English (2001, 337) elaborates on the notion that Western Europe must be united and backed by the British and Americans.

22. A recent discussion of the effect of the Czech coup on the Brussels pact negotiations and ultimately the North Atlantic Treaty negotiations is offered by Svik (2016).

23. Svik 2016, 152. Further details available in Kaplan (1987), which is also cited by Svik.

24. Transcript of Oral History Interview with John D. Hickerson, January 26, 1973, Truman Library and Museum, https://www.trumanlibrary.org/oralhist/hickrson.htm (accessed on January 15, 2018).

25. Quoted in Svik 2016, 153.

26. See The Ambassador in the United Kingdom (Douglas) to the Secretary of State, February 26, 1948, *Foreign Relations of the United States* 3:32–33.

27. Quoted in English 2001, 338.

28. Quoted in Bagnato 1991, 85. While the note was a private letter from Bidault to Marshall, it expressed views supported by the French Ministry of Foreign Affairs, notably Secretary-General Jean Chauvel (see Wall 1991, 133–34).

29. The Ambassador in France (Caffery) to the Secretary of State, March 2, 1948, *Foreign Relations of the United States* 3:34–35.

30. The official U.S. airbases in Europe as of 1948 were Hellenikon airbase in Greece, Keflavik airbase in Iceland, Lajes Field in the Azores, Lindsey Air Station in West Germany, RAF Greenham in the United Kingdom; RAF Lakenheath in the United Kingdom; Rhein-Main Air Base in Germany, Sondrestrom Air Base in Greenland, and Tempelhof Central Airport in West Germany. See Fletcher 1993.

31. Quoted in Cook 1989, 115–16.

32. Memorandum by Mr. George H. Butler of the Policy Planning Staff, March 19, 1948, *Foreign Relations of the United States* 3:58–59.

33. Quoted in Cook 1989, 117.

34. Trachtenberg (1999) argues that cooperation against a German threat was really a pretext for cooperation against the Russian threat.

35. The British motivation for a two-level system was captured well in a November 1948 U.S. Office of Intelligence Research report (Report by the Office of Intelligence Research, November 17, 1948, *Foreign Relations of the United States* 3:274). The report mentions a fear, held especially by the British, "that a large-scale defense and rearmament burden will undermine the foundations of British and European economic recovery."

36. Memorandum by Kennan to Secretary of State Marshall, January 20, 1948, *Foreign Relations of the United States* 3:7–8.

37. Secretary of State Marshall to British Ambassador Inverchapel, January 20, 1948, *Foreign Relations of the United States* 3:8–9.

38. Memorandum of Conversation, by the Director of the Office of European Affairs (Hickerson), January 21, 1948, *Foreign Relations of the United States* 3:9–12.

39. Memorandum of Conversation, by the Director of the Office of European Affairs (Hickerson).

40. Memorandum of Conversation, by the Director of the Office of European Affairs (Hickerson).

41. Memorandum of Conversation, by Undersecretary of State (Lovett), January 27, 1948, *Foreign Relations of the United States* 3:12–14.

42. Memorandum of Conversation, by Undersecretary of State (Lovett).

43. See "The Pentagon Talks of 1947" between the United States and the United Kingdom Concerning the Middle East and the Eastern Mediterranean, *Foreign Relations of the United States*, 1947, vol. 5, ed. John G. Reid and Herbert A. Fine (Washington, DC: Government Printing Office, 1971).

44. Memorandum of Conversation, by Undersecretary of State (Lovett), January 27, 1948, *Foreign Relations of the United States* 3:13. The NSC was created in 1947. The secretaries of state, defense, the navy, the army, and the air force; the chairman of the National Security Resources Board; and the president sat on the NSC until 1949, when the service secretaries were replaced by the Joint Chiefs of Staff.

45. Ibid.

46. The Acting Secretary of State to the Embassy in the United Kingdom, April 6, 1948, *Foreign Relations of the United States* 3:78–79. See also Editor footnote 1 for Memorandum of Conversation by the Chief of the Division of Western European Affairs (Achilles), April 5, 1948, *Foreign Relations of the United States* 3:76–78.

47. The Secretary of State to the Embassy in France, March 12, 1948, *Foreign Relations of the United States* 3 (1948): 50.

48. Memorandum by the Secretary of State to President Truman March 12, 1948, *Foreign Relations of the United States* 3 (1948): 49–50.

49. See The Ambassador in the United Kingdom (Douglas) to the Secretary of State, May 14, 1948, *Foreign Relations of the United States* 3:123–26.

50. According to Hickerson, this comment by Lovett was made to Inverchapel "one week before Mr Bevin's speech of January 22nd." See Memorandum of Conversation, by

the Director of the Office of European Affairs (Hickerson), February 7, 1948, *Foreign Relations of the United States* 3:21–23.

51. Transcript of Oral History Interview with John D. Hickerson, January 26, 1973, Truman Library and Museum, https://www.trumanlibrary.org/oralhist/hickrson.htm (accessed on January 15, 2018).

52. There is a small debate about the origins of these options. Mackenzie (2004/05, 97) claims that Pearson identified three options available to the United States, while Wiebes and Zeeman (1983, 353) state that the British laid out the options several days earlier to the United States (in a March 11 memo from the British secretary of state for foreign affairs, Ernest Bevin). However, Wiebes and Zeeman (1983, 354) acknowledge that Bevin's March 11 proposal induced the Canadian delegation to bring "the most elaborate ideas to Washington."

53. See MacKenzie 2004, 97; and Wiebes and Zeeman 1983, 356.

54. Quotes from Minutes of the Second Meeting of the United States-United Kingdom-Canada Security Conversations, March 23, 1948, *Foreign Relations of the United States* 3:61–64. Quoted in MacKenzie 2004, 97.

55. Minutes of the Second Meeting of the United States-United Kingdom-Canada Security Conversations, March 23, 1948, *Foreign Relations of the United States* 3:65. See also Memorandum from Undersecretary of State for External Affairs to Prime Minister, *Documents on Canadian External Relations* 14, no. 322, chap. 6.

56. Memorandum from Undersecretary of State for External Affairs to Prime Minister, March 29, 1948, *Documents on Canadian External Relations*, vol. 14, chap. 6, no. 322.

57. Ibid. Text for both draft proposals found in *Documents on Canadian External Relations*, vol. 14, chap. 6, no. 319 (the United States draft statement) and no. 320 (Canadian draft statement).

58. Memorandum from Undersecretary of State for External Affairs to Prime Minister, March 29, 1948, *Documents on Canadian External Relations*, vol. 14, chap. 6, no. 322. An editor's footnote in the *Foreign Relations of the United States* entry for the minutes of March 24, 1948, meeting acknowledges that a draft paper was not included in the State Department files (*Foreign Relations of the United States* 3:66).

59. The final draft of the Pentagon Paper was included with the Minutes of the Sixth Meeting of the United States-United Kingdom-Canada Security Conversations, April 1, 1948, *Foreign Relations of the United States*, 1948, vol. 2, ed. William Slany and Charles S. Sampson (Washington, DC: Government Printing Office, 1973), 71–75.

60. According to the U.S. minutes of the March 31, 1948, meeting, it was Hickerson who introduced a new draft with the changed wording and additional provisions. Minutes of the Fifth Meeting of the United States-United Kingdom-Canada Security Conversations, March 31, 1948, *Foreign Relations of the United States* 2:7–71.

61. Memorandum from Undersecretary of State for External Affairs to Prime Minister, March 29, 1948, *Documents on Canadian External Relations*, vol. 14, chap. 4, no. 322.

62. Memorandum from Undersecretary of State for External Affairs to Prime Minister.

63. Memorandum from Undersecretary of State for External Affairs to Prime Minister.

64. Memorandum from Undersecretary of State for External Affairs to Prime Minister.

65. Reference to the islands was included because, at the time, U.S. strategic bombers had a range that required the use of such islands as "stepping stones" in order to conduct operations in Europe (Wiebes and Zeeman 1983, 360).

66. Memorandum from Undersecretary of State for External Affairs to Prime Minister, March 29, 1948, *Documents on Canadian External Relations*, vol. 14, chap. 4, no. 322.

67. Memorandum from Undersecretary of State for External Affairs to Prime Minister.

68. An outstanding account of NATO (and Warsaw pact) war planning and war plans throughout the Cold War is in Mastny et al. (2008).

69. Article 7 of the Brussels pact established the council. Upon the formation of the Brussels pact, the council immediately established a permanent military committee (The Ambassador in the United Kingdom [Douglas] to the Secretary of State, July 2, 1948, *Foreign Relations of the United States* 3:143). The military committee was officially established on April 30, 1948 (see "Britain's Rearmament Policy: Political and Economic Implications," November 17, 1948, in Report by the Office of Intelligence Research, *Foreign Relations of the United States* 3:273–77).

70. "Britain's Rearmament Policy: Political and Economic Implications."

71. "Britain's Rearmament Policy: Political and Economic Implications."

72. Memorandum of Conversation, by Acting Secretary of State (Lovett), April 11, 1948, *Foreign Relations of the United States* 3:82–84.

73. Transcript of Oral History Interview with John D. Hickerson, January 26, 1973, Truman Library and Museum, https://www.trumanlibrary.org/oralhist/hickrson.htm (accessed on January 15, 2018).

74. Transcript of Oral History Interview with John D. Hickerson.

75. Comments by the Secretary of State on Mr. Bevin's Message of May 14, May 28, 1948, *Foreign Relations of the United States* 3:132–34.

76. U.S. Senate Resolution 239, 80th Congress, 2nd Session, June 11, 1948, available through the Avalon Project, Yale Law School, http://avalon.law.yale.edu/20th_century/decad040.asp (accessed on February 1, 2018).

77. It should be noted that Luxembourg was represented at the talks by the Belgian ambassador (Achilles 1985, 34).

78. Transcript of Oral History Interview with John D. Hickerson, January 26, 1973, Truman Library and Museum, https://www.trumanlibrary.org/oralhist/hickrson.htm (accessed on January 15, 2018).

79. Memorandum of Conversation, by the Director of the Office of European Affairs (Hickerson), January 3, 1949, *Foreign Relations of the United States*, 1949, vol. 4, ed. David H. Stauffer, Frederick Aandahl, Charles S. Sampson, Howard McGaw Smyth, and Joan Ellen Corbett (Washington, DC: Government Printing Office, 1974), 1.

80. Memorandum by the Participants in the Washington Security Talks, July 6 to September 9, Submitted to Their Respective Governments for Study and Comment, September 9, 1948, *Foreign Relations of the United States* 3:237–48.

81. This includes both countries that would eventually be part of the Warsaw pact and countries that would not (i.e., Tito's Yugoslavia).

82. For a discussion of the importance of military installations in Iceland, see The Secretary of State to the Legation in Iceland, January 27 1949, *Foreign Relations of the United States* 4:50.

83. Making the treaty "Atlantic" was vital for its acceptance in the United States. The same also pertains to why Canada's inclusion was important to the Americans from the beginning.

84. The third paragraph specifies that the article applies to attack on the territory of a member or the region defined by Article 4. The fourth article specifies that the acts of self-defense can continue until the UN Security Council takes measures to maintain peace.

85. Text of the 1947 Inter-American Treaty of Reciprocal Assistance, available via the Organization of American States website, http://www.oas.org/juridico/english/treaties/b-29.html (accessed on December 24, 2016).

86. Text of the 1948 Treaty of Economic, Social and Cultural Collaboration and Collective Self-Defence, North Atlantic Treaty Organization website, http://www.nato.int/cps/en/natohq/ official_texts_17072.htm (accessed on December 24, 2016).

87. Little additional insight is offered by the December 24 report produced at the second round of the talks. Annex B, which provides comments on each provision, only shows

that there was disagreement about the territories to be covered by Article 5. It says nothing about how agreement on Article 5's final wording was reached.

88. Article 5, Annex B, 247.

89. Memorandum by the Participants in the Washington Security Talks, July 6 to September 9, Submitted to Their Respective Governments for Study and Comment, September 9, 1948, *Foreign Relations of the United States* 3:244.

90. Memorandum by the Participants in the Washington Security Talks.

91. Memorandum by the Participants in the Washington Security Talks, 245.

92. This was the first time Acheson met with the ambassadors, as he was being confirmed as secretary of state during the month of January (Insall and Salmon 2015, xxiii).

93. Minutes of the Twelfth Meeting of the Washington Exploratory Talks on Security, February 8, 1949, *Foreign Relations of the United States* 4 (1949): 73.

94. Minutes of the Twelfth Meeting of the Washington Exploratory Talks on Security.

95. Minutes of the Twelfth Meeting of the Washington Exploratory Talks on Security, 74–75.

96. Minutes of the Twelfth Meeting of the Washington Exploratory Talks on Security.

97. Minutes of the Twelfth Meeting of the Washington Exploratory Talks on Security, 76.

98. Minutes of the Twelfth Meeting of the Washington Exploratory Talks on Security.

99. Minutes of the Ninth Meeting of the Washington Exploratory Talks on Security, December 13, 1948, *Foreign Relations of the United States* 3:316.

100. Minutes of the Twelfth Meeting of the Washington Exploratory Talks on Security, February 8, 1949, *Foreign Relations of the United States* 4:77.

101. Memorandum of Conversation by the Secretary of State, February 14, 1949, *Foreign Relations of the United States* 4:107.

102. Transcript of "1949: NATO's Anxious Birth" lecture by Jamie Shea, Deputy Assistant Secretary General for Emerging Security Challenges, March 5, 2009, NATO's Experts' Corner on the Founding Treaty, https://www.nato.int/cps/en/natohq/opinions _139301.htm (accessed on February 5, 2018).

103. Transcript of Oral History Interview with John D. Hickerson, January 26, 1973, Truman Library and Museum, https://www.trumanlibrary.org/oralhist/hickrson.htm (accessed on January 15, 2018).

104. Memorandum of Conversation by Secretary of State, February 14, 1949, *Foreign Relations of the United States* 4:108–10.

105. Memorandum of Conversation by Secretary of State, 109.

106. Memorandum of Conversation by Secretary of State.

107. Memorandum by the Counselor of the Department of State (Bohlen) to the Secretary of State and the Undersecretary of State (Webb), February 16, 1949, *Foreign Relations of the United States* 4:113–15.

108. Memorandum by the Counselor of the Department of State (Bohlen) to the Secretary of State and the Undersecretary of State (Webb).

109. Memorandum by the Counselor of the Department of State (Bohlen) to the Secretary of State and Undersecretary of State (Webb), February 16, 1949, *Foreign Relations of the United States* 4:115–16.

110. Memorandum by the Counselor of the Department of State (Bohlen) to the Secretary of State and Undersecretary of State (Webb).

111. See Henderson 1983, 93.

112. This is consistent with the reflections of Achilles. According to him, agreement was possible because while the words "such action as it deems necessary" appeased the U.S. senators, the words "forthwith" and "including the use of armed force" showed that the United States was willing to take immediate military action (Achilles 1985, 35). Acheson

observed that the European ambassadors accepted the wording because it left "no doubt that armed force was contemplated" (Acheson 1969, 280).

113. Minutes of the Ninth Meeting of the Washington Exploratory Talks on Security, December 13, 1948, *Foreign Relations of the United States* 3:318.

114. Minutes of the Tenth Meeting of the Washington Exploratory Talks, December 22, 1948, *Foreign Relations of the United States* 3:325.

115. Minutes of the Tenth Meeting of the Washington Exploratory Talks on Security, December 22, 1948, *Foreign Relations of the United States* 3:328.

116. Along with Silvercruys (Belgium).

117. Le Gallis of Luxembourg abstained. Minutes of the Tenth Meeting of the Washington Exploratory Talks on Security, 326.

118. See Memorandum of the Sixth Meeting of the Working Group Participating in the Washington Exploratory Talks on Security, July 26, 1948, *Foreign Relations of the United States* 3:201–4.

119. See Memorandum of the Sixth Meeting of the Working Group Participating in the Washington Exploratory Talks on Security, 203–4.

120. Memorandum of Conversation (regarding Twelfth Meeting of the Working Group), by Undersecretary of State (Lovett), August 20, 1948, *Foreign Relations of the United States* 3:218.

121. Memorandum of Conversation (regarding Twelfth Meeting of the Working Group), by Undersecretary of State (Lovett).

122. Memorandum of the Thirteenth Meeting of the Working Group Participating in the Washington Exploratory Talks on Security, September 2, 1948, *Foreign Relations of the United States* 3:227.

123. Memorandum of the Thirteenth Meeting of the Working Group Participating in the Washington Exploratory Talks on Security, September 2, 1948, *Foreign Relations of the United States* 3:227.

124. Minutes of the Sixth Meeting of the Washington Exploratory Talks on Security, September 3 1948, *Foreign Relations of the United States* 3:232.

125. Memorandum by the Participants in the Washington Security Talks, July 6 to September 9, Submitted to Their Respective Governments for Study and Comment, September 9, 1948, *Foreign Relations of the United States* 3:241.

126. Memorandum by the Participants in the Washington Security Talks.

127. Memorandum by the Participants in the Washington Security Talks.

128. Report of the International Working Group to the Ambassador's Committee, December 24, 1948, *Foreign Relations of the United States* 3:333.

129. The Secretary of State to the Embassy in Belgium, January 21, 1949, *Foreign Relations of the United States* 4:41–42.

130. Annex C to Report of the International Working Group to the Ambassador's Committee, *Foreign Relations of the United States* 3:339–42.

131. Indeed, there was a concern that it might serve as a drain on the allies' military assets. This was a concern of British officials, namely, Foreign Minister Ernest Bevin. See The Chargé in the United Kingdom (Holmes) to the Secretary of State, January 24, 1949, *Foreign Relations of the United States* 4:44.

132. The Secretary of State to the Embassy in Belgium, January 21, 1949, *Foreign Relations of the United States* 4:41–42.

133. Acheson 1969, 279.

134. Acheson.

135. Acheson.

136. The U.S. ambassador to France, Caffery, informed Acheson that at the Brussels Pact Consultative Council meeting of January 27–28, "nobody objected to inclusion of

Italy in Atlantic Pact" (The Ambassador in France [Caffrey] to the Secretary of State, *Foreign Relations of the United States* 4:53).

137. The Ambassador in Belgium (Kirk) to the Secretary of State, January 22, 1949, *Foreign Relations of the United States* 4:43–44.

138. Minutes of the Twelfth Meeting of the Washington Exploratory Talks on Security, February 8, 1949, *Foreign Relations of the United States* 4:87.

139. Bevin to Harvey, February 27, 1949, in *Documents on British Policy Overseas*, series 1, vol. 10, ed. Tony Insall and Patrick Salmon (Tony Insall and Patrick Salmon), 402–3.

140. Bevin to Harvey.

141. Bevin to Harvey.

142. The instructions given to Bonnet by the French foreign minister Shuman were that France "would not object to immediate admission of Norway to the Washington discussions, but would be forced to reconsider this action if the question of similar participation by Italy were not made" (see Secretary of State to the Embassy in France, February 25, 1949, *Foreign Relations of the United States* 4:124n4).

143. Secretary of State to the American Embassy in France, February 25, 1949, *Foreign Relations of the United States* 4:123.

144. Secretary of State to the American Embassy in France.

145. Franks to Bevin, February 26, 1949, in *Documents on British Policy Overseas*, series 1, 10:400–401.

146. Position stated by Roland J. Margerie of the French Foreign Office to the British ambassador to France, Sir Oliver Harvey. Harvey to Bevin, February 27, 1949, in *Documents on British Policy Overseas*, series 1, 10:401–42.

147. Position stated by Roland J. Margerie of the French Foreign Office to the British ambassador to France.

148. Bevin to Harvey, February 27, 1949, in *Documents on British Policy Overseas*, series 1, 10:402–3.

149. Minutes of the Fourteenth Meeting of the Washington Exploratory Talks on Security, March 1, 1949, *Foreign Relations of the United States* 4:129.

150. Minutes of the Fourteenth Meeting of the Washington Exploratory Talks on Security, 134.

151. Minutes of the Fifteenth Meeting of the Washington Exploratory Talks on Security, March 1, 1949, *Foreign Relations of the United States* 4:151–63.

152. Minutes of the Fifteenth Meeting of the Washington Exploratory Talks on Security, 156.

153. Minutes of the Fifteenth Meeting of the Washington Exploratory Talks on Security.

154. Minutes of the Fifteenth Meeting of the Washington Exploratory Talks on Security, 157.

155. Memorandum by the Secretary of State: Memorandum of Discussion with the President, March 2, 1949, *Foreign Relations of the United States* 4:141.

156. Memorandum by the Secretary of State: Memorandum of Discussion with the President.

157. Memorandum by the Secretary of State: Memorandum of Discussion with the President, 142.

158. Memorandum by the Secretary of State: Memorandum of Discussion with the President, 142.

159. Memorandum by the Secretary of State: Memorandum of Discussion with the President.

160. Minutes of the Sixteenth Meeting of the Washington Exploratory Talks on Security, March 7, 1949, *Foreign Relations of the United States* 4:166–74.

161. Minutes of the Eleventh Meeting of the Washington Exploratory Talks on Security, January 14, 1949, *Foreign Relations of the United States* 4:27–34.

162. Minutes of the Tenth Meeting of the Washington Exploratory Talks on Security, December 22, 1948, *Foreign Relations of the United States* 3:325.

163. Minutes of the Twelfth Meeting of the Washington Exploratory Talks on Security, February 8, 1949, *Foreign Relations of the United States* 4:73–88.

164. Minutes of the Twelfth Meeting of the Washington Exploratory Talks on Security, 86. Some of the negotiation participants suspected that France was motivated to gain support either against nationalistic uprisings in Algeria or against attacks by armed forces from nearby Arab states (Reid 1977, 218).

165. Minutes of the Twelfth Meeting of the Washington Exploratory Talks on Security, 86–87.

166. Minutes of the Twelfth Meeting of the Washington Exploratory Talks on Security, 87.

167. Minutes of the Fourteenth Meeting of the Washington Exploratory Talks on Security, March 1, 1949, *Foreign Relations of the United States* 4:131.

168. Text of the North Atlantic Treaty, NATO website, http://www.nato.int/nato_static /assets/pdf/stock_publications/20120822_nato_treaty_en_light_2009.pdf (accessed on June 15, 2016).

169. Reid 1977, 217. Stone was Ambassador Wrong's second in command at the Canadian embassy.

170. Acheson 1969, 278.

171. Paraphrase of a telegram from the British Secretary of State for Foreign Affairs (Bevin), April 9, 1948, *Foreign Relations of the United States* 3:79.

172. Minutes of the Fifth Meeting of the Washington Exploratory Talks on Security, July 9, 1948, *Foreign Relations of the United States* 3:176. Note that throughout the negotiations the participants referred to the governing and organizing bodies as the alliance's "machinery."

173. Memorandum by the Participants in the Washington Security Talks, July 6 to September 9, Submitted to Their Respective Governments for Study and Comment, September 9, 1948, *Foreign Relations of the United States* 3:243–44.

174. Memorandum by the Participants in the Washington Security Talks, annex, 248. The article also mentions that "any two or more Parties might establish or maintain special machinery between themselves to facilitate execution of the agreement." However, this would be dropped from subsequent drafts of the treaty.

175. Interestingly, the article actually cites Article 8 of the Brussels pact, not Article 7. But article 8 only refers to using the ICJ to settle disputes between members. It is Article 7 that states, "For the purpose of consulting together on all the questions dealt with in the present Treaty, the High Contracting Parties will create a Consultative Council, which shall be so organised as to be able to exercise its functions continuously." Text of the 1948 Brussels Pact, NATO online archives, http://www.nato.int/cps/en/natohq/official_texts_17072.htm (accessed on December 21, 2016).

176. Annex A of Report of the International Working Group to the Ambassadors' Committee, December 24, 1948, *Foreign Relations of the United States* 3:334–37.

177. Annex A of Report of the International Working Group to the Ambassadors' Committee.

178. See Minutes of the Twelfth Meeting of the Washington Exploratory Talks on Security, February 3, 1949, *Foreign Relations of the United States* 4:87.

179. Minutes of the Fifteenth Meeting of the Washington Exploratory Talks on Security, March 4, 1949, *Foreign Relations of the United States* 4:161.

180. Minutes of the Fifteenth Meeting of the Washington Exploratory Talks on Security, 162. The details of the views of the U.S. military officials is conveyed in a February 17,

1949, memorandum by Hickerson to Acheson (see Memorandum by the Director of the Office of European Affairs [Hickerson] to the Secretary of State, February 17, 1949, *Foreign Relations of the United States* 4:120–21).

181. Minutes of the Fifteenth Meeting of the Washington Exploratory Talks on Security.

182. In January 1949, a report from the Joint Chiefs of Staff to Secretary of Defense Forrestal recommended adding the words "general" between "recommend" and "measures." However, this was not pursued, and the word was not included in the draft treaty. See Memorandum by the Joint Chiefs of Staff for Secretary of Defense (Forrestal), January 5, 1949, *Foreign Relations of the United States* 4:12–13.

183. The minutes in the *Foreign Relations of the United States* do not explicitly state Bonnet's response, but the final text did not include the phrase "prepare plans." From the minutes of the February 3 meeting of the exploratory talks, it is clear that Bonnet viewed the Article 8 request and Algeria as the two points on which the French government "had strong views." See Minutes of the Twelfth Meeting of the Washington Exploratory Talks on Security, February 3, 1949, *Foreign Relations of the United States* 4:77.

184. Memorandum of Conversation, by Secretary of State, February 14, 1949, *Foreign Relations of the United States* 4:107–8.

185. Memorandum of Conversation, by Secretary of State.

186. Memorandum of Conversation, by Secretary of State.

187. Memorandum of Conversation, by Secretary of State.

188. Memorandum of Conversation, by Secretary of State.

189. Bland (1991, 119–44) offers an excellent discussion of the debates and negotiations leading to the adoption of an initial military structure for NATO.

190. For example, see Kaplan 2013, 2.

CONCLUSION. NEGOTIATIONS AND THE FUTURE OF ALLIANCE STUDIES

1. See Ambrose 1969, 571.

2. For example, post-formation performance of alliances has been a major focus of Ashley Leed's research. See Leeds, Long, and Mitchell 2000; Leeds 2003a; Leeds 2003b; Leeds and Anac 2005; Leeds and Savun 2007; Fang, Johnson, and Leeds 2014.

3. "Military Convention between the Kingdom of Greece and the Kingdom of Serbia, May 19, 1913," Official Documents Supplement, *American Journal of International Law* 12, no. 2 (1913): 96.

4. Text from response to question 18 in ATOP codesheet for ATOP ID#2055.

5. See ATOP codesheet for ATOP ID #1475.

6. Provision reproduced on ATOP codesheet for ATOP Treaty ID #1350.

7. See question 18 in codesheet for ATOP ID #2075.

8. ATOP alliance #1075. Quotations from the alliance found in this paragraph are from this treaty's ATOP codesheet.

9. According to Article 2 of the 1833 treaty, the treaty applies to any state that "shall attempt to annex or occupy, or to take military possession of, even temporarily, any part whatever of the territory of the Balkan peninsula now under Turkish domination."

10. See question 18 in codesheet for ATOP ID #2330. However, the treaty goes on to provide details by stating, "If one of the parties is the victim of aggression on the part of any other non-Balkan power, and a Balkan state associates itself with such aggression, whether at the time or subsequently, the pact shall be applicable in its entirety in relation to such Balkan state."

11. Identified using the *DEFCONADV, OFFCONADV, DEFCONLOC,* and *OFFCONLOC* variables in the member-level data of ATOP 3.0.

12. Notice, however, the state's hands are not tied out of fear of reputational costs for breaking the treaty. Instead, the state's hands are tied because failure to follow through with a costly peacetime action could nullify the treaty (or, at minimum, weaken the alliance relationship).

13. For more on the Methuen treaties, see Chalmers 1790, 296–306.

14. These new terms can include greater material and political concessions from the guest country and new restrictions on the scope of the basing activity.

15. A full account is offered in Poast and Urpelainen (2018).

16. Associated Press, "Concern of Russian Rightists Key to Caution over Expanding NATO," *The Item*, January 4, 1994, http://news.google.com/newspapers?nid=1980&dat=19940104&id= XosiAAAAIBAJ&sjid=Iq8FAAAAIBAJ&pg=1366,823031 (accessed on June 4, 2014).

17. Quoted in Paljak 2013, 206.

18. Interestingly, Kinne (2018) points out that NATO members rarely sign DCAs with one another because of NATO's broad mandate (i.e., functions served by DCAs are fulfilled by the NATO secretariat).

19. Joel Guinto, Margaret Talev, and Phil Mattingly, "U.S., Philippines Sign Defense Pact amid China Tensions," Bloomberg, April 28, 2014, https://www.bloomberg.com/news/articles/2014-04-27/philippines-to-sign-defense-deal-with-u-s-amid-china-tensions (accessed on August 14, 2018).

20. Statement of ROK Foreign Ministry spokesman Cho Byung-jae. Quoted in "S. Korea Postpones Signing Controversial Military Pact with Japan," Yonhap News Agency, June 29, 2012, http://english.yonhapnews.co.kr/national/2012/06/29/57/0301000000AEN2012062 9008900315F.HTML (accessed on August 14, 2018).

21. See Michishita (2012) for more on the divergent perception of the two countries vis-à-vis China.

22. Martin Fackler, "Japan and South Korea Vow to Share Intelligence about North via the U.S.," *New York Times*, December 29, 2014, https://www.nytimes.com/2014/12/30/world/asia/japan-south-korea-north-intelligence.html (accessed on August 14, 2018).

23. Anna Fifield, "Japan and South Korea Sign Long-Awaited Intelligence-Sharing Deal," *Washington Post*, November 23, 2016, https://www.washingtonpost.com/world/japan-and-south-korea-sign-long-awaited-intelligence-sharing-deal/2016/11/23/bcad8c3f-9c4d-4eff-b41a–4d8ee2ab7035_story.html?utm_term=.068617df8f8f (accessed on August 14, 2018).

24. Article 1, in *Die Grosse Politik* 19, chap. 138, 465.

25. Not to mention the history of military affairs. See Cowley 1999.

Bibliography

Abadie, Alberto, and Imbens Guido. 2002. "Simple and Bias-Corrected Matching Estimators." Working paper, Department of Economics, UC Berkeley.

Abadie, Alberto, and Imbens, Guido. 2006. "Large Sample Properties of Matching Estimators for Average Treatment Effects." *Econometrica* 74, no. 1: 235–67.

Abadie, Alberto, and Javier Gardeazabal. 2003. "The Economic Costs of Conflict: A Case Study of the Basque Country." *American Economic Review* 93, no. 1: 113–32.

Abadie, Alberto, Alexis Diamond, and Jens Hainmueller. 2015. "Comparative Politics and the Synthetic Control Method." *American Journal of Political Science* 59, no. 2: 495–510.

Abadie, Alberto, David Drukker, Jane Herr, and Guido Imbens. 2004. "Implementing Matching Estimators for Average Treatment Effects in Stata." *STATA Journal* 4, no. 3: 290–311.

Abbott, Kenneth W., and Duncan Snidal. 2000. "Hard and Soft Law in International Governance." *International Organization* 54, no. 3: 421–56.

Achen, Christopher H. 1986. *The Statistical Analysis of Quasi-Experiments*. Berkeley: University of California Press.

——. 2002. "Toward a New Political Methodology." *Annual Review of Political Science* 5:423–50.

——. 2005. "Let's Put Garbage-Can Regressions and Garbage-Can Probits Where They Belong." *Conflict Management and Peace Science* 22, no. 4: 327–39.

Acheson, Dean. 1969. *Present at the Creation: May Years in the State Department*. New York: W. W. Norton.

Achilles, Theodore C. 1985. "The Omaha Milkman: The Role of the United States." In *NATO's Anxious Birth: The Prophetic Vision of the 1940s*, ed. Nicholas Sherwen, 34–35. New York: St. Martin's Press.

Adcock, Robert, and David Collier. 2001. "Measurement Validity: A Shared Standard for Qualitative and Quantitative Research." *American Political Science Review* 95, no. 3: 529–46.

Albrecht-Carreé, René. 1972. *A Diplomatic History of Europe since the Congress of Vienna*. New York: Harper and Row.

Al-Najjar, Nabil I., and Jonathan Weinstein. 2009. "Rejoinder: The Ambiguity Aversion Literature: A Critical Assessment." Special issue, *Economics and Philosophy* 25, no. 3: 357–69.

Ambrose, Stephen E. 1970. *The Supreme Commander: The War Years of General Dwight D. Eisenhower*. Garden City, NY: Double Day.

Arnold, Jeffrey. 2014. "CDB90 Variable Levels CSV File." Gitbub.com, October 17, 2014. https://github.com/jrnold/CDB90/blob/master/src-data/variable_levels.json. Accessed August 19, 2016.

Auerswald, David P., and Stephen M. Saideman. 2014. *NATO in Afghanistan: Fighting Together, Fighting Alone*. Princeton, NJ: Princeton University Press.

Avant, Deborah. 1993. "The Institutional Sources of Military Doctrine: Hegemons in Peripheral Wars." *International Studies Quarterly* 37, no. 4: 409–30.

Axelrod, Robert, and Robert Keohane. 1985. "Achieving Cooperation under Anarchy: Strategies and Institutions." *World Politics* 38, no. 1: 226–54.

Baylis, John. 1984. *Anglo-American Defence Relations, 1939–1984.* London: Macmillan.

Bean, Richard. 1973. "War and the Birth of the Nation State." *Journal of Economic History* 33, no. 1: 203–21.

Beckley, Michael. 2015. "The Myth of Entangling Alliances: Reassessing the Security Risks of US Defense Pacts." *International Security* 39, no. 4: 7–48.

Benians, E. A., James Bulter, and C. E. Carrington. 1959. *The Cambridge History of the British Empire.* Vol. 3. *The Empire-Commonwealth, 1870–1919.* London: Cambridge University Press.

Bennett, Andrew. 2004. "Case Study Methods: Design, Use, and Comparative Advantages." In *Models, Numbers, and Cases: Methods for Studying International Relations*, ed. Detlef F. Sprinz and Yael Wolinsky-Nahmias, 19–55. Ann Arbor: University of Michigan Press.

Bennett, Andrew, and Colin Elman. 2006. "Qualitative Research: Recent Developments in Case Study Methods." *Annual Review of Political Science* 9: 455–76.

Bennett, D. Scott. 1996. "Security, Bargaining, and the End of Interstate Rivalry." *International Studies Quarterly* 40, no. 2: 157–83.

——. 1997a. "Democracy, Regime Change, and Rivalry Termination." *International Interactions* 22, no. 4: 369–97.

——. 1997b. "Measuring Rivalry Termination, 1816–1992." *Journal of Conflict Resolution* 41, no. 2: 227–54.

——. 1998. "Integrating and Testing Models of Rivalry Duration." *American Journal of Political Science* 42, no. 4: 1200–232.

Bennett, D. Scott, and Allan Stam. 1996. "The Duration of Interstate Wars, 1816–1985." *American Political Science Review* 90, no. 2: 239–57.

Bensahel, Nora. 2007. "International Alliances and Military Effectiveness: Fighting alongside Allies and Partners." In *Creating Military Power: The Sources of Military Effectiveness*, ed. Risa Brooks and Elizabeth Stanley, 186–206. Stanford, CA: Stanford University Press.

Benson, Brett. 2012. *Constructing International Security.* New York: Cambridge University Press.

Benson, Brett, Adam Meirowitz, and Kris Ramsay. 2014. "Inducing Deterrence through Moral Hazard in Alliance Contracts." *Journal of Conflict Resolution* 58, no. 2: 307–35.

Berk, Richard A. 1983. "An Introduction to Sample Selection Bias in Sociological Data." *American Sociological Review*, June, 386–98.

Biddle, Stephen. 2004. *Military Power.* Princeton, NJ: Princeton University Press.

Biddle, Stephen, and Stephen Long. 2004. "Democracy and Military Effectiveness: A Deeper Look." *Journal of Conflict Resolution* 48, no. 4: 525–46.

Bland, Douglas. 1991. *The Military Committee of the North Atlantic Alliance: A Study of Structure and Strategy.* New York: Praeger.

Bloch, Marc. 1968 [1946]. *Strange Defeat: A Statement of Evidence Written in 1940.* New York: W. W. Norton.

Bohlen, C. E. 1969. *The Transformation of American Foreign Policy.* New York: W. W. Norton.

Brady, Henry E., David Collier, and Jason Seawright. 2004. "Refocusing the Discussion of Methodology." In *Rethinking Social Inquiry: Diverse Tools, Shared Standards*, ed. Henry E. Brady and David Collier, 3–20. Lanham, MD: Rowman & Littlefield.

Brooks, Risa. 2003. "Making Military Might: Why Do States Fail and Succeed?" *International Security* 28:149–91.

Buben, Jan. 1999. "Mediterranean Agreement of Great Britain, Italy and Austria-Hungary from February–March 1887." *Prague Papers on History of International Relations*. Prague: Institute of World History.

Bueno de Mesquita, Bruce, and J. David Singer. 1973. "Alliances, Capabilities, and War: A Review and Synthesis." *Political Science Annual: An International Review* 4:237–80.

Bushway, Shawn, Brian D. Johnson, and Lee Ann Slocum. 2007. "Is the Magic Still There? The Use of the Heckman Two-Step Correction for Selection Bias in Criminology." *Journal of Quantitative Criminology* 23, no. 2: 151–78.

Cameron, A. Colin, and Pravin K. Trivedi. 2005. *Microeconometrics: Methods and Applications*. New York: Cambridge University Press.

Capoccia, G., and R. D. Kelemen. 2007. "The Study of Critical Junctures: Theory, Narrative, and Counterfactuals in Historical Institutionalism." *World Politics* 59, no. 3: 341–69.

Carnegie, Allison. 2015. *Power Plays: How International Institutions Reshape Coercive Diplomacy*. New York: Cambridge University Press.

Cecil, Lady Gwendolen. 1921. *Life of Robert Maquis of Salisbury*. Vol. 2. London: Hodder and Stoughton.

Chayes, Abram, and Antonia Handler Chayes. 1993. "On Compliance." *International Organization* 47, no. 2: 175–205.

Chiba, Daina, Carla Martinez Machain, and William Reed. 2014. "Major Powers and Militarized Conflict." *Journal of Conflict Resolution* 58, no. 6: 976–1002.

Choi, Seung-Whan, and Patrick James. 2008. "Civil-Military Structure, Political Communication, and the Democratic Peace." *Journal of Peace Research* 45, no. 1: 37–53.

Christensen, Thomas, and Jack Snyder. 1990. "Chain Gangs and Passed Bucks: Predicting Alliance Patterns in Multipolarity." *International Organization* 44, no. 2: 137–68.

Clare, Joe. 2013. "The Deterrent Value of Democratic Allies." *International Studies Quarterly* 57, no. 3: 545–55.

Clark, Christopher. 2012. *The Sleepwalkers: How Europe Went to War in 1914*. New York: Penguin.

Clarke, Kevin A. 2005. "The Phantom Menace: Omitted Variable Bias in Econometric Research." *Conflict Management and Peace Science* 22, no. 4: 341–52.

Clayton, Govinda, and Kristian Skrede Gleditsch. 2014. "Will We See Helping Hands? Predicting Civil War Mediation and Likely Success." *Conflict Management and Peace Science* 31, no. 3: 265–84.

Cline, Kirssa, Patrick Rhamey, Alexis Henshaw, Alesia Sedziaka, Aakriti Tandon, and Thomas J. Volgy. 2011. "Identifying Regional Powers and Their Status." In *Major Powers and the Quest for Status in International Politics*, ed. Thomas Volgy, Renato Corbetta, Keith Grant, and Ryan Baird, 133–57. New York: Palgrave Macmillan.

Clodfelter, Michale. 1993. *Warfare and Armed Conflicts*. 2 vols. Jefferson, NC: McFarland.

Colaresi, Michael, Karen A. Rasler, and William R. Thompson. 2007. *Strategic Rivalries in World Politics*. Cambridge: Cambridge University Press.

Collier, D. 1999. "Data, Field Work and Extracting New Ideas at Close Range." *APSA-CP Newsletter*, Winter, 1–6.

Cook, Don. 1989. *Forging the Alliance: NATO, 1945–1950*. New York: Arbor House.

Cooley, Alexander, and Hendrick Spruyt. 2009. *Contracting States: Sovereign Transfers in International Relations*. Princeton, NJ: Princeton University Press.

Cowles, Loyal. 1990. "The Failure to Restrain Russia: Canning, Nesselrode, and the Greek Question, 1825–1827." *International History Review* 12, no. 4: 688–720.

Cowley, Robert. 1999. *What If? The World's Foremost Military Historians Imagine What Might Have Been.* New York: G. P. Putnam's Sons.

Cranmer, Skyler, Bruce A. Desmaris, and Elizabeth J. Menninga. 2012. "Complex Dependencies in the Alliance Network." *Conflict Management and Peace Science* 29, no. 3 (July): 279–313.

Crawford, Timothy W. 2008. "Wedge Strategy, Balancing, and the Deviant Case of Spain, 1940–41." *Security Studies* 17, no. 1: 1–38.

——. 2011. "Preventing Enemy Coalitions: How Wedge Strategies Shape Power Politics." *International Security* 35, no. 4: 155–89.

Crawford, Vincent P., and Joel Sobel. 1982. "Strategic Information Transmission." *Econometrica: Journal of the Econometric Society* 50, no. 6: 1431–51.

Crescenzi, Mark J. C., Jacob D. Kathman, Katja B. Kleinberg, and Reed M. Wood. 2012. "Reliability, Reputation, and Alliance Formation." *International Studies Quarterly* 56, no. 2: 259–74.

Dafoe, Allan, and Nina Kelsey. 2014. "Observing the Capitalist Peace: Examining Market- Mediated Signaling and Other Mechanisms." *Journal of Peace Research* 51, no. 5: 619–33.

Dakin, Douglas. 1962. "The Diplomacy of the Great Powers and the Balkan States, 1908–1914." *Balkan Studies* 3, no. 2: 327–74.

Dai, Xinyuan. 2005. "Why Comply? The Domestic Constituency Mechanism." *International Organization* 59, no. 2: 363–98.

Davis, Christina. 2004. "International Institutions and Issue Linkage: Building Support for Agricultural Trade Liberalization." *American Political Science Review* 98, no. 1: 153–69.

——. 2009. "Linkage Diplomacy: Economic and Security Bargaining in the Anglo-Japanese Alliance, 1902–23." *International Security* 33, no. 3: 143–79.

Davis, Clarence B., and Robert J. Gowen. 2000. "The British at Weihaiwei: A Case Study in the Irrationality of Empire." *Historian* 63, no. 1: 87–104.

Dempsey, Guy. 2008. *Albuera 1811: The Bloodiest Battle of the Peninsular War.* London: Frontline Books.

Desch, Michael C. 1989. "The Keys That Lock Up the World: Identifying American Interests in the Periphery." *International Security* 14, no. 1: 86–121.

——. 2002. "Democracy and Victory: Why Regime Type Hardly Matters." *International Security* 27, no. 2: 5–47.

Diamond, Alexis, and Jasjeet S. Sekhon. 2013. "Genetic Matching for Estimating Causal Effects: A General Multivariate Matching Method for Achieving Balance in Observational Studies." *Review of Economics and Statistics* 95, no. 3: 932–45.

Diehl, Paul, and Gary Goertz. 2000. *War and Peace in International Rivalry.* Ann Arbor, MI: University of Michigan Press.

DiGiuseppe, Mathew, and Paul Poast. 2018. "Arms and Democratic Allies." *British Journal of Political Science* 48, no. 4: 981–1003.

Downs, George W., David M. Rocke, and Peter N. Barsoom. 1996. "Is the Good News about Compliance Good News about Cooperation?" *International Organization* 50:379–406.

Drezner, Daniel. 2009. *All Politics Is Global.* Princeton, NJ: Princeton University Press.

Dupuy, R. Ernest, and Trevor N. Dupuy. 1986. *The Encyclopedia of Military History from 3500 B.C. to the Present.* 2nd rev. ed. New York: Harper & Row.

Dupuy, Trevor N., Grace P. Hayes, C. Curtiss Johnson, Charles R. Smith, Brian Bader, Edward Oppenheimer, and Arnold Dupuy. 1984. *Military History: A Data Base of Selected Battles, 1600–1973,* vol. 1, main report. Bethesda, MD: U.S. Army Concepts Analysis Agency.

Eckardstein, Baron Von Hermann. 1922. *Ten Years at the Court of St. James, 1895–1905.* New York: Dutton.

Ellenberg, Jonas H. 1994. "Selection Bias in Observational and Experimental Studies." *Statistics in Medicine* 13, nos. 5–7: 557–67.

English, John. 2001. "'Who Could Ask for Anything More?' North American Perspectives on NATO's Origins." In *A History of NATO—The First Fifty Years*, vol. 2, ed. Gustav Schmidt, 305–20. London: Palgrave.

Fang, Songying, Jesse C. Johnson, and Brett Ashley Leeds. 2014. "To Concede or to Resist? The Restraining Effect of Military Alliances." *International Organization* 68, no. 4: 775–809.

Farrell, Joseph, and Robert Gibbons. 1989. "Cheap Talk with Two Audiences." *American Economic Review* 79, no. 5: 1214–23.

Fearon, James D. 1994. "Signaling versus the Balance of Power and Interests: An Empirical Test of a Crisis Bargaining Model." *Journal of Conflict Resolution* 38, no. 2: 236–69.

——. 1995. "Rationalist Explanations for War." *International Organization* 49, no. 3: 379–414.

——. 1997. "Signaling Foreign Policy Interests: Tying Hands and Sinking Costs." *Journal of Conflict Resolution* 41, no. 1: 68–90.

——. 1998. "Bargaining, Enforcement, and International Cooperation." *International Organization* 52, no. 2: 269–306.

Feis, H. 1970. *From Trust to Terror.* New York: Norton.

Ferguson, Naill. 1999. *The Pity of War.* New York: Basic Books.

Ferris, John. 1993. "'Worthy of Some Better Enemy?': The British Estimate of the Imperial Japanese Army, 1919–41, and the Fall of Signapore." *Canadian Journal of History* 28, no. 2 (August): 223–56.

Fisher, R., and William Ury. 1981. *Getting to Yes: Negotiating Agreement without Giving In.* Boston: Houghton Mifflin.

Fletcher, Harry R. 1993. *Air Force Bases.* Vol 2, *Air Bases Outside the United States of America.* Washington, DC: Center for Air Force History.

Fordham, Benjamin. 1998. "Economic Interests, Party, and Ideology in Early Cold War Era U.S. Foreign Policy." *International Organization* 52, no. 2: 359–96.

——. 2011. "Who Wants to Be a Major Power? Explaining the Expansion of Foreign Policy Ambition." *Journal of Peace Research* 48, no. 5: 587–603.

Fordham, Benjamin, and Paul Poast. 2016. "All Alliances Are Multilateral: Rethinking Alliance Formation." *Journal of Conflict Resolution* 60, no. 5: 840–65.

Freedman, David A., and Jasjeet S. Sekhon. 2010. "Endogeneity in Probit Response Models." *Political Analysis* 18, no. 2: 138–50.

Fudenberg, Drew, and Jean Tirole. 1991. *Game Theory.* Cambridge, MA: MIT Press.

Fuhrmann, Matthew, and Todd S. Sechser. 2014. "Signaling Alliance Commitments: Hand-Tying and Sunk Costs in Extended Nuclear Deterrence." *American Journal of Political Science* 58, no. 4: 919–35.

Fukuyama, Francis. 2011. *The Origins of Political Order: From Prehuman Times to the French Revolution.* New York: Farrar, Straus, and Giroux.

Gardner, Hall. 2015. *The Failure to Prevent World War I.* Burlington, VT: Ashegate.

Gartner, Scott S. 1997. *Strategic Assessment in War.* New Haven, CT: Yale University Press.

Gartzke, Erik. 1999. "War Is in the Error Term." *International Organization* 53, no. 3: 567–87.

Gartzke, Erik, and Kristian Skrede Gleditsch. 2004. "Why Democracies May Actually Be Less Reliable Allies." *American Journal of Political Science* 48, no. 4: 775–95.

Gaubatz, Kurt Taylor. 1996. "Democratic States and Commitment in International Relations." *International Organization* 50, no. 1: 109–39.

George, Alexander L. 1979. "Case Studies and Theory Development." In *Diplomacy: New Approaches in Theory, History, and Policy*, ed. Paul Gordon Lauren, 43–68. New York: Free Press.

Gerring, J. 2017. *Case Study Research: Principles and Practices*. 2nd ed. Cambridge, NY: Cambridge University Press.

Gerring, J., and Lee Cojocaru. 2016. "Selecting Cases for Intensive Analysis: A Diversity of Goals and Methods." *Sociological Methods and Research* 45, no. 3: 392–423.

Gerring, J., and J. Seawright. 2017. "Case Selection Techniques in Case Study Research: A Menu of Qualitative and Quantitative Options." *Political Research Quarterly* 61, no. 2: 294–308.

Ghosn, Faten, Glenn Palmer, and Stuart Bremer. 2004. "The MID3 Data Set, 1993–2001: Procedures, Coding Rules, and Description." *Conflict Management and Peace Science* 21:133–54.

Gibler, D. M. 2008. "The Costs of Reneging: Reputation and Alliance Formation." *Journal of Conflict Resolution* 52, no. 3: 426.

——. 2009. *International Military Alliances, 1648–2008*. Washington, DC: CQ Press.

Gibler, D. M., and M. R. Sarkees. 2004. "Measuring Alliances: The Correlates of War Formal Interstate Alliance Dataset, 1816–2000." *Journal of Peace Research* 41, no. 2: 211.

Gibler, D. M., and Scott Wolford. 2006. "Alliances, Then Democracy: An Examination of the Relationship between Regime Type and Alliance Formation." *Journal of Conflict Resolution* 50, no. 1: 129–53.

Gilpin, Robert. 1971. "The Politics of Transnational Economic Relations." *International Organization* 25, no. 3: 398–419.

Glantz, David M. 2010. *Barbarossa Derailed: The Battle for Smolensk, 10 July–10 September 1941*. Vol. 1. Solihull: Helion.

Goemans, Henk E., Kristian Skrede Gleditsch, and Giacomo Chiozza. 2009. "Introducing Archigos: A Dataset of Political Leaders." *Journal of Peace Research* 46, no. 2: 269–83.

Goertz, Gary. 2012. "Case Studies, Causal Mechanisms, and Selecting Cases." Unpublished manuscript, version 5.

Goertz, Gary, and Paul F. Diehl. 1993. "Enduring Rivalries: Theoretical Constructs and Empirical Patterns." *International Studies Quarterly* 37, no. 2: 147–71.

——. 1995. "The Initiation and Termination of Enduring Rivalries: The Impact of Political Shocks." *American Journal of Political Science* 39, no. 1:30–52.

Goertz, Gary, Paul F. Diehl, and Alexandru Klein. 2016. *The Puzzle of Peace: The Evolution of Peace in the International System*. New York: Oxford University Press.

Goldstein, Avery. 1995. "Discounting the Free Ride: Alliances and Security in the Postwar World." *International Organization* 49, no. 1: 39–71.

Goodlad, Graham. 2000. *British Foreign and Imperial Policy, 1865–1919*. London: Routledge.

Gowa, Joanne. 1989. "Bilpolarity, Multipolarity, and Free Trade." *American Political Science Review* 83, no. 4: 1245–56.

Gowa, Joanne, and Edward Mansfield. 1993. "Power Politics and International Trade." *American Political Science Review* 87, no. 2: 408–20.

Greene, William H. 2011. *Econometric Analysis.* 7th ed. Upper Saddle River, NJ: Pearson.

Gross Stein, Janice.1989. "Getting to the Table: Processes of International Prenegotiation." *International Journal* 44, no. 2: 231–36.

Guisinger, Alexandra, and Alastair Smith. 2002. "Honest Threats: The Interaction of Reputation and Political Institutions in International Crises." *Journal of Conflict Resolution* 46, no. 2: 175–200.

Guzman, Andrew T. 2009. "How International Law Works: A Response to Commentators." *International Theory* 1, no. 2: 335.

Hakki, Murat Metin. 2007. *Cyprus Issue: A Documentary History, 1878–2006.* London: I. B. Tauris.

Hall, Christopher. 1992. *British Strategy During the Napoleonic War, 1803–1815.* Manchester: Manchester University Press.

Harder, Anton. 2015. "Not at the Cost of China: New Evidence Regarding US Proposals to Nehru for Joining the United Nations Security Council." CWIHP Working Paper Series, no. 76, Woodrow Wilson International Center for Scholars, Washington, DC, March.

Herwig, Holger. 2003. "Germany." In *The Origins of World War I,* ed. Richard Hamilton and Holger Herwig, 150–87. New York: Cambridge University Press.

Hamilton, Richard, and Holger Herwig. 2010. *War Planning 1914.* New York: Cambridge University Press.

Harkavy, Robert E. 2007. *Strategic Basing and the Great Powers, 1200–2000.* London: Routledge.

Hayashi, Count Tadasu. 1915. *The Secret Memoirs of Count Tadasu Hayashit.* New York: G. P. Putnam's Sons.

Heckman, James J. 1979. "Sample Selection Bias as a Specification Error." *Econometrica* 47, no. 1: 153–61.

Hemmer, Christopher, and Peter J. Katzenstein. 2002. "Why Is There No NATO in Asia? Collective Identity, Regionalism, and the Origins of Multilateralism." *International Organization* 56, no. 3: 575–607.

Henderson, Nicholas. 1983. *The Birth of NATO.* Boulder, CO: Westview Press.

Henke, Marina. 2019. *Constructing Allied Cooperation: Diplomacy, Payments and Power in Multilateral Military Coalitions.* Ithaca, NY: Cornell University Press.

Ho, Daniel, Kosuke Imai, Gary King, and Elizabeth Stuart. 2007. "Matching as Nonparametric Preprocessing for Reducing Model Dependence in Parametric Causal Inference." *Political Analysis* 15:199–236.

Holland, T. E. 1885. *The European Concert in the Eastern Question: A Collection of Treaties and Other Public Acts.* Oxford: Clarendon Press.

Holsti, Kalevi J. 1991. *Peace and War: Armed Conflicts and International Order.* Cambridge: Cambridge University Press.

Horowitz, Michael C., Allan C. Stam, and Cali M. Ellis. 2015. *Why Leaders Fight.* Cambridge, NY: Cambridge University Press.

Horowitz, Michael C., Paul Poast, and Allan C. Stam. 2017. "Domestic Signaling of Commitment Credibility: Military Recruitment and Alliance Formation." *Journal of Conflict Resolution* 61, no. 8: 1682–710.

Howard, Michael. 1984. "Men against Fire: Expectations of War in 1914." *International Security* 9, no. 1: 41–57.

Hughes, Michael. 2000. *Diplomacy before the Russian Revolution: Britain, Russia, and the Old Diplomacy, 1894–1917.* New York: St. Martin's Press.

Hurst, Michael, ed. 1972. *Key Treaties for the Great Powers 1814–1914.* Vol. 2. St. Martin's Press, 735–38.

Imai, Kosuke, Gary King, and Elizabeth Stuart. 2008. "Misunderstandings between Experimentalists and Observationalists about Causal Inference." *Journal of the Royal Statistical Society* 171, part 2: 1–22.

Insall, Tony, and Patrick Salmon, eds. 2015. *Documents on British Policy Overseas: The Brussels and North Atlantic Treaties, 1947–1949.* Foreign and Commonwealth Office. London: Routledge.

Jönsson, Christer. 2002. "Diplomacy, Bargaining, and Negotiation." In *Handbook of International Relations,* ed. Walter Carlsnaes, Thomas Risse, and Beth A. Simmons, 212–34. London: Sage Publications.

Jackson, Aaron P. 2013. *The Roots of Military Doctrine: Change and Continuity in Understanding the Practice of Warfare.* Fort Leavenworth, KS: Combat Studies Institute Press.

Jelavich, Barbara. 2004. *Russia's Balkan Entanglements, 1806–1914.* New York: Cambridge University Press.

Jervis, Robert. 1970. *The Logic of Images in International Politics.* Princeton, NJ: Princeton University Press.

——. 1976. *Perception and Misperception in International Politics.* Princeton, NJ: Princeton University Press.

——. 1997. *System Effects: Complexity in Political and Social Life.* Princeton, NJ: Princeton University Press.

——. 2002. "Signaling and Perception: Drawing Inferences and Projecting Images." In *Political Psychology,* ed. Kristen Renwick Monroe, 293–314. London: Erlbaum.

Johnsen, William T. 2016. *The Origins of the Grand Alliance: Anglo-American Military Collaboration from the Panay Incident to Pearl Harbor.* Lexington: University of Kentucky Press.

Johnson, Jesse C. 2017. "External Threat and Alliance Formation." *International Studies Quarterly* 61:736–45.

Johnson, Jesse C., and Brett Ashley Leeds. 2011. "Defense Pacts: A Prescription for Peace?" *Foreign Policy Analysis* 7, no. 1: 45–65.

Johnson, Jesse C., Brett Ashley Leeds, and Ahra Wu. 2015. "Capability, Credibility, and Extended General Deterrence." *International Interactions* 41, no. 2: 309–36.

Jones, Spencer. 2012. *From Boer War to World War: Tactical Reform of the British Army, 1902–1914.* Norman: University of Oklahoma Press.

Kadera, Kelly M., and Sara McLaughlin Mitchell. 2005. "Heeding Ray's Advice: An Exegesis on Control Variables in Systemic Democratic Peace Research." *Conflict Management and Peace Science* 22, no. 4: 311–26.

Kaplan, Karel. 1987. *The Short March: The Communist Takeover in Czechoslovakia, 1945–1948.* New York: St. Martin's Press.

Kaplan, Lawrence. 2007. *NATO 1948: The Birth of the Transatlantic Alliance.* New York: Rowman and Littlefield.

——. 2013. *NATO before the Korean War: April 1949–June 1950.* Kent, OH: Kent State University Press.

Kappler, Dietrich. 2001. "Texts in Diplomacy." In *Language and Diplomacy,* ed. Jovan Kurbalija and Hannah Slavik, 201. Malta: DiploProjects.

Kawai, Kazuo. 1939. "Anglo-German Rivalry in the Yangtze Region, 1895–1902." *Pacific Historical Review* 8, no. 4: 413–33.

Kennan, George. 1984. *The Fateful Alliance: France, Russia, and the Coming of the First World War.* New York: Pantheon Books.

Kennedy, Paul M. 1976. *The Rise and Fall of British Naval Mastery.* New York: Cambridge University Press.

———, ed. 1979. *War Plans of the Major Powers*. London: Allen and Unwin.

———. 1980a. *The Rise of The Anglo-German Antagonism, 1860–1914*. London: Allen and Unwin.

———. 1980b. "Editor's Introduction." In *War Plans of the Great Powers, 1880–1914*, ed. Paul Kennedy, 1–22. London: George Allen and Unwin.

Kertzer, Joshua D., and Ryan Brutger. 2016. "Decomposing Audience Costs: Bringing the Audience Back into Audience Cost Theory." *American Journal of Political Science* 60, no. 1: 234–49.

Khong, Y. F. 1992. *Korea, Munich, Dien Bien Phu, and the Vietnam Decisions of 1965*. Princeton, NJ: Princeton University Press.

Kier, Elizabeth. 1997. *Imagining War: French and British Military Doctrine Between the Wars*. Princeton, NJ: Princeton University Press.

Kim, Tongfi. 2011. "Why Alliances Entangle but Seldom Entrap States." *Security Studies* 20, no. 3: 350–77.

Kimball, Warren F., ed. 1984. *Churchill and Roosevelt: The Complete Correspondence: Vol I. Alliance Emerging*. Princeton, NJ: Princeton University Press.

King, Gary, Robert O. Keohane, and Sidney Verba. 1994. *Designing Social Inquiry: Scientific Inference in Qualitative Research*. Princeton, NJ: Princeton University Press.

Kinne, Brandon J. 2016. "Agreeing to Arm: Bilateral Weapons Agreements and the Global Arms Trade." *Journal of Peace Research* 53, no. 3: 359–77.

———. 2018. "Defense Cooperation Agreements and the Emergence of a Global Security Network." *International Organization* 72, no. 4: 799–837.

Kinne, Brandon J., and Jonas Bunte. Forthcoming. "Guns or Money? Defense Cooperation and Bilateral Lending as Coevolving Networks." *British Journal of Political Science*.

Klein, James P., Gary Goertz, and Paul F. Diehl. 2006. "The New Rivalry Dataset: Procedures and Patterns." *Journal of Peace Research* 43, no. 3: 331–48.

Koch, H. W. 1969. "The Anglo-German Alliance Negotiations: Missed Opportunity or Myth?" *History* 54, no. 182: 378–92.

Kolodziej, Edward A. 2005. *Security and International Relations*. New York: Cambridge University Press.

Koremenos, Barbara. 2005. "Contracting around International Uncertainty." *American Political Science Review* 99, no. 4: 549–65.

Koremenos, Barbara, Charles Lipson, and Duncan Snidal. 2001. "The Rational Design of International Institutions." *International Organization* 55, no. 4: 761–99.

Kreps, Sarah E. 2011. *Coalitions of Convenience: United States Military Interventions after the Cold War*. New York: Oxford University Press.

Kuneralp, Sinan, ed. 2009. *The Queen's Ambassador to the Sultan: Memoirs of Sir Henry A. Layard's Constantinople Embassy, 1877–1880*. Istanbul: ISIS Press.

Kydd, Andrew. 2009. "Reputation and Cooperation: Guzman on International Law." *International Theory* 1, no. 2: 295–305.

Lai, Brian, and Dan Reiter. 2000. "Democracy, Political Similarity, and International Alliances, 1816–1992." *Journal of Conflict Resolution* 44, no. 2: 203–27.

Lake, David A. 1996. "Anarchy, Hierarchy, and the Variety of International Relations." *International Organization* 50, no. 1: 1–33.

———. 1999. *Entangling Relations*. Princeton, NJ: Princeton University Press.

Langer, William. 1951. *The Diplomacy of Imperialism: 1890–1902*. New York: Knopf.

———. 1966. *European Alliances and Alignments*. New York: Alfred A. Knopf.

Lansdowne to Salisbury, May 24, 1901, in British Documents, vol. 2, no. 82 (enclosure).

Lee, Dwight E. 1931. "A Memorandum Concerning Cyprus, 1878." *Journal of Modern History* 3, no. 2: 235–41.

———. 1934. *Great Britain and the Cyprus Convention Policy of 1878*. Cambridge, MA: Harvard University Press.

Leeds, Brett Ashley. 1999. "Domestic Political Institutions, Credible Commitments, and International Cooperation." *American Journal of Political Science* 43, no. 4: 979–1002.

———. 2003a. "Alliance Reliability in Times of War: Explaining State Decisions to Violate Treaties." *International Organization* 57, no. 4: 801–27.

———. 2003b. "Do Alliances Deter Aggression? The Influence of Military Alliances on the Initiation of Militarized Interstate Disputes." *American Journal of Political Science* 47, no. 3: 427–39.

Leeds, Brett Ashley, and Burcu Savun. 2007. "Terminating Alliances: Why Do States Abrogate Agreements?" *Journal of Politics* 69, no. 4: 1118–32.

Leeds, Brett Ashley, and Sezi Anac. 2005. "Alliance Institutionalization and Alliance Performance." *International Interactions* 31, no. 3: 183–202.

Leeds, Brett Ashley, Andrew G. Long, and Sara McLaughlin Mitchell. 2000. "Reevaluating Alliance Reliability Specific Threats, Specific Promises." *Journal of Conflict Resolution* 44, no. 5: 686–99.

Leeds, Brett Ashley, Michaela Mattes, and Jeremy S. Vogel. 2009. "Interests, Institutions, and the Reliability of International Commitments." *American Journal of Political Science* 53, no. 2: 461–76.

Leeds, Brett Ashley, Jeffrey M. Ritter, Sara McLaughlin Mitchell, and Andrew G. Long. 2002. "Alliance Treaty Obligations and Provisions, 1815–1944." *International Interactions* 28, no. 3: 237–60.

LeVeck, Brad L., and Neil Narang. "How International Reputation Matters: Revisiting Alliance Violations in Context." *International Interactions* 43, no. 5 (2017): 797–821.

Levendusky, Matthew S., and Michael C. Horowitz. 2012. "When Backing Down Is the Right Decision: Partisanship, New Information, and Audience Costs." *Journal of Politics* 74, no. 2: 323–38.

Leventoğlu, Bahar, and Ahmer Tarar. 2008. "Does Private Information Lead to Delay or War in Crisis Bargaining." *International Studies Quarterly* 52, no. 3: 533–53.

Levy, Jack. S. 1981. "Alliance Formation and War Behavior: An Analysis of the Great Powers, 1495–1975." *Journal of Conflict Resolution* 25, no. 4: 581–613.

———. 1982. *War in the Great Power System*. Lexington: University of Kentucky Press.

———. 1984. "The Offensive/Defensive Balance of Military Technology: A Theoretical and Historical Analysis." *International Studies Quarterly* 28, no. 2: 219–38.

———. 1986. "Organizational Routines and the Causes of War." *International Studies Quarterly* 30, no. 2: 193–222.

———. 2003. "Economic Interdependence, Opportunity Costs, and Peace." In *Economic Interdependence and International Conflict: New Perspectives on an Enduring Debate*, ed. Edward D. Mansfield and Brian Pollins, 127–47. Ann Arbor: University of Michigan Press.

———. 2008. "Case Studies: Types, Designs, and Logics of Inference." *Conflict Management and Peace Science* 25, no. 1: 1–18.

———. 2011. "Preventive War: Concept and Propositions." *International Interactions* 37, no. 1: 87–96.

———. 2013. "Psychology and Foreign Policy Decision-Making." In *The Oxford Handbook of Political Psychology*, 2nd ed., ed. Leonie Huddy, David O. Sears, and Jack S. Levy, 301–33. Oxford: Oxford University Press.

Levy, Jack S., and Joseph R. Gochal. 2001. "Democracy and Preventive War: Israel and the 1956 Sinai Campaign." *Security Studies* 11, no. 2: 1–49.

Levy, Jack S., and William Thompson. 2010. "Balancing on Land and at Sea: Do States Ally against the Leading Global Power?" *International Security* 35, no. 1: 7–43.

Levy, Jack S., Michael McKoy, Paul Poast, and Geoffrey P. R. Wallace. 2015. "Backing Out or Backing In? Commitments and Consistency in Audience Costs Theory." *American Journal of Political Science* 59, no. 4: 988–1001.

Lieberman, E. S. 2005. "Nested Analysis as a Mixed-Method Strategy for Comparative Research." *American Political Science Review* 99, no. 3: 435–52.

Lipscy, Phillip. 2015. "Explaining Institutional Change: Policy Areas, Outside Options, and the Bretton Woods Institutions." *American Journal of Political Science* 59, no. 2: 341–56.

Liska, George. 1962. *Nations in Alliance: The Limits of Interdependence*. Baltimore: Johns Hopkins Press.

Lukes, Igor. 1996. *Czechoslovakia between Hitler and Stalin: The Diplomacy of Edvard Benes in the 1930s*. Oxford: Oxford University Press.

Lupu, Yonatan. 2013. "Best Evidence: The Role of Information in Domestic Judicial Enforcement of International Human Rights Agreements." *International Organization* 67, no. 3: 469–503.

Lupu, Yonatan, and Paul Poast. 2016. "Team of Former Rivals: A Multilateral Theory of Non-aggression Pacts." *Journal of Peace Research* 53:344–58.

Luvaas, Jay. 1959. *The Military Legacy of the Civil War: The European Inheritance*. Chicago, IL: University of Chicago Press.

Lyall, Jason. 2010. "Do Democracies Make Inferior Counterinsurgents? Reassessing Democracy's Impact on War Outcomes and Duration." *International Organization* 64, no. 1: 167–92.

MacMurray, John V., ed. 1921. *Treaties and Agreements with and concerning China, 1894–1919*. Vol. 1. New York: Oxford University Press.

Mahoney, James, and Gary Goertz. 2006. "A Tale of Two Cultures: Contrasting Quantitative and Qualitative Research." *Political Analysis* 14, no. 3: 227–49.

Manne, Robert. 1974. "The British Decision for Alliance with Russia, May 1939." *Contemporary History* 9, no. 3: 3–26.

Mansfield, Edward D., and Eric Reinhardt. 2003. "Multilateral Determinants of Regionalism: The Effects of GATT/WTO on the Formation of Preferential Trading Arrangements." *International Organization* 57, no. 4: 829–62.

Mansfield, Edward D., and Jon C. Pevehouse. 2008. "Democratization and the Varieties of International Organizations." *Journal of Conflict Resolution* 52, no. 2: 269–94.

Manski, Charles F. 1995. *Identification Problems in the Social Sciences*. Cambridge, MA: Harvard University Press.

——. 2007. *Identification for Prediction and Decision*. Cambridge, MA: Harvard University Press.

Maoz, Zeev. 1996. *Domestic Sources of Global Change*. Ann Arbor: University of Michigan Press.

Maoz, Zeez, and B. Russett. 1993. "Normative and Structural Causes of Democratic Peace, 1946–1986." *American Political Science Review* 87, no. 3: 624–38.

Maoz, Zeev, Lesley Terris, Ranan Kuperman, and Ilan Talmud. 2007. "What Is the Enemy of My Enemy? Causes and Consequences of Imbalanced International Relations, 1816–2001." *Journal of Politics* 69, no. 1: 100–115.

March, Peter. 1972. "Lord Salisbury and the Ottoman Massacres." *Journal of British Studies* 11, no. 2: 63–83.

Marder, Arthur Jacob. 1940. *The Anatomy of British Sea Power: A History of British Naval Policy in The Pre-dreadnought Era, 1880–1905*. New York: A. A. Knopf.

Marshall, Monty G., and Keith Jaggers. 2002. "Polity IV Project: Political Regime Characteristics and Transitions, 1800–2002." Dataset users' manual, Center for International Development and Conflict Management, University of Maryland, College Park, MD.

Martin, Lisa L. 2000. *Democratic Commitments: Legislatures and International Cooperation.* Princeton, NJ: Princeton University Press.

Mastny, Vojtech, Sven G. Holtsmark, and Andreas Wenger, eds. 2006. *War Plans and Alliances in the Cold War: Threat Perceptions in the East and West.* London: Routledge.

Matloff, Maurice, and Edwin M. Snell. 1953. *Strategic Planning for Coalition Warfare, 1941–1942.* Center of Military History, United States Army. Washington, DC: US Government Printing Office.

Mattes, Michaela. 2012a. "Democratic Reliability, Precommitment of Successor Governments, and the Choice of Alliance Commitment." *International Organization* 66, no. 1: 153–72.

——. 2012b. "Reputation, Symmetry, and Alliance Design." *International Organization* 66, no. 4: 679–707.

Maurer, John H. 1995. *The Outbreak of the First World War: Strategic Planning, Crisis Decision Making, and Deterrence Failure.* London: Praeger.

McKibben, Heather Elko. 2013. "The Effects of Structures and Power on State Bargaining Strategies." *American Journal of Political Science* 57, no. 2: 411–27.

——. 2015. *State Strategies in International Bargaining: Play by the Rules or Change Them?* New York: Cambridge University Press.

McManus, Roseanne, and Keren Yarhi-Milo. 2017. "The Logic of 'Backstage' Signaling: Domestic Politics, Regime Type, and Major Power-Protégé Relations." *International Organization* 71, no. 4: 701–33.

Mearsheimer, John J. 1983. *Conventional Deterrence.* Ithaca, NY: Cornell University Press.

——. 1989. "Assessing the Conventional Balance: The 3:1 Rule and Its Critics." *International Security* 13, no. 4: 54–89.

——. 1990. "Back to the Future: Instability in Europe after the Cold War." *International Security* 15, no. 1: 5–56.

——. 1994. "The False Promise of International Institutions." *International Security* 19, no. 3: 5–49.

——. 2001. *The Tragedy of Great Power Politics.* New York: Norton.

Mebane, Walter R., and Paul Poast. 2013. "Causal Inference without Ignorability: Identification with Nonrandom Assignment and Missing Treatment Data." *Political Analysis* 21, no. 2: 233–51.

Michon, Georges. (1929) 1969. *The Franco-Russian Alliance, 1891–1917.* New York: Howard Fertig.

Michishita, Narushige. 2014. "Changing Security Relationship between Japan and South Korea: Frictions and Hopes." *Asia-Pacific Review* 21, no. 2: 12–32.

Mill, John Stuart. 1843. *System of Logic, Ratiocinative and Inductive.* Vol. 1. (London: John Parker West).

Miller, Gregory D. 2003. "Hypotheses on Reputation: Alliance Choices and the Shadow of the Past." *Security Studies* 12, no. 3: 40–78.

——. 2012. *The Shadow of the Past: Reputation and Military Alliances before the First World War.* Ithaca, NY: Cornell University Press.

Millett, Allan R., Williamson Murray, and Kenneth H. Watman. 1986. "The Effectiveness of Military Organizations." *International Security* 11, no. 1: 37–71.

Miner, Steven. 2015. Review and comments on Roger Moorhouse. "The Devil's Alliance: Hitler's Pact with Stalin, 1939–1941." H-DIPLO Blog, January 2015. https://networks.h-net.org/node/28443/discussions/58075/miner-moorhouse-devils -alliance-hitlers-pact. Accessed on May 14, 2015.

Mitzen, Jennifer, and Randall L. Schweller. 2011. "Knowing the Unknown Unknowns: Misplaced Certainty and the Onset of War." *Security Studies* 20, no. 1: 2–35.

Modelski, George, and William R. Thompson. 1988. *Seapower in Global Politics, 1494–1993.* London: Macmillan Press.

——. 1999. "The Long and the Short of Global Politics in the Twenty-First Century: An Evolutionary Approach." *International Studies Review* 1, no. 2: 109–40.

Molinari, Francesca. 2010. "Missing Treatments." *Journal of Business and Economic Statistics* 28, no. 1: 82–95.

Mombauer, Annika. 2014. "The Moltke Plan: A Modified Schlieffen Plan with Identical Aims?" In *The Schlieffen Plan: International Perspectives on the German Strategy for World War I*, ed. Hans Ehlert, Gerhard Gross, and Michael Epkenhans, 43–66. Lexington, KY: University Press of Kentucky.

Monger, George W. 1963. *The End of Isolation: British Foreign Policy, 1900–1907.* London: T. Nelson.

Morewood, Steven. 1996. "Appeasement from Strength: The Making of the 1936 Anglo- Egyptian Treaty of Friendship and Alliance." *Diplomacy and Statecraft* 7, no. 3: 530–62.

Morgan, Stephen L., and Christopher Winship. 2007. *Counterfactuals and Causal Inference.* New York: Cambridge University Press.

Morgenthau, Hans. 1948. *Politics Among Nations.* New York: Knopf.

Morrow, James D. 1987. "On the Theoretical Basis of a Measure of National Risk Attitudes." *International Studies Quarterly* 31, no. 4: 423–38.

——. 1989 "Capabilities, Uncertainty, and Resolve: A Limited Information Model of Crisis Bargaining." *American Journal of Political Science* 33: 941–72.

——. 1991. "Alliances and Asymmetry: An Alternative to the Capability Aggregation Model of Alliances." *American Journal of Political Science* 35, no. 4: 904–33.

——. 1992. "Signaling Difficulties with Linkage in Crisis Bargaining." *International Studies Quarterly* 36, no. 2: 153–72.

——. 1993. "Arms versus Allies: Tradeoffs in the Search for Security." *International Organization* 47, no. 2: 207–33.

——. 1994. "Alliances, Credibility, and Peacetime Costs." *Journal of Conflict Resolution* 38, no. 2: 270–97.

——. 1997. "When Do 'Relative Gains' Impede Trade?" *Journal of Conflict Resolution* 41, no. 1: 12–37.

——. 2000. "Alliances: Why Write Them Down?" *Annual Review of Political Science* 3, no. 1: 63–83.

Most, B. A., and H. Starr. 1989. *Inquiry, Logic, and International Politics.* Columbia: University of South Carolina Press.

Murray, Willamson. 2000. "Comparative Approaches to Interwar Innovation." *Joint Force Quarterly* 25: 83–90.

Nagler, Jonathan. 1994. "Scobit: An Alternative Estimator to Logit and Probit." *American Journal of Political Science* 38, no. 1: 230–55.

Neilson, Keith. 1993. "Pursued by a Bear: British Estimates of Soviet Military Strength and Anglo-Soviet Relations, 1922–1939." *Canadian Journal of History* 28, no. 2: 180–22.

Newell, Clayton R. 1991. *The Framework of Operational Warfare.* London: Routledge.

Newton, Thomas Wodehouse Legh. 1929. *Lord Lansdowne: A Biography*. London: Macmillan.

Nye, Joseph. 2012. "The Twenty-First Century Will Not Be a 'Post-American' World." *International Studies Quarterly* 56, no. 1: 215–17.

Odell, John. 2000. *Negotiating the World Economy*. Ithaca, NY: Cornell University Press.

——. 2005. "Three Islands of Knowledge about Negotiation in International Organizations." *Journal of European Public Policy* 17, no. 5: 619–32.

Olekalns, Mara, and Philip L. Smith. 2009. "Mutually Dependent: Power, Trust, Affect and the Use of Deception in Negotiation." *Journal of Business Ethics* 85, no. 3: 347–65.

Olson, Mancur, and Richard Zeckhauser. 1967. "Collective Goods, Comparative Advantage, and Alliance Efficiency." In *Issues of Defense Economics*, ed. Roland McKean, 25–63. New York: NBER.

Oneal, J., and B. Russett. 1997. "The Classic Liberals Were Right: Democracy, Interdependence, and Conflict, 1950–1985." *International Studies Quarterly* 41, no. 2: 267–93.

——. 2005. "Rule of Three, Let It Be? When More Really Is Better." *Conflict Management and Peace Science* 22, no. 4: 293–310.

Osgood, R. E. 1962. *NATO: The Entangling Alliance*. Chicago: University of Chicago Press.

Otte, T. G. 1995. "Great Britain, Germany, and the Far-Eastern Crisis of 1897–1898." *English Historical Review* 110, no. 439: 1157–79.

——. 2007. *The China Question: Great Power Rivalry and British Isolation, 1894–1905*. Oxford: Oxford University Press.

Park, Jaehan, and Sangyoung Yun. 2016. "Korea and Japan's Military Information Agreement: A Final Touch for the Pivot?" *The Diplomat*, November 24, 2016. https://thediplomat.com/2016/11/korea-and-japans-military-information-agreement-a-final-touch-f. Accessed on July 2, 2018.

Pahre, Robert. 2008. *Politics and Trade Cooperation in the Nineteenth Century: The "Agreeable Customs" of 1815–1914*. Cambridge: Cambridge University Press.

Palmer, Glenn, and Clifford Morgan. 2006. *A Theory of Foreign Policy*. Princeton, NJ: Princeton University Press.

Parent, Joseph, and Sebastian Rosato. 2015. "Balancing in Neorealism." *International Security* 40, no. 2: 51–86.

Poast, Paul. 2004. "The Wall and Maastricht: Exogenous Shocks and the Initiation of the EMU and EPU IGCs." *Journal of European Integration* 26, no. 3: 281–307.

——. 2010. "(Mis)Using Dyadic Data to Analyze Multilateral Events." *Political Analysis* 18, no. 4: 403–25.

——. 2012. "Does Issue Linkage Work? Evidence from European Alliance Negotiations, 1860 to 1945." *International Organization* 66, no. 2: 277–310.

——. 2013. "Can Issue Linkage Improve Treaty Credibility." *Journal of Conflict Resolution* 57, no. 5: 739–64.

——. 2015. "Central Banks at War." *International Organization* 69, no. 1: 63–95.

Poast, Paul, and Johannes Urpelainen. 2015. "How International Organizations Support Democratization: Preventing Authoritarian Reversals or Promoting Consolidation?" *World Politics* 67, no. 1: 72–113.

——. 2018. *Organizing Democracy: How International Organizations Assist New Democracies*. Chicago, IL: University of Chicago Press.

Porter, Andrew N. 1980. *The Origins of the South African War: Joseph Chamberlain and the Diplomacy of Imperialism, 1895–1899.* Manchester: Manchester University Press.

Posen, Barry R. 1984. *The Sources of Military Doctrine: France, Britain, and Germany between the World Wars.* Ithaca, NY: Cornell University Press.

———. 1993. "Nationalism, The Mass Army, and Military Power." *International Security* 18, no. 2: 80–124.

Pouliot, Vincent, and Jérémie Cornut. 2015. "Practice Theory and the Study of Diplomacy: A Research Agenda." *Cooperation and Conflict* 50, no. 3: 297–315.

Powell, Robert. 1999. *In the Shadow of Power.* Princeton, NJ: Princeton University Press.

———. 2002. "Bargaining Theory and International Conflict." *Annual Review of Political Science* 5, no. 1: 1–30.

Pressman, Jeremy. 2008. *Warring Friends: Alliance Restraint in International Politics.* Ithaca, NY: Cornell University Press.

Putnam, Robert D. 1988. "Diplomacy and Domestic Politics: The Logic of Two-Level Games." *International Organization* 42, no. 3: 427–60.

Ralston, D. B. 1990. *Importing the European Army: The Introduction of European Military Techniques and Institutions into the Extra-European World, 1600–1814.* Chicago: University of Chicago Press.

Ramsay, Kristopher C. 2008. "Settling It on the Field: Battlefield Events and War Termination." *Journal of Conflict Resolution* 52, no. 6: 850–79.

Ramsay, Kristopher W. 2011. "Cheap Talk Diplomacy, Voluntary Negotiations, and Variable Bargaining Power." *International Studies Quarterly* 55, no. 4: 1003–23.

Rathbun, Brian C. 2011. *Trust in International Cooperation: International Security Institutions, Domestic Politics and American Multilateralism.* New York: Cambridge University Press.

Ray, James L. 2003. "Explaining Interstate Conflict and War: What Should Be Controlled For?" *Conflict Management and Peace Science* 20, no. 2: 1–31.

Reid, Escott. 1977. *Time of Fear and Hope.* Toronto: McClelland and Stewart.

Reiter, Dan. 1995. "Exploding the Powder Keg Myth: Preemptive Wars Almost Never Happen." *International Security* 20, no. 2: 5–34.

———. 1996. *Crucible of Beliefs: Learning, Alliances, and World Wars.* Ithaca, NY: Cornell University Press.

Reiter, Dan, and Allan C. Stam. 1998. "Democracy, War Initiation, and Victory." *American Political Science Review* 92, no. 2: 377–89.

Reiter, Dan, and Curtis Meek. 1999. "Determinants of Military Strategy, 1903–1994: A Quantitative Empirical Test." *International Studies Quarterly* 43, no. 2: 363–87.

Reynolds, David. 1993. "Churchill in 1940: The Worst and Finest Hour." In *Churchill,* ed. Robert B. Blake and William Roger Louis, 241–56. Oxford: Clarendon Press.

Rich, Norman. 1965. *Friedrich von Holstein, Politics and Diplomacy in the Era of Bismarck and Wilhelm II.* 2 vols. Cambridge: Cambridge University Press.

Roberts, Geoffrey. 1992. "The Soviet Decision for a Pact with Nazi Germany." *Soviet Studies* 44, no. 1: 57–78.

Röhl, John C. G. 2014. *Wilhelm II: Into the Abyss of War and Exile, 1900–1941.* Cambridge: Cambridge University Press.

Rosenbaum, Peter. 2005. "Sensitivity Analysis in Observational Studies." In *Encyclopedia of Statistics in Behavioral Science,* ed. Brian Everitt and David C. Howell, 1809–14. New York: Wiley.

Rubin, Donald B. 1976. "Inference and Missing Data." *Biometrika* 63, no. 3: 581–92.

———. 2006. *Matched Sampling for Causal Effects.* New York: Cambridge University Press.

Rubinstein, Ariel. 1982. "Perfect Equilibrium in a Bargaining Model." *Econometrica* 50, no. 1: 97–109.

Russett, Bruce, and Harvey Starr. 1989. *World Politics: The Menu for Choice*. 3rd ed. New York: W. H. Freeman.

Sagan, Scott D. 1986. "1914 Revisited: Allies, Offense, and Instability." *International Security* 11, no. 2: 151–75.

Sandler, Todd. 1977. "Impurity of Defense: An Application to the Economics of Alliances." *Kyklos* 30, no. 3: 443–60.

Sandler, Todd, and John F. Forbes. 1980. "Burden Sharing, Strategy, and the Design of NATO." *Economic Inquiry* 18, no. 3: 425–44.

Sandler, Todd, and Keith Hartley. 2001. "Economics of Alliances: The Lessons for Collective Action." *Journal of Economic Literature* 39, no. 3: 869–96.

Sarkees, Meredith R., and Frank W. Wayman. 2010. *Resort to War, 1816–2007*. Correlates of War Series. Washington, D.C.: CQ Press.

Sartori, Anne E. 2003. "An Estimator for Some Binary Outcome Selection Models without Exclusion Restrictions." *Political Analysis* 11, no. 2: 111–38.

———. 2005. *Deterrence by Diplomacy*. Princeton, NJ: Princeton University Press.

Saunders, David. 1992. *Russia in the Age of Reaction and Reform 1801–1881*. London: Routledge.

Saville, A. R. 1878. *Cyprus*. London: H. M. Stationery Office.

Schelling, Thomas. 1960. *The Strategy of Conflict*. Boston: Harvard University Press.

———. 1966. *Arms and Influence*. New Haven, CT: Yale University Press.

Schmitt, Oliver. 2018. *Allies That Count*. Washington, DC: Georgetown University Press.

Schroeder, Paul W. 1994. *The Transformation of European Politics, 1763–1848*. London: Oxford University Press.

Schroeder, Paul W. 2004. "Alliances, 1815–1945: Weapons of Power and Tools of Management." In *Systems, Stability, and Statecraft: Essays on the International History of Modern Europe*, ed. David Wetzel, Robert Jervis, and Jack S. Levy, 195–222. New York: Palgrave Macmillan.

Schultz, Kenneth. 2001. "Looking for Audience Costs." *Journal of Conflict Resolution* 45, no. 1: 32–60.

———. 2012. "Why We Needed Audience Costs and What We Need Now." *Security Studies* 21, no. 3: 369–75.

Schweller, Randall L. 2004. "Unanswered Threats: A Neoclassical Realist Theory of Underbalancing." *International Security* 29, no. 2: 159–201.

Sebenius, James K. 1983. "Negotiation Arithmetic: Adding and Subtracting Issues and Parties." *International Organization* 37, no. 2: 281–316.

———. 2009. "Negotiation Analysis: From Games to Inferences to Decisions to Deals." *Negotiation Journal* 25, no. 4: 449–65.

Sechrest, Lee. 2005. "Validity of Measures Is No Simple Matter." *Health Services Research* 40, no. 5: 1584–1604.

Seton-Watson, Robert W. 1934. *Disraeli, Gladstone, and the Eastern Question*. London: Macmillan.

Sheen, Seongho, and Jina Kim. 2012. "What Went Wrong with the ROK-Japan Military Pact?" *Asia Pacifica Bulletin*, no. 176 (July 31, 2012).

Signorino, Curtis S., and Jeffrey M. Ritter. 1999. "Tau-b or Not Tau-b: Measuring the Similarity of Foreign Policy Positions." *International Studies Quarterly* 43, no. 1: 115–44.

Simmons, Beth A., and Daniel J. Hopkins. 2005. "The Constraining Power of International Treaties: Theory and Methods" *American Political Science Review* 99, no. 4: 623–31.

Siverson, Randolph, and Harvey Starr. 1991. *The Diffusion of War.* Ann Arbor: University of Michigan Press.

Slantchev, Branislav L. 2004. "How Initiators End Their Wars: The Duration of Warfare and the Terms of Peace." *American Journal of Political Science* 48, no. 4: 813–29.

———. 2006. "Politicians, the Media, and Domestic Audience Costs." *International Studies Quarterly* 50, no. 2: 445–77.

———. 2011. *Military Threats: The Costs of Coercion and the Price of Peace.* New York: Cambridge University Press.

Small, Melvin, and J. D. Singer. 1966. "Formal Alliances, 1815–1939: A Quantitative Description." *Journal of Peace Research* 3, no. 1: 1–31.

———. 1982. *Resort to Arms: International and Civil Wars, 1816–1980.* Beverly Hills, CA: Sage Publications.

Smith, Alastair. 1995. "Alliance Formation and War." *International Studies Quarterly* 40, no. 1: 133–53.

———. 1998. "Extended Deterrence and Alliance Formation." *International Interactions* 24, no. 4: 315–43.

Smith, Alastair, and Allan C. Stam. 2004. "Bargaining and the Nature of War." *Journal of Conflict Resolution* 48, no. 6: 783–813.

Snyder, Glenn H. 1984a. "The Security Dilemma in Alliance Politics." *World Politics* 36, no. 4: 461–95.

———. 1991. "Alliances, Balance, and Stability." *International Organization* 45, no. 1: 121–42.

———. 1997. *Alliance Politics.* Ithaca, NY: Cornell University Press.

Snyder, Jack. 1984. "Civil-Military Relations and the Cult of the Offensive, 1914 and 1984." *International Security* 9, no. 1: 108–46.

———. 1989. *Ideology of the Offensive.* Ithaca, NY: Cornell University Press.

Spence, Michael. 1973. "Job Market Signaling." *Quarterly Journal of Economics* 87, no. 3: 355–74.

Stam, Allan. 1996. *Win, Lose, or Draw: Domestic Politics and the Crucible of War.* Ann Arbor: University of Michigan Press.

Stein, Janice Gross. 2013. "Threat perception in international relations." In *The Oxford handbook of political psychology*, ed. Leonie Huddy, David O. Sears, and Jack S. Levy, 364–94 (New York: Oxford University Press).

Steiner, Zara S. 2005. *The Lights That Failed: European International History, 1919–1933.* New York: Oxford University Press.

Stevenson, David. 1999. "War by Timetable? The Railway Race before 1914." *Past and Present* 162: 163–94.

Stinnett, Douglas M., Jaroslav Tir, Philip Schafer, Paul F. Diehl, and Charles Gochman. 2002. "The Correlates of War Project Direct Contiguity Data, Version 3." *Conflict Management and Peace Science* 19, no. 2: 58–66.

Svik, Peter. 2016. "The Czechoslovak Factor in Western Alliance Building, 1945–1948." *Journal of Cold War Studies* 18, no. 1: 133–60.

Tang, Shiping. 2005. "Reputation, Cult of Reputation, and International Conflict." *Security Studies* 14, no. 1: 34–62.

Taylor, A. J. P. 1934. *The Italian Problem in European Diplomacy.* Manchester: Manchester University Press.

———. 1954. *The Struggle for Mastery in Europe.* Oxford: Oxford University Press.

———. 1961 *The Origins of the Second World War.* New York: Simon and Schuster.

———. 1966. *The First World War: An Illustrated History.* Harmondsworth: Penguin.

Taylor, R. K. 2001. "2020 Vision: Canadian Forces Operational-Level Doctrine." *Canadian Military Journal* 2, no. 3: 35–42.

Temperley, Harold. 1925. *The Foreign Policy of Canning, 1822–1827*. London: G. Bell and Sons.

———. 1931. "Disraeli and Cyprus." *English Historical Review* 46, no. 182: 274–79.

Thies, Wallace J. 1987. "Alliances and Collective Goods: A Reappraisal." *Journal of Conflict Resolution* 31, no. 2: 298–332.

———. 2003. *Friendly Rivals: Bargaining and Burden-Sharing in NATO*. Armon, NY: M. E. Sharpe.

Thompson, Julian. 1991. *The Lifeblood of War: Logistics in Armed Conflict*. London: Brassey's.

Thompson, William R. 2001. "Identifying Rivals and Rivalries in World Politics." *International Studies Quarterly* 45, no. 4: 557–86.

Tomz, Michael. 2007. "Domestic Audience Costs in International Relations: An Experimental Approach." *International Organization* 61, no. 4: 821–40.

Toscano, Mario. 1966. *The History of Treaties and International Politics*. Baltimore: Johns Hopkins University Press.

Trachtenberg, M. 1999. *A Constructed Peace: The Making of the European Settlement, 1945–1963*. Princeton, NJ: Princeton University Press.

Trager, Robert F. 2010. "Diplomatic Calculus in Anarchy: How Communication Matters." *American Political Science Review* 104, no. 2: 347–68.

Travers, T. H. E. 1978. "The Offensive and the Problem of Innovation in British Military Thought, 1870–1915." *Journal of Contemporary History* 13, no. 3: 531–53.

Tuchman, Barbara. 1962. *The Guns of August*. London: Random House.

Tversky, Amos, and Daniel Kahneman. 1974. "Judgment under Uncertainty: Heuristics and Bias." *Science* 185, no. 4157: 1124–31.

Underdal, Arild. 1983. "Causes of Negotiation 'Failure.'" *European Journal of Political Research* 11, no. 2: 183–95.

Urpelainen, Johannes. 2012. "How Uncertainty about Outside Options Impedes International Cooperation." *International Theory* 4, no. 1: 133–63.

Van Creveld, Martin. 2004. *Supplying War: Logistics from Wallenstein to Patton*. New York: Cambridge University Press.

Van Evera, Stephen. 1984. "The Cult of the Offensive and the Origins of the First World War." *International Security* 9, no. 1: 58–107.

———. 1998. "Offense, Defense, and the Causes of War." *International Security* 22, no. 4: 5–43.

———. 1999. *Causes of War*. Ithaca, NY: Cornell University Press.

Valeriano, Brandon, and John A. Vasquez. 2010. "Identifying and Classifying Complex Interstate Wars." *International Studies Quarterly* 54, no. 2: 561–82.

Voeten, Erik. 2001. "Outside Options and the Logic of Security Council Action." *American Political Science Review* 95, no. 4: 845–58.

Von Stein, Jana. 2005. "Do Treaties Constrain or Screen? Selection Bias and Treaty Compliance." *American Political Science Review* 99, no. 4: 611–22.

Wagner, R. Harrison. 2007. *The Theory of International Politics: War and the State*. Ann Arbor: University of Michigan Press.

Wallace, Geoffrey P. R. 2008. "Alliances, Institutional Design, and the Determinants of Military Strategy." *Conflict Management and Peace Science* 25, no. 3: 224–43.

Walpole, Spencer. 1889. *The Life of Lord John Russell*. Vol. 2. New York: Longmans, Green.

Walt, Stephen M. 1985. "Alliance Formation and the Balance of World Power." *International security* 9, no. 4: 3–43.

———. 1987. *The Origins of Alliances*. Ithaca, NY: Cornell University Press.

Waltz, Kenneth. 1979. *Theory of International Politics*. Boston: McGraw-Hill.

Warren, T. Camber. 2010. "The Geometry of Security: Modeling Interstate Alliances as Evolving Networks." *Journal of Peace Research* 47, no. 6: 697–709.

Watson, Mark Skinner. 1950. *Chief of Staff: Prewar Plans and Preparations*. Center of Military History, United States Army. Washington, DC: Government Printing Office.

Weeks, Jessica. 2008. "Autocratic Audience Costs: Regime Type and Signaling Resolve." *International Organization* 62, no. 1: 35–64.

Weisiger, Alex. 2013. *Logics of War: Explanations for Limited and Unlimited Conflicts*. Ithaca, NY: Cornell University Press.

——. 2016. "Learning from the Battlefield: Information, Domestic Politics, and Interstate War Duration." *International Organization* 70, no. 2: 347–75.

Weitsman, Patricia A. 2004. *Dangerous Alliances: Proponents of Peace, Weapons of War*. Stanford, CA: Stanford University Press.

——. 2014. *Waging War: Alliances, Coalitions, and Institutions of Interstate Violence*. Stanford, CA: Stanford University Press.

Wendt, Alexander. 1992. "Anarchy Is What States Make of It: The Social Construction of Power Politics." *International Organization* 46, no. 2: 391–425.

Wiens, David, Paul Poast, and William Roberts Clark. 2014. "The Political Resource Curse: An Empirical Re-evaluation." *Political Research Quarterly* 67, no. 4: 783–94.

Williamson, S. J. 1979. "Joffre Reshapes French Strategy, 1911–1913." In *The War Plans of the Great Powers*, ed. Paul Kennedy, 133–54. London: Routledge.

Wohlforth, William C. 2012. "How Not to Evaluate Theories." *International Studies Quarterly* 56, no. 1: 219–22.

Wolford, Scott. 2015. *Politics of Military Coalitions*. New York: Cambridge University Press.

Wolford, Scott, Dan Reiter, and Clifford J. Carrubba. 2011. "Information, Commitment, and War." *Journal of Conflict Resolution* 55, no. 4: 556–79.

Wooldridge, Jeffrey M. 2002. *Econometric Analysis of Cross Section and Panel Data*. Cambridge: Massachusetts Institute of Technology.

Yarhi-Milo, Keren. 2014. *Knowing the Adversary: Leaders, Intelligence, and Assessment of Intentions in International Relations*. Princeton, NJ: Princeton University Press.

Zartman, William. 1987. *The 50% Solution*. New Haven, CT: Yale University Press.

——. 2010. "Negotiation Pedagogy: International Relations." *International Negotiation* 15, no. 2: 229–46.

Index

1868 (Wellington), 189n99–110

Abadie, Alberto, 94, 104
Achen, Christopher, 197n24
Acheson, Dean, 137, 153, 157, 160–63, 165, 211n112
Achilles, Theodore C., 137, 150, 211n112
Adcock, Robert, 99
Albrecht-Carrie, René, 48
Alexander I (Tsar), 36
Alexander II (Tsar), 28, 49, 189n91–92
Alliance Politics (Snyder), 3
alliance treaty negotiations: ad hoc coalitions and, 2, 68–70, 181n9; agreement and, 1–11, 27–32, 43–44, 66–80, 107–9, 137—145, 151–64, 168–72, 178; alliance treaty design and, 6, 42–44, 172–74, 182n18; Alliance Treaty Obligation and Provision (ATOP) data and, 79, 191n10; asymmetric alliance and, 54, 72–74, 85, 87–88, 97; attractiveness of outside options and, 15–16, 29–32, 39, 41, 101, 103, 170–71, 185n39, 187n64; bargaining and, 7–9, 15–18, 31, 133, 181n11, 182n26, 185n39, 185n42, 185n44; bilateral negotiations and, 50, 73, 98–101, 122, 131, 143–44, 200n63; Britain and, 3, 18, 20, 34–41, 51–57, 110–20, 190n115; buck passing and, 4, 29, 38, 99, 105, 187n58; capitulation and, 16, 38–39, 43, 135, 170; coalition members and, 6, 70, 181n9, 196n11; coding and, 48–49, 105, 170; collapse and, 5, 38–40, 43, 100, 107, 115, 170; colonies and, 54, 57, 115, 119–20, 131–33, 160–61, 193n29, 206n7; comparability of ideal war plans and, 16, 32, 107–8; compromise and, 7, 16, 33, 37–40, 43, 131, 135, 170; Defense Cooperation Agreements and, 177–78; democratic regimes and, 75–78, 201n12; diplomacy and, 6, 30, 48, 50, 201n8; economics and, 39–40, 73, 98–99, 183n5, 190n119; enforcement and, 182n31, 183n32, 183n34; entrapment and, 9, 11–12, 136, 168, 182n28; France and, 1–3, 19–21, 25–27, 37–38, 49–54; Future Research and, 172–74; Germany and, 19–27, 113–15, 119–20; ideal war plan compatibility and, 4–9, 28–32, 45, 65–70, 80–86, 96–103, 170–71, 195n2, 200n72; ideal war plans and, 2, 8–9, 17–18, 25–28, 171; joint war planning and, 7, 9–10, 14–20, 41, 164, 171, 182n19; major powers and, 40, 72–74, 139, 181n14, 192n17, 192n21, 192n23, 193n23, 199n58; military capabilities and, 4, 8–9, 68, 89, 169, 174, 181n12; minor powers and, 67–68, 72–74; multipolar systems and, 12, 98, 182n26, 183n36; nonagreement and, 4–11, 27–36, 42–44, 107–33, 169–71, 187n72; partners and, 14, 72; Pleasant Surprise and, 16, 32, 36–38, 102, 170, 200n68; reliability concerns and, 8–9, 74–76, 78–79, 136, 174–75, 182n24, 187n61; Revealed Deadlock and, 16, 33, 37–38, 102, 170, 200n67; reverse causality and, 195n2; Russia and, 19, 21, 27, 36–37, 50, 80, 87, 93–95, 112–14; Same Page and, 16, 32–36, 38, 102, 170, 172; signaling and, 2, 89, 144, 165, 175, 181n7, 190n112–13; Standard Bargaining and, 16, 33, 38–41, 101–2, 134, 170, 172; threats and, 2–9, 32–35, 53–54, 135–42, 169–73, 183n1, 193n24–25; unilateral action and, 16, 29, 37–39, 105, 142–43, 170; United States and, 12, 34–35, 70, 177–78; USSR/Soviet Union and, 1, 40–41, 139–42; watered-down agreements and, 47, 126

Alliance Treaty Obligation and Provision (ATOP) data, 10, 46–47, 63, 79, 181n14, 188n74, 191n5, 191n10
American-British-Conversations (ABC) report, 34–35, 150, 188n88
American-British-Conversations (ABC) talks, 140, 142, 145–46, 164
American-Dutch-British (ADB) report, 188n81
Andrassy, Gyula, 49, 191n6
Anglo-American Atlantic Charter, 34
Anglo-American negotiations (1941), 34, 77

237